EXPERIENC[E]
AND THE
CURRICULUM

edited by
Bert Horwood

Center for Teaching Library
The Westminster Schools
1424 West Paces Ferry Road, N.W.
Atlanta, Georgia 30327

ASSOCIATION FOR EXPERIENTIAL EDUCATION

2885 Aurora Ave., #28   Boulder, CO 80303-2252   303-440-8844

KENDALL/HUNT PUBLISHING COMPANY
4050 Westmark Drive   Dubuque, Iowa 52002

Cover design
by Bert Horwood
& Renée Meyer
Illustrations by Jan Swaren

Dedicated to the Memory of
Robert J. (Bob) Pieh

1916-1993

Athlete, teacher, headmaster, founder, trickster;
a man who led others by giving them confidence in themselves
and who always held true to his own rule:

Be tough yet gentle, humble yet bold,
swayed always by beauty and truth.

The traditional way of education
   was by example and experience
      and by story telling.

The first principle involved was total respect
   and acceptance of the one to be taught.
And that learning was a continuous process
   from birth to death.
         It was a total continuity without interruption.
Its nature was like a fountain
   that gives many colours and flavours of water
      and that whoever chose could drink as much or as little
         as they wanted to and whenever they wished.
The teaching strictly adhered
   to the sacredness of life whether of human
      or animals or plants. . . .

Arthur Solomon, a Nishnawbe spiritual teacher

In this program you don't learn from one teacher and one text-book, you learn from everything. You learn from your experience; you learn from observing and asking questions; you learn from everything you do and people you meet. This is what life's about: You make friends, you work together, you learn. You go out into the world and you . . . live life.

High school student's self-evaluative statement

TABLE OF CONTENTS

About the Association for Experiential Education

The Association for Experiential Education (AEE) is a not-for-profit, international, professional organization with roots in adventure education, committed to the development, practice, and evaluation of experiential learning in all settings.

AEE sponsors local, regional, and international conferences, projects, seminars, and institutes, and publishes the *Journal of Experiential Education,* the *Jobs Clearinghouse,* directories of programs and services, and a wide variety of books and periodicals to support educators, trainers, practitioners, students, and advocates.

AEE's diverse membership consists of individuals and organizations with affiliations in education, recreation, outdoor adventure programming, mental health, youth service, physical education, management development training, corrections, programming for people with disabilities, and environmental education.

To receive additional information about the Association for Experiential Education call or write AEE, 2885 Aurora Avenue, Ste. #28, Boulder, CO USA 80303-2252. Phone (303) 440-8844, FAX (303) 440-9581, e-mail AEEMikal@Nile.com

About the AEE Schools
and Colleges Professional Group

The Schools and Colleges Professional Group is committed to the development and promotion of experiential learning in school and college settings. The Schools and Colleges PG seeks to serve members and those beyond its membership in public and private settings, at all age levels. Through a newsletter, workshops, and conference offerings, it networks experiential educators who are interested in applying the principles of experiential education to schooling. Members of the Schools and Colleges PG work in many areas of expertise, but share a common philosophy and use a humanistic approach to formal education.

PREFACE

This book emerged with the support and encouragement of the Schools and Colleges Professional Group within the Association for Experiential Education (AEE). With that support, I sought to assemble a set of essays which would illustrate the best of practice, offer encouragement to teachers everywhere, and point the way to the future of experiential education in schools. The idea was to elicit teacher's voices and display the power and dilemmas of practice.

AEE publications invited members and subscribers to submit essays. I also sent invitations to other educators known to be working at the cutting edge of experiential education in a wide variety of settings. Two teachers anonymously reviewed each submission and made recommendations. Authors rewrote their chapters to reflect the reviewers' opinions. In some cases, potentially valuable contributions could not be rewritten due to pressures of other commitments. The accumulating collection reflected considerations of quality, relevance, and diversity.

The panel of reviewers included M. J. Barrett, Caroline Conzelman, Anne Davies, Stephanie Doll, Doug Gray, Glenda Hanna, Daniel Kirkpatrick, Heidi Mack, Christine Robertson, and Alan Warner. I am grateful to these reviewers who provided thoughtful and detailed feedback on the submissions. Heidi Mack and Christine Robertson did extra duty in consulting with me from time to time when I felt the need for advice. Jan Carrick provided efficient typing and grammatical assistance.

Late in the editing process, a review subcommittee of AEE's Publications Advisory Committee read the manuscript. Under the able leadership of James Raffan, the review group supported and criticized the manuscript and stimulated improvements. Nina Roberts also made helpful suggestions. Jan Swaren, artist and teacher, drew the illustrations. Production of the book was overseen by Pia Renton, for AEE, and Kendall/Hunt Publishing.

Notwithstanding all that help, the responsibility for any errors in judgment or editing which may persist is strictly my own.

Bert Horwood

Chapter 1

OF STONES AND STRANDS: AN INTRODUCTION

Bert Horwood

This chapter sets the stage for the rest of the book. The remaining chapters are entirely independent from each other, yet, paradoxically, they are linked at many levels by common themes which run among them. To outline some of the major themes and suggest ways to extract the greatest value from the rest of the book, Bert Horwood, as editor, uses an analogy which compares the chapters to stones on the shores of an arctic river.

The river shore was lined with stones. As far as I could see, nothing but stones. There was every colour, shape, and texture imaginable. Billions upon billions of stones. One of them glinted in my eye in the thin arctic sun. I stooped, fingered it into my palm, and marvelled.

The brown, elongated pebble fitted perfectly on my curled forefinger. My thumb rested in the polished groove on its upper surface and easily caressed the silky smooth surface. I cannot explain, with any certainty, how that stone came to me, but I have it still.

Of course there are explanations. One belongs to the random chance school of thought. The original rock, polished by ages of tumbling, was the mother of tons of sand and gravel, leaving this shiny morsel to reflect the sun which by chance was just rightly placed to beam into my eye. Pure chance. Another possible explanation is more mystical. Perhaps the stone called out to me, having lessons to teach about the land, or because of its feminine shape, to teach me, a privileged male, to nurture my vulnerability and to see that the variety visible at my feet represented the invisible, greater diversity of the whole. Sermons in stones.

At the same time, some of my companions also found stones to marvel over. We had all walked by them, but only one of us at a time had seen a particular stone. One, a smooth, dull, ochre disk, was pierced by a hole. Another, just fist-sized, was chocolate brown streaked with an intricate network of creamy lines. The provenance of each called forth worlds of speculation.

The chapters in this book are rather like those special stones which somehow came to the attention of passers-by. Each chapter has called itself to my attention somehow. Each is as different from the others as are the stones along the Horton River. Some are small gems, polished in intervals between the daily demands of teaching. Others are larger and multifaceted. Some tell of teaching the young; others pertain to adult learning. There are chapters which emphasize practice and those which stress theory.

And like river stones, the chapters have common features. All are written by practising teachers. All contain accounts of practice that fall within the general realm of experiential education. All have inspiring aspects but also point to problems and dilemmas in the field of experiential education.

If one lies down on the stony shore of the Horton River and looks out along the tops of the stones with unfocused gaze, the visual effect is almost the same as looking closely along the surface of a woven fabric. The totally independent stones form rounded mounds which seem to rise and fall into each other, much as strands of woven fibre do. In the same way there are strands of thought and experience which interweave through the independent chapters of this book. In this introduction, I will identify some threads that link the chapters together and suggest ways of approaching the collection most beneficially. In the concluding chapter, I will reflect on the meaning of the collection and explore its implications.

Of numerous possible connecting threads, I will mention only four. These are teacher voice, active and responsible students, diversity, and experience as a bridge linking the school curriculum with the rest of the world. There are two reasons for highlighting these strands: First, they are central to understanding the place of experience in the curriculum, and second, they are the lines which extend from the local specifics of time and setting to any of the myriad teaching contexts in which readers find themselves. In short, these strands provide both internal and external connections and applicability.

The literature of education is full of inquiry and opinion *about* teaching. The voices of social scientists claim to be detached from the teaching process and assert their objectivity in attempting descriptions or drawing conclusions. This kind of outside view has qualities which may be desirable in certain circumstances. By contrast, in the chapters which follow, a strong theme is reflection from *within* teaching. Teachers' voices, raised out of hard-won experience and filtered through thoughtful, critical perspectives, provide insiders' views of practice. These voices claim close attachment to the process of teaching and produce a rich counterpoint to the literature which, otherwise, tends to treat teaching and learning as remote subjects of science.

Each chapter contains an element of narrative. Each is a story, or series of stories, of practice. The writers speak for themselves as teachers, whether in elementary, secondary, or university settings. The voices are grounded in their own practices as teachers, but they also are informed by scholarship and awareness that keeps them from being self-centred. Most chapters, for example, cite literature in order to link the individual story to the body of academic and professional knowledge. The voices are enthusiastic. Even stories of failure are framed positively as opportunities for learning. The thread of teacher voice links the chapters together and yields a kind of positive harmony, a major chord as it were, that augurs well for the teachers themselves and their students. Given that the writers of these chapters are but a small sampling of many thousands of similar teachers all over the world, the overall weave gives cause for optimism.

A second thread that weaves through the chapters is the persistent image of active students. It is easy to misunderstand that expression, "active students." As Joanna Allen wrote on the internet (AEEList, 19 February, 1995), "So often we are fooled into thinking an activity is experiential when it's only busywork or doing. Experience means the whole person is involved, especially the emotions and an actively involved mind. . . . A key factor is how open the person is to experience and not only how good the . . . teacher . . . is." The activity which marks so many of these chapters makes large demands on the students for autonomy, social interaction, and responsibility. An ironic comment on the state of education in general is that, in these pages, university teachers report that some adult students had great difficulty in acting in the independent and responsible way that their teachers demanded. It is as though the adult students were saying, "Tell us what you want us to do and we'll do it. But don't ask us to figure out what it's important for us to do." The irony lies in the fact that, if docility and willing compliance are desired ends of education, then these adults display its success. On the other hand, if the capability for creative, inventive independence is a desired end, then education has, in these cases, failed.

Autonomy, imagination, and responsibility are common features in the active-student strand. There is also much variation, as though the thread were multicoloured. Unlike the restricted notion that the "experience" in experiential education must comprise some kind of physical adventure, in these stories, active experience includes reading and writing, and classroom work as well as out-of-school events. Action, as portrayed in this thread, includes families, the community, and beyond.

It is paradoxical to claim that diversity is a third strand linking the chapters. Yet, just as biologists observe that unity in diversity is a principle in living things, so the presence of diversity is a valued quality found in experiential education. The practice of experiential teaching is not limited to a particular age group, nor to a particular geographic region. Taking the school into the community, and the community into the school does not depend on socioeconomic status. The chapters to come are diverse within themselves, dealing with a variety of school subjects and perspectives. Yet the power of each chapter is that it deals with some particularity which the author knows intimately. That makes for conviction. The challenge for the reader is to recognize the aspects of those particularities which allow transfer to other settings. In most cases, the authors have indicated transferable points.

Each chapter is unique. Yet the accumulated effect is one of accord and relationship. That is the essence of diversity as a unifying strand. This collection, like a collection of stones from one beach, is exemplary and illustrative of a larger diversity and a greater relationship to be found in the many beaches of experiential education.

A fourth strong strand weaving through the chapters is the curriculum. Curriculum can be interpreted broadly as all the things a school is trying to do, or it may be more narrowly limited to the specific requirements of various government mandates. In either case, these stories reveal serious attempts by teachers to help their students have a lively experience of the curriculum. Curriculum is not seen as a school thing so much as a part of life. These teachers treat curriculum as something to be lived, something to be experienced directly by the students and themselves. Experiences, and the thoughts that surface from them, serve as bridges between the curriculum, as a school phenomenon, and the rest of the world in which the students will eventually live their lives. This is a centrally important function of experience in the curriculum whether in a middle-class suburban school, an inner-city alternative learning community, or a traditional healing program in a Third World village.

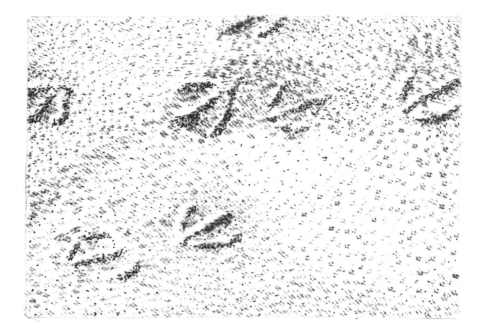

Curriculum is commonly expressed in terms of school subjects. The authors in this book do refer to particular subjects, sometimes as a central feature of their story, sometimes more peripherally. Mathematics, history, English, building trades, outdoor education, and science are specifically included. But more significantly, for me, is the fact that the thread of experience as a bridge between curriculum and the rest of the world leads to inevitable erosion of subject boundaries. Through the experiential practice of curriculum, active students in these chapters link classical literature with physics, mathematics with crafts, building trades with gender issues, and science with earth wisdom. Experience, when fully developed, integrates a fragmented curriculum.

Given the diversity of chapters and the multiple strands which pass among them, there is no more a way of arranging them logically than there is of arranging the stones on the river shore. I have selected a sequence that emphasizes contrast, leaving the most comprehensive chapters for the end. In these final chapters, all the threads are in evidence and very beautifully interwoven. This means that there is no reason to read the chapters in any particular sequence. But there is good reason to read them with an eye open for the many motifs and strands, other than those already mentioned, which give unity and broad applicability within the diversity to the collection.

Because this is a book of narratives of practice, of experiences of experience in teaching, the stories cry out to be compared with the practices of those who read them. For many there will be affirmation and validation; for some there will be inspiration and encouragement; for others there will be challenges and puzzlement in the problems and dilemmas of practice. Professional dialogue should be one of the consequences of reading, but before that, simple enjoyment of sharing the working lives of courageous and articulate fellow teachers should prevail. As Robert Fulghum said of his book, *All I Really Need to Know I Learned in Kindergarten*, "Read a little bit at a time—there's no hurry and no resolution of the plot at the end." Like the stones along the Horton River, the stories in this book should be savoured, appreciated, and taken into each reader's understanding of experience in education.

Chapter 2

EXPERIENTIAL EDUCATION IN THE ENGLISH CLASSROOM

Gail C. Simmons

Gail C. Simmons holds a BA with honours in English and a BEd from Queen's University at Kingston, Ontario. She is licensed as an Ontario teacher with the Honours Specialist Certificate in English. Currently she is Head of English at Gananoque Secondary School in Gananoque, Ontario. She also leads the outdoor adventure club in the school.

Gail's story is appealing because of the vividness with which she describes a peak experience in her classroom. Gail goes on to reflect on the processes by which she found out how to implement experiential learning in the English curriculum. She describes her role, after starting students on their own paths, as one of supplying support and confidence. Here, a neglected aspect of teaching is articulated, namely, the importance of the teacher instilling confidence in students who are about to embark on risky ventures into the unknown. Author Mary Stewart, in her Arthurian trilogy, says that a leader is one who, with a word, can confer or withhold confidence. Gail's story shows that a teacher is the same.

Silence fell as she entered the classroom; wheels clicked as veined hands clawed for the elusive chrome rim. Head shaking, she haltingly rolled to the front of the class and fumbled with papers, eyes downcast, searching for just the right order before starting her speech. An outlet to plug in her tape recorder was stubbornly out of her grasp. "Here, let me help you," I offered, springing to life. As if in slow motion, her head lifted, heavy with age, and I was paralyzed by the strong, steady stare of eyes that denied her years. They defied me to ignore the magnificence of the person trapped within the body which was confined to the chair. Stunned, I returned to my seat like a scolded child, and waited.

Taking what seemed like forever to shuffle and re-shuffle her papers, the silence persisted, and this class of usually restless senior students was still. "Let's get on with it!" my teacher's mind pleaded, eyes on the clock. Finally a strong, clear voice, a foil to the woman's failing body, freed her listeners with a question: "What did you feel when you realized that an older woman would be talking to you today?"

Students fidgeted self-consciously.

She began again: "When you first looked at me, did you think I'd be feeble-minded and forgetful, and that youth is the most desirable thing? You know," she added, "we are all in the process of aging."

The eyes of all students were, like mine, downcast, avoiding the truths we were hearing.

"What do you think of me?" she asked, with calculated accusation in her voice. Teacher-like she waited for a response from some reticent student, and I looked up to see who she had singled out. Panic gripped my insides when I met her stare straight on.

"That you are old," I blurted.

I couldn't believe my stupidity at replying in such a shallow, no-mind manner. At least it was the truth. Surveying the young people before her, and lingering purposely on each syllable for effect, she said, "I feel I am wise, open-minded, alert, and very good at getting things done. So, you see, the way *you* think of me and the way *I* think of me are very different."

Now, with every eye on the visitor, she explained how frightening it was when her body would limit what her mind wanted to do. She spoke of the frustrations of relying on others to do what she had always been able to do for herself, and of the impatience of sharp-tongued young people who viewed her more as an imposition than as a human being. With that, she leaned forward to impart what we thought would be another frustration of old age. Lined lips hissed: "Sex! Yes, well, I don't know how it is nowadays, but when I was a little younger, this was a personal interaction with another person; something you shared with someone you cared about." With that same accusatory tone creeping back into her voice, she continued, "Younger people seem to think that this doesn't matter any more in a person's senior years."

The woman paused at this point as though to catch her breath. I wondered if she were about to single me out again. But then she hardened her jaw and announced, "Well, let me tell you people. I'm a person too, and if I wish to spend some romantic evening with some tall, grey, handsome man, I do not wish to broadcast it!" Convinced that she would explain further, we waited silently while she composed herself. I marvelled at the bittersweet passion in this small person before us, and wondered, only for a moment, if she were about to cry. Then, lowering her voice, she assured us that when someone wishes to spend some time alone with someone else in a residence, there is a facility provided. "There is a room . . . *one* room . . . designated for *all* residents who wish to spend some time alone." Prompting each and every one of us to think deeply about her next question, she asked, "Do you realize how humiliating this is?" I was just trying to imagine what it would be like when she snapped, "How would you feel if somebody, the whole world, could tell you what time you were with whom, and what you were doing, and for how long?" Uncertain laughter rippled through the room. Was this comic relief? Nervous energy resulting from having to face the indignities suffered by a generation who was well aware of our narrow-minded view of the elderly? It was almost as though she knew us better than we knew ourselves—as though she had not lost contact with the young woman she had been.

Then, she caught us again with an account of a married couple being "allowed" to live in the same room together but having to sleep in separate beds. With incredulity in her voice, she asked, "Do younger people feel that these two people are not responsible enough? After all, these are the same two people who were responsible enough to get married, raise a family, and take care of mortgages and bills. Are these two people all of a sudden unable to be trusted? Think about it!" she encouraged us.

I could feel a heaviness come upon me, a sense of hopelessness at the magnitude of the wrongs that seniors faced every day. The gentle hush in the room assured me that I was not alone with these feelings. It was this wonderful woman before us, Ethel Sherman, who set our minds at ease, assuring us that our time would come when we, too, would face the prejudices of the younger generation. She went on: "Old age is not a time to be agreeable but, rather, a time to be a rebel; a time to get out of life what you are willing to put into it." And again she illustrated that youth and age share similar experiences: loves, regrets, and plans for the future.

I had never really thought about an older person having a future. In fact, I had to confess that I hadn't given much thought at all to the realities of old age. Ethel's talk was good for us. As though we were coming to the end of an intense journey together, Ethel said, "We have touched hearts today, and for a few moments our minds became one." We knew that her time with us was about to end, and I felt, as I know others did, the heaviness which comes with saying goodbye to someone you care about. She reached haltingly for her tape recorder, and explained to us that before she went she would like us to hear a poem that was written by a friend of hers; a poem found on her closet floor after her friend had died. The tape recorder clicked on and, with gentle music in the background, Ethel read an intensely personal poem.

At this point, tears streaming down her face, tears mirrored in the faces of each one of my English students, Ethel Sherman took off her hat, reached for the elastic binding her powdered hair, and shook it free with a youthful flip of her head. With steady hands she peeled off the mask of age from her face to reveal the 18-year-old Penny Burnham, a member of the class. Her seminar complete, Penny waited, not knowing what to do next. Her classmates sat stunned by the intensity of the last hour. As her teacher, it was all I could do to contain the emotions which Penny's presentation had stirred within me. I, too, watched, waiting for the spell to break.

Suddenly, applause. Some students cried openly, or rushed up to hug the friend who had touched them so deeply; others remarked to anyone who was listening that Penny had really reached them, that she had certainly brought her experience to the classroom.

It was the singularly most powerful moment of my teaching career.

On first reflection, I couldn't believe that Penny's gripping presentation had anything to do with me or the changes I had made in my English curriculum, but it did. I marvelled at her passion and her commitment to her topic, and wondered why I had not had a similar experience during my own high school career, or university career, for that matter. I also wondered how I had learned to teach in such a powerful fashion, so different from my own experiences as a student.

I had decided early in life that I wanted to be a teacher, and I had experienced high school with that goal in mind. I could have observed my own teachers' successes and failures and tried to remember those methods which worked. After five years of university, I faced my first classes of Grade 10 students, thinking I knew quite a bit about teaching, and was shocked to learn that the students knew far more about effective and ineffective teaching methods than I did.

Paradoxically, it was teaching a geography course (not a strong subject of mine) which showed me the path I eventually followed in English teaching. Being a new teacher in the early 1980s demanded flexibility and willingness to teach out of your subject area; hence, I found myself struggling to teach a geography course which contained a unit on marine life. The challenge was to find a way to connect these young people, in the centre of the continent, to the bounty of the sea. Somehow, I knew that the textbook wasn't going to do it.

Inadvertently, I stumbled on the basis of what I now know to be experiential learning by asking the students to each choose a sea creature that we might eat, and then to find a recipe for serving it. The results were marvellous. Parents helped with recipes and volunteered to purchase the sea food at a nearby market. Students researched origins and market value of their fish in preparation for written and oral presentations. When the fish were delivered to the classroom, there was a wonderful hubbub of questions, suppositions, and explanations that I had never observed when working with the usual question-and-answer of textbook work. The next day, we feasted and made connections between the food we were eating and the places the food came from.

That was all very well for geography, but would it work in my English classes? The challenge was to figure out exactly what could be gleaned from my experiences with the geography class that could apply to a curriculum of literature and language, so I asked my students what made a lesson or a unit work for them.

The main message was that the curriculum was secondary to the methods of delivery; that learning happened when the teacher instilled in students a desire to learn; that every meeting with their teacher and peers should have personal meaning of some kind. The students were right. The geography students were directly involved in the marine life unit, and because they were making personal choices and decisions, they became curious and dedicated explorers. They were learning because they *wanted* to learn, not because they *had* to learn. The traditional role of the teacher as the person who imparted information to a disinterested audience was replaced by a teacher who worked with students who had taken some control of their own learning. My new task was to adopt a supportive role that would give students the direction and confidence they needed, emphasizing the process rather than the content of the English curriculum. It was these realizations that led to the Senior English Independent Study Program in which Penny Burnham found a place to shine.

The official government curriculum for this Senior English course reads, in part:

> Students ... are at an important stage in their personal development, a stage that will continue in their university years and beyond. [The courses] refine and extend skills and knowledge in the following areas:
>
> • speaking and writing proficiency;
>
> • response to literature and the articulation of this response;
>
> • enjoyment and appreciation of literature and the development of a reading habit;
>
> • understanding of language, its nature and functions;

- independence in reading, thought, and expression.

(Ministry of Education, Ontario Academic Courses, Senior Division Guidelines, 1984)

Ironically, the vagueness of the mandated English guidelines provided me with the opportunity to try out some of the methods that worked with my geography class. Other than the stipulations quoted above, the document instructs that topics should be developed from students' special interests, in consultation with the teacher, and that topics should arise out of the literature at hand or from the wide reading encouraged by the course. Worth 20% of the course weight, the independent study unit is to culminate in a formal report that includes an oral and a written component. It was here that I saw the potential to make English personally relevant to my students' lives. I created a standard independent study unit—selecting a topic, reading novels, writing an essay, and making an oral presentation—but added to these was the requirement that the students get involved personally with their topics through an experience of some sort. In their oral presentations, they were to discuss the novels they read and bring their experiences to life for their classmates. Penny's wasn't the only superb response to this challenge.

For example, Mary Anne explored her Italian roots through visual art. She used literature based on the life story of Michelangelo and began her moving presentation with a slide show of his art, interspersed with quotations from the literature. The highlight, however, was when she proudly unveiled her own oil painting and explained to the class how she had tried to imitate the master's style and technique.

Then there was Trevor, a student who openly disliked English and preferred to be working with his hands. He said that he wished we could do more hands-on things, as he was doing in his physics class. He was making a windmill out of bicycle tires, pulleys, and an old barrel cut in two. Trevor was able to combine his interest in physics and engineering with the classic novel, *Don Quixote*, and he dazzled the class with an oral presentation which addressed humanity's mechanical and metaphoric use of the windmill. He included a reading from the literature, a video of a play about Don Quixote, and a demonstration of his windmill. Here was an unabashed, reluctant student of English who talked authoritatively about human dreams using symbol and metaphor within the context of a complex piece of literature that would have been too difficult for him had he not had the personal connection through his interest in wind power.

Finally, I come back to Penny Burnham. Penny took a part-time job in a local nursing home and reached the hearts of the elderly residents there. For her project, she said that she was interested in reading about old age in order to better understand what her elderly friends were going through. She read a novel about an elderly woman who had been institutionalized; she interviewed nurses and residents in the home; she read locally available literature about services provided for the elderly, and she made good use of local libraries to further research gerontology. Penny used her experiences with drama to create Ethel Sherman, a composite of the character in the novel and the people she worked with at the home for the aged. She learned how to operate a wheelchair and, in order to become one with her character, she chose to wheel herself to school on the day of her oral presentation. She later explained to the class how disappointed she was when one of her own classmates walked by her on her way to school, choosing to ignore the old woman in the chair who needed help at the curb.

In Penny's presentation, I saw experiential education at its best. Penny was committed to learning; curious about her world, she went into the community to learn more about old age. She contacted experts and was current in her research; she was also able to unearth the poem that had brought the house down. Penny escaped the confining boundaries of conventional methods of learning, gaining the confidence to push herself beyond the limits of her own knowledge. She used the freedom to explore her choice of literature, and her risk taking was supported by a teacher committed to the process. She was naturally taking control of her own learning and, in doing so, learning became exciting, energizing, and pertinent because she could make her own insightful connections between real life and literature.

Successes like Penny's, Trevor's, and Mary Anne's have become part of my own experiential learning process. Through them I am able to reaffirm that meaningful and lasting education starts with people rather than curriculum. It is easier now to say "No" occasionally to lists of mandatory units and to embrace the extra time and energy this kind of teaching requires. Admittedly, we all need parameters; however, within these boundaries there is still ample room to see into the faces of each of our students and to realize that real learning for them will come when they are able to internalize facts and ideas through personal experience. Whether a student is struggling with a disability, wrestling with theoretical concepts, learning outdoors, or sitting at a desk, I am convinced that experiential education will bring to each a personal connection to the curriculum reminiscent of Ethel Sherman.

Chapter 3

EXPERIENTIAL LEARNING: A TEACHER'S PERSPECTIVE

Tom Herbert

Tom Herbert graduated from Cornell College with a BA in History and Education. Later, he gained an MS in Education from Oregon State. While teaching at Concord (New Hampshire) High School over some 25 years, Tom has started two different experiential courses and has worked to "experientialize" traditional classes. His mentor in experiential education was Keith King. Tom has received several state awards for his teaching.

In his chapter, which is both personal and professional, Tom provides a picture of a thoughtful and successful teacher making sense out of his practice. He demonstrates the meeting of theory and practice, not as one driving the other, but rather as a kind of dialogue. Tom's great contribution is in expanding the notion of adventure beyond wilderness travel and ropes courses. In doing this, he gives many practical hints for practice in any subject in any school. A similar version of this chapter appears in Kraft and Kielsmeier, *Experiential Learning in Schools and Higher Education* (Boulder, Association for Experiential Education, 1995).

When I first came across the idea of experiential learning, I thought it took place only at a ropes course or in the woods. As a classroom teacher I struggled to make my classes more experiential, but found that this limiting idea made it difficult to do. Then I modified my working definition to be "active learning." With this definition, I started to make changes in my teaching techniques. But I still had numerous questions, such as, if it was active, did it automatically mean it was experiential? Could an outdoor program not be experiential?

I took a sabbatical leave to try and answer just two of my questions. These were: "What is experiential learning?" and "How can the experiential process be applied to the classroom?" This paper presents some of my findings.

What is Experiential Learning?

Originally, I viewed experiential learning in an either/or framework. Either a teaching strategy was experiential or it was not. Upon reflection, I realized that this was false. It is much more accurate to look at it as a continuum or sliding scale. One end of the scale has passive students receiving transmitted knowledge and the other end has active students deeply involved in generating knowledge from their own experiences.

I looked for answers to my questions in research literature. Gibbons and Hopkins (1985) and Warren (1988) describe students' involvement in their learning. At one extreme is the transmission of information, where students passively receive the experience of others as interpreted by the teacher. This learning is second- or third-hand. Sometimes this type of learning is important. For example, teachers would not want their students to learn to cross streets safely by walking in front of cars. At the other end of this continuum, students experience learning firsthand and draw meaning and information from their own experiences. The teacher's role is one of guide, resource, and clarifier (Warren, 1988).

Mosston and Ashworth (1990) write about teaching and learning styles. They visualize two separate tracks that can, but do not necessarily, intersect. Both tracks involve decision making—what kinds of decisions are made and who makes them? In some situations, teachers make the decisions about major issues. In others, it is the students who decide. The same goes for other types of problems facing the class. Mosston and Ashworth attach no moral value to either end, or to the middle, of the spectrum of styles. They do point out that all styles have implications for students becoming independent and critical thinkers. Mosston's work enables a teacher to understand the process of transferring more decisions to students while at the same time changing the quality of those decisions.

The two models described above are important when thinking about experiential learning because of the importance of active involvement in the learning process. When students are encouraged to make more decisions, especially important ones about meaning, interpretation, and content, the learning is more directly experiential. When important decisions are to be made, and the students make fewer of them and the teacher more, the experiential base for learning tends to diminish. It is possible to have students be very active, but not make many decisions. "Active" does not translate into "experiential." The central distinction is the responsibility assigned to the students to derive meaning from what they have done.

There are five variables that helped me explore the range of experiential learning. They are reality, risk, responsibility, predictability, and reflection. Each deserves a closer look.

Reality of Experience

The impact of learning depends on the amount of reality involved, the directness of the experience, and the number of senses used. Interviewing a former prisoner of war, for example, is going to result in longer lasting learning than reading an interview conducted by someone else. Neither will have the impact of actually being a prisoner of war.

Jernstedt (1980) studied the psychology of experiential learning in academic courses at college. He found that active learning is more effective than passive learning.

Students who use information they are trying to learn, who challenge and grapple with their new knowledge, or who use it to solve new problems, tend to learn more effectively than students who passively read, memorize or merely absorb that to which they have been exposed. . . . Learners remember not what they encounter while learning, so much as what they do while learning. (p. 12)

Vicarious experiences, for example, relevant stories and movies, have a kind of reality which helps to secure learning. Jernstedt (1980) reported that "tying information to be learned to experience, even when the experience is purely hypothetical, can preserve learning within the mind and prime the mind for new learning more effectively than other techniques" (p. 13).

Jernstedt's investigation of the contribution of vicarious experience to the perception of reality in an academic context can be summarized as follows:

1. Whole-class experiences, such as reading a novel or taking a trip, are better than individual experiences because they have been shared by the class and can be validated.

2. Printed handouts and examples drawn from real life are remembered more accurately and longer than information taught without them.

3. Demonstrations are remembered best and for the longest periods of time, and they should be chosen for their intellectual value and not simply as motivational aids.

4. Modeling, in which the instructor actually engages in the behavior which the students are trying to learn, has a powerful, positive effect on learning.

The pioneer research of Jernstedt (1980) has been richly amplified in other work. Finkel and Monk (1985), Warren (1988), and Biedler (1987), to mention only a few, all give examples which put principles articulated by Jernstedt into practice. Other research, such as that of Allen (1987), Yerkes (1988), and Horwood (1994), shows that these principles apply at the elementary and secondary levels as well as at college.

Levels of Risk

The condition of reality helps generate a sense of risk and uncertainty for the learner. John Dewey (1938) states that ". . . growth depends upon the presence of difficulty to be overcome by the exercise of intelligence" (p. 79). The difficulty Dewey refers to can be physical, emotional, social, or intellectual. It could be the result of having to make a speech on a personally important issue, finding oneself in what is perceived to be a dangerous situation, or being relied upon by other class members to complete a task.

In using this discordant atmosphere, the teacher must also take care to create an environment of trust and support, without which the learner will not risk anything. For example, my high school sociology class discussed different types of risk in class participation. The class concluded that being called on by a teacher was of relatively little risk because your opinion was being solicited. You were not being given a choice of expressing it or not. To volunteer an opinion involved more risk—what you said had to have some value to you because you were offering it. Class discussions and opinion sharing are important to our class. Therefore, we do not allow "killer statements" or put-downs. We disagree, but disagree without personal judgments. To do otherwise would be to foster a climate where only a few would be willing to risk.

This concept of risk has been defined as a "vigorous environment … any place in which you are uncomfortable, or any place in which you have not learned to behave [competently]" (King, 1981, p. 1). Thus, there can be risk involved on the dance floor or on a rock wall, spending time alone or standing in front of a group, or working in a day care center or an old age home. Vigorous environments vary for the individual.

The greater the level of risk, the more real one perceives the consequences of one's actions to be. The sense of reality in those consequences helps to involve the entire person in the experience. It is no longer solely a physical or intellectual exercise. The reality of the consequences that arises from the uncertainty is the glue that cements the learning for the individual.

Sense of Responsibility

In experiential learning, there is a feeling of personal investment in what is being undertaken. The learner is involved in decisions leading up to the experience. He or she chooses the course, the assignment, or method of presentation, helps in the construction of the test, and participates in the decision of what should be covered in the unit of study. This establishes a high level of responsibility and expectation on the part of the student.

Once students have been involved in the decision making, they also have a responsibility to help carry it through. Instead of remaining on the sidelines as a recipient of someone else's decisions, the learner is now responsible for implementing them. Eliot Wigginton (1978) once advised staff members of a basic belief at Foxfire: "Before you start to do anything related to your work in this organization, ask yourself first why a student is not doing it instead. If you don't have a good reason, then go and find a student —preferably one who has not done it before" (p. 30). In experiential learning, teachers are not responsible for their students' learning so much as they are responsible to their students to help them learn.

Students involved in experiential learning make decisions that affect their learning. A teacher committed to experiential learning must be willing to accept the consequences of those student decisions. The only exceptions to this are decisions that affect the safety of an individual or group. In these cases, student decisions must be carefully monitored and may be occasionally overruled by the teacher.

The commitment by the teacher to the student's exposure to the consequences of his or her own decisions is sufficiently difficult and important to warrant two examples from my own practice. In planning a March trip to a mountain lake, a student in the ROPE class (a modified Outward Bound course at Concord High School, New Hampshire) asked to take along his fishing pole. Our response was that as long he had the proper licenses it was not a problem. We did not tell him of the thick layer of ice that we expected to find. When we arrived, he went down to the lake with his small hatchet to chop a hole in the ice. Before we left the next day, he was still chopping in the hole, visible only from the waist up.

The point here is that the staff expected an impossibly thick layer of ice. Yet we made it possible for him to learn this for himself in a far more meaningful way than if we had told him that bringing fishing gear would not be useful. He ended up bringing fishing tackle on every subsequent trip, as a matter of pride, I suspect. On the last trip, a bike tour, he finally managed to hook something—his hand—while riding his bike.

The second example is from an oral history class, called "Homegrown," that I used to teach. Each year, the class took a 12-day trip to another part of the country, not to sightsee, but to learn from local people in other regions. On one occasion, the class had set up a seminar with a local resource person from a college. He was an extremely easygoing and humorous person, until he got in front of a group. In that formal situation he became boring, reading verbatim from his notes. True to form, this trip he had nearly half the class nodding off within 20 minutes. When we went for a break, I asked the class if everyone had liked the first half of his presentation. After a few initial grumbles and foot shuffles, someone, in understatement, said, "Uh, I think he's a bit dry." I then asked if there was any way they could change his method of presentation to make him feel more comfortable. After talking for a few minutes, they decided to ask him questions and get him telling stories. The second half was much more interesting and the speaker enjoyed it more, too, because he could feel the students' interest through their questions.

In this example, I asked a question to determine if the students were dissatisfied with the presentation. If they had been content, I would have let the issue drop. I could not impose my opinion at this point without undermining students' responsibility. In later discussion, if they continued to have positive reactions to the session, contrary to my own experience of boredom, I would let the matter rest. Otherwise, it would be an opportunity to hold a discussion on how they might deal with boring presentations another time. In this example, it was the students who said that the presentation was boring. I was not imposing my evaluation. This is not to say that the teacher must never express his or her opinions. On the contrary, the teacher must be responsible to the class to reveal insights and understandings but always in a context and at a time which supports the pattern of decision making and student responsibility. Teachers must always be aware of the special weight which their opinions carry and how expressing them can unduly influence students' decisions.

In these examples, carrying a fishing pole and not taking initiative to alter a boring, guest speaker's presentation are not "mistakes." The only true mistakes are experiences one doesn't learn from, or that don't lead to further learning. What is ordinarily perceived to be a mistake in school is better understood as an acceptable part of experiential learning because the focus of learning is on the process of achieving a goal, as well as on the goal itself.

Predictability and Planning

In experiential learning, the specific outcome is not always predictable. This is a result of the students' involvement in decision making and the teacher's role being that of clarifier, rather than leader, and the overall value of process in preference to product. The wide range of student options requires the teacher to plan for an equally wide range of possible outcomes. Each possibility must be anticipated and researched. Student choices should not be limited by inadequate planning on the part of the teacher. At the same time, enthusiasm should not be tempered by overplanning.

Anticipating every possible outcome and planning for it removes some of the adventure and discovery for the teacher. Nothing can replace that genuine shared enthusiasm between teacher and class. This is a fine line for the teacher to walk: how much to plan and how much to leave to circumstance depends on both the teacher's experience and confidence in being able to adjust to the moment.

It is tempting for the teacher to try to manipulate the students to select one plan for which the teacher is ready. It can also be frustrating for the teacher to plan for five possibilities, knowing full well that only one of them may be selected. It is important for the teacher to appreciate the significance of choice in experiential learning in order to keep his or her frustration at manageable levels.

An example of this kind of prediction and planning in my practice comes from students making decisions about the format of their reports. Thinking about it, I anticipate that some students will write, as usual. What other options are there? Tape record it! Are tape recorders available for students to use? Videotape it! Is there someone available to instruct students in use of the camcorders? A photographic essay! Can students get materials and help from the school's photography lab? Once answers to these and related questions are determined, the teacher knows what is possible. Without this knowledge, there are really no options for students at all. But all this background information is not passed on to the students because it is up to them to make their choices and find out the needed resources on their own. If they get stymied, the teacher may offer hints or possibilities without robbing the student of the central experience.

Sometimes a student will propose an option that has not been expected. Rather than reject it, the teacher should encourage the student to develop the idea further. Perhaps the student will discover that it is truly unreasonable. On the other hand, perhaps the teacher will learn that it is possible.

Reflection

In experiential learning, the student decides what he or she has learned from the experiences. One method of learning is reflection on the experience, thinking about what happened and one's position in the process. Reflection includes separating elements in the experience (analysis) and connecting those elements with other experiences and knowledge (synthesis), as well as other mental activities, such as feeling emotions. Reflection can be verbal or nonverbal, alone or as a group, or alone with the instructor or with the class and the instructor. There are many effective ways. It should also be understood that analysis and reflection does not take place only after the planned activity. It takes place when it is needed during the activity. The goal is to achieve learning and it doesn't matter at which points in the educational sequence learning happens. The critical thing is that experience alone is not necessarily educative— it must be turned into learning by thought.

To be effective facilitators of reflection, teachers must be keen observers of events and people. Then, at appropriate times, observations may be offered, questions asked, or feelings explored.

Teachers should also be able to vary the methods of helping students analyze what has taken place. The choice of methods depends on the personalities and the situations involved. At times it might be necessary to be blunt and honest with feedback. At other times, questions, discussions, or a gentle approach will enable students to discover for themselves the significance of what they have done and how they are perceived. Sometimes nothing needs to be said. It is difficult for teachers to know which method is the ideal one to use. Experience, with reflection, is a good teacher.

Another stimulus for reflection and connection in experiential learning is the application of newly learned material, such as a skill, in another demanding situation. Repeated re-application of learning helps to reinforce it and also helps to ensure that students have not made the learning in isolation. Applications in other contexts help to integrate learning. Without such bridge-building, what is learned in the woods will stay in the woods, what is learned in science will stay in science, and what is learned in school will stay in school.

An example of forging this sort of connection is found in the speech requirement of the ROPE class in Concord High School. I am often asked, "Why require a five-minute prepared speech as part of an outdoor adventure class?" The reasons are twofold. First, it helps students to recognize that fear is fear, whether it is on a rock face or in front of a group of people. If you use your inner strength to overcome fear in one place, the same source of strength is available to help in the other. And why stop tapping that strength in only those two fearful settings? The second reason is so that those students who felt little or no fear on the rock face can understand something about those people who did, when the roles are exchanged and they stand alone in front of the class, sharing a part of themselves. These repeated applications of experience go beyond metaphoric implications of a single experience and seek to make the connections concrete.

Pulling it Together

The interrelationship of the above five factors is complex. It is impossible to modify one without affecting the others. The level of risk is at least partially determined by the reality of the experience and vice versa. Student responsibility for learning makes it less predictable. Students' reflection determines what meaning emerges from all the others.

The first three factors (reality, risk, and responsibility) work in parallel. The greater the reality, the higher the level of risk, and the more responsible the students are, the more directly experiential is the learning process. Movement on these scales influences predictability. In general, the higher any of the first three, the less predictability there is. The methods and timing of reflection will depend on all four factors. The teacher must be prepared to deal with considerable ebb and flow.

There have been numerous attempts to explain these complexities by placing them into flow charts. One of the earliest (Gager, 1977) shows a flow sequence in which the learner, placed in a demanding reality context, must master a new skill and apply it with reflection in a challenging setting. The result is that the students "learn" through a reorganization of their individual understandings. Another widely used experiential learning cycle has been developed by Kolb (1974). In this cycle, four phases are connected in a continuous cycle of learning. Concrete experience flows into reflective observation and the resulting thought generates abstract conceptualization, the implications of which are tested by active experimentation. The cycle is completed as the results of active experimentation become a new set of concrete experiences.

Joplin (1981) has developed a widely cited model. Her flow path is through a spiraling sequence of focus, challenging action, and debriefing (reflection) which leads to another round. For Joplin, it is essential that these actions be embedded in a climate of support and feedback.

In practice, each of these models helps our understanding of some aspects of the experiential learning process. But each one also fails to meet the rich complexities of human interaction and individuality.

The teacher should use insights from such mechanical models and then be ready to flow with events in a more organic way.

How Can Experiential Learning Be Applied in the Classroom?

The problems of application are not only with the limitations of the classroom itself. Rather, they are the other restrictions that go along with being part of a school: noise level, time constraints, student and teacher responsibilities in other classes, and transportation, to name a few. Also, it is a problem to create a vigorous environment, as defined by King (1981), in a place where students already have an established pattern of behavior. Finally, it must be remembered that students have very little choice whether to be in school or not. Since student choice is an important part of experiential learning, this is an almost impossible problem to overcome for students who don't want to be in school at all.

Here are some of the ways I have found to work around these restrictions. No doubt there are other ways I have yet to learn. Students have to be in school. Without getting into the merits of the issue here, I simply deal with the law by accepting it as a given in my work.

I tend to view concerns like noise, time, outside commitments, and transportation simply as problems to be dealt with. They are difficult but not insurmountable. They can be overcome. It helps me to be flexible, reasonable, and good-humored in what I do. I try very hard not to impinge too much or too often on other teachers and I find that with these operating principles, I can usually teach as experientially as I want. A classic example is the "seats-in-a-row" problem. I like moving desks around to fit what the class does. Other teachers with whom I share the room (and the desks) don't. Instead of a cold war, we have established the "Concord High Compromise": they put the desks in a circle for me and I replace the rows for them. The point is that different lessons occupy different places on the various spectrums and require different arrangements. It is not a matter of right and wrong, but a matter of mutual accommodation.

It is also possible to create vigorous environments where students can be challenged within a behaviorally acceptable climate. First I determine the students' behavioral norms, the ways in which they are accustomed to act in various parts of school work. Then the way is clear to begin the process of changing expectations. For example, students accustomed to a large amount of teacher decision making will find the shift to student decision making a vigorous environment. Students used to individual tests will find that group tests challenge their ways of acting. Since there are many students in a class with different school experiences, what counts as a vigorous environment for some may not have vigor for others. I meet this need by changing the pattern on an irregular and unpredictable basis. One of my favorite bits of feedback from my students is that they come to class because they don't know what to expect.

The concept of adventure is also helpful when one is faced with these restrictions. Lentz, Smith, Stentowski, and Seidman (1976) identify four elements that comprise adventure education. One of these, the idea of having an adventure, is different from the stereotype of adventure programs which seems confined to wilderness travel or high ropes courses. Many adventurous people have not been adventurers in the wilderness travel sense of the word. Yet they have been on an adventure in different ways. These adventures could be the development of their first photograph, writing a book review and sending it to the book's author, reading one's own poetry in public, or discovering a possible solution to a problem facing a social agency in one's community. It is not necessary to go to the top of a mountain to have an adventure.

There are essential elements common to all adventures. Three of them are the same as the first three factors in experiential learning: reality, risk, and responsibility. As a general operating principle, having an adventure in school supports experiential learning by creating conditions in which students feel that their work is real, that they are exposed to some risk and have ownership for the situation and the outcomes.

There are three ways to build adventure into the school curriculum, depending on the amount of time available. One of the most obvious adventures is for the class to go on an extended field trip. The duration could be for the weekend or for as long as several weeks. It could be a trip to the ocean or the mountains to study ecology, a sociological study in a large city neighborhood, or a history class reenacting a long march across a state. Preparations in the classroom focus on the trip and become part of the adventure. Fund raising, development of the areas of study, logistics, relations with the rest of the school, and media contacts are only a few of the activities that can become part of the set of learning experiences.

The second adventure curriculum is planned to take a few hours. Here the time available limits not only what can be done, but also where. The advantage is that it can be more easily negotiated within the school's time and budget framework. Half-day field trips to a funeral home or to a prison are examples of adventures in vigorous environments for most students, and they contribute to experiential learning in the social sciences. An English class that presents an act of a play being studied to a school assembly or to a local nursing home is having an adventure. The French class that uses the school's home economics facilities to prepare (and eat!) French pastries, while speaking only French, is having an adventure. The possibilities, limited only by imagination, apply to every subject.

The third time interval is the class period. It is the most accessible but also the most constrained as to content and place. Reality and risk in these short adventures are reduced, but the experiential teacher should not be deterred because the opportunities are many, and significant experiences as part of the day-in and day-out schedule are critical and cumulative. It may be discouraging not to be able to pull off the big adventure, but the accumulating impact of daily lessons is equally important in the long run.

Within a classroom period, adventures can be provided that sustain direct experience. A lesson on trust will emerge from a blindfolded Trust Walk in or around the school. A study of prisons will become more real following a period of sensory deprivation. An important decision in history will gain focus by a related problem-solving task with which students must grapple. An English teacher uses obscure facts and little known people to create a mystery which students can only solve by learning how to use the reference section of the library. Routine testing becomes an adventure when half a class creates a test for the other half to take, and vice versa.

In my sociology classes, it was possible to use repeated single-class periods and homework time for a sustained exploration of social agencies in our town. Students determined that they were responsible for contacting an agency and spending ten hours of service time there. Then, they were expected to determine what social problems the agency was trying to deal with and suggest some practical solutions for them. Students prepared reports for the class and for the agency's reaction. Other small group and individual projects that call on reality, risk, and responsibility can be organized to fit the time available in class periods.

Conclusion

In trying to answer the two questions I posed at the outset, I have come to realize two central and critical points. First, it is absolutely essential to the implementation of experiential learning to work at understanding its flow and process. Second, experiential learning can happen in any place and subject where people are interested in having it.

It is easy for busy teachers to latch on to the superficial or symbolic aspects of an educational process without understanding the underlying philosophy. Their efforts fail and they return to what they were doing before because the newly adopted methods are not supported by adoption of related values. Without the principles of experiential learning, it is not possible to successfully translate classical experiential symbols such as ropes courses and cultural journalism magazines into each teacher's unique setting.

Romantic and large-scale experiential programs cloud the fact that ordinary classroom teachers can implement experiential learning on a small scale within their schools and within their subjects. An adventure does not have to be monumental to count. Leo Buerman, a person with severe birth defects and sheltered for most of his life, said in a film on his life, "Courage is a factor in many things that are seemingly insignificant." It is one of the jobs of the experiential teacher to find those things and arrange events so that students learn from them.

For me, as teacher, experiential learning is an adventure in and of itself. I feel the reality, risk, and responsibility just as my students do. Although it is hard to plan for all the various options, to deal with the unexpected, and to remain flexible to students' needs, the results can be worth it. Please note that I did not write "will be" worth it in the previous sentence. In experiential learning and teaching there are no guarantees, for if there were, reality, risk, and responsibility would be lost. But if I, and others like me, can run the risk of failure and determine to learn from it, then, as teachers, we become learners, too, and have the best of both worlds.

References

Allen, J. (1987). Gunpowder River project: Experiential education in a large public school system. *Journal of Experiential Education, 10*(3), 11-15.

Biedler, P. (1987). Bee weekend. *Journal of Experiential Education, 10*(3), 23-27.

Dewey, J. (1938). *Experience and education.* New York: Collier.

Finkel, D. L. and Monk, S. G. (1985). The design of intellectual experience. In R. Kraft and M. Sakofs (Eds.), *The theory of experiential education* (2nd ed.) (pp. 183-190). Boulder, CO: Association for Experiential Education.

Gager, R. (1977). Experiential learning process flow. *Voyageur Reports of the Association for Experiential Education, 1*(1).

Gibbons, M., & Hopkins, D. (1985). How experiential is your experience-based program? In R. Kraft and M. Sakofs (Eds.), *The theory of experiential education* (2nd ed.) (pp. 135-140). Boulder, CO: Association for Experiential Education.

Horwood, B. (1994). Integration and experience in the secondary curriculum. *McGill Journal of Education, 29*(1), 89-102.

Jernstedt, G. (1980). Experiential components in academic courses. *Journal of Experiential Education, 3*(2).

Kolb, D. A. (1974). On management and the learning process. In D. A. Kolb, I. M. Rubin, & J. M. McIntyre (Eds.), *Organizational psychology. A book of readings* (2nd ed.) (pp. 27-42). Englewood Cliffs, NJ: Prentice Hall.

Lentz, B., Smith, M., Stentowski, A., & Seidman, M. (1976). *Teaching through adventure: A practical approach.* Hamilton, MA: Project Adventure.

Mosston, M., & Ashworth, S. (1990). *The spectrum of teaching styles: From command to discovery.* White Plains, NY: Longman.

Warren, K. (1988). The student directed classroom: A model for teaching experiential education theory. *Journal of Experiential Education, 11*(1), 4-9.

Yerkes, R. (1988). What about the young child? *Journal of Experiential Education, 11*(2), 21-25.

Chapter 4

HISTORY COMES ALIVE

Gary Shultz

Gary Shultz was educated at Queen's University in Kingston, Ontario, with a BA, BPHE, and BEd. He has taken a strong lead in developing experiential curricula within his school district, specializing in programs which build on cooperative interaction among schools, community, and government agencies. With 18 years of teaching experience in the intermediate grades and his current experience as an elementary school vice-principal, Gary is well qualified to tell the story of experiential programs in history.

This chapter outlines the development of history programs based at heritage sites. The programs are of particular importance in the way that they demonstrate the creation and maintenance of wide-ranging cooperation among various heritage organizations and groups. The chapter also makes a strong contribution to the experiential teaching of history. As Gary would be the first to point out, cooperation among agencies is of little value if it fails to excite interest and knowledge in the pupils. Gary's enthusiastic account does not hide the difficulties to be overcome and should serve to inspire history teachers everywhere to explore the heritage potential within their own communities.

Introduction

"History" is boring. We teachers have lived with this common, and sometimes justified, complaint from all levels and abilities of students. Realizing that my school system was not using the wealth of historical opportunities that existed in our own communities, I undertook to make history exciting by using community resources as the sites for students to truly experience history. The set of programs called *History Comes Alive* was designed and piloted as a series of historical simulations and activities in local heritage sites. The sites were developed to be the tools for direct experiential learning. Textbooks, the focus of so many complaints about memorization of unimportant facts, became secondary resources. Students from kindergarten to college were about to find out that history relived is history discovered. And it is far from boring.

This chapter demonstrates how local historical sites were developed to provide interactive experiences for students. These experiences led to exciting accomplishments and learning covering all areas of student achievement. Sample activities are described, and student and teacher responses are outlined as examples of experiential learning in a historical context.

Developing the Programs

Assumptions

Students learn best by doing. But how can grade school children "do" history? I decided that students could learn to understand and appreciate their heritage by reliving the past. This is achieved by simulating, as realistically as possible, life in a specific historical setting, like living for three days and two nights aboard a decommissioned icebreaker. Spending at least one overnight period seemed necessary to gain the full benefit of reliving the historical setting. Students also use these experiences to explore their present social contexts.

History Comes Alive is more than a set of history lessons. There is a firm curriculum connection covering all subject areas in each package including music, technology, drama, and computers. Although central importance is given to the on-site experiential field trip, I assume that the best learning takes place when students apply knowledge and have motivation across a variety of subject areas.

Programs involving out-of-school sites must engage the classroom teachers and site interpreters in cooperative and clearly defined roles. An important assumption is that the programs have to make sense to the people both in the schools and in the heritage sites and that clear, functional roles have to be defined for them.

Another mandate of *History Comes Alive* is the stimulation of each individual student, the development of motivation and self-direction as they learn to appreciate their heritage. At the same time, working cooperatively within a healthy social structure is also valued.

The Inventory

The first task was to establish an inventory of possible historical opportunities for learning. The list of possible resources turned out to be staggering. Imagine the chance to set programs of study comparing a 17th-century fur trading post with a 19th-century British fort staffed by uniformed interpreters. A museum of marine history had potential for studying firsthand the archaeology of our past as a shipbuilding centre, trans-shipment port, and the only inland British naval dockyard in the Empire. There was a 200-mile waterway and a canal system engineered and constructed through primeval bush 150 years ago. Finally, there was a fully interpreted 19th-century residence of our country's founding Prime Minister, a National Historic Site managed by Parks Canada, the federal agency responsible for National Parks. With this wealth of experiential learning possibilities, the challenge was not to find sites but to prioritize their relevance in providing situational learning experiences matched to the school's curriculum.

Designing the Activities

The next task was to get cooperation from the federal, provincial, and private agencies who operate the sites to design hands-on experiences for student excursions. This meant going beyond the more usual, forgettable outings: "Walk through, listen, and do not touch anything." Another change for the agencies was to connect proposed activities with learning outcomes required by the government-authorized curriculum.

Initially, I undertook to develop the educational potential in one of Canada's foremost historical fortifications, Fort Henry. The development matched the Ontario Ministry of Education history curriculum guidelines for Grades 7-9 students, entitled "Early Canadian Communities" and "Building the Nation." It took a year of challenging negotiations with the personnel who manage and operate Fort Henry to organize and prepare a set of activities. At the same time, a working relationship between school teachers and interpreters at the Fort was established which promised to continue the program for a long period.

I quickly learned that developing these activities would require overcoming red tape which had little to do with curriculum. It was necessary to convince the Fire Marshal's Office that fortifications built of huge limestone blocks would not be burned down by careless youth. The Health Department officials had to be persuaded that washroom and cooking facilities would not cause scurvy, smallpox, or other diseases of the time period of study. With patience, it was possible to receive splendid cooperation from all parties and agencies involved. Today, thousands of students from our own county, other parts of Ontario, and neighbouring New York State participate in the Fort Henry educational programs.

A similar set of negotiations was conducted to establish each of the other programs. One of the most productive ones involved establishing a working partnership among our School Board, Parks Canada (the national parks service) and its local interpreters, the Rideau Canal Museum Board, and community residents in Chaffey's Locks, a small village on the Rideau Canal. It is a remarkable contribution to education when agencies and individuals like these work together with students in such a direct and positive manner. These partnerships are constantly being updated and sustained at meetings with all parties involved.

These successful negotiations with multiple agencies and individuals gave me the experience I needed to develop a set of activities where students would relive the marine past of the Great Lakes through investigative research and archaeological study of local shipbuilding. If red tape seemed to be a stumbling block earlier, imagine trying to convince officials that 36 students could live aboard a moored, decommissioned, 210-ft. Coast Guard vessel of 1,607 tons, using it as a classroom for two or three days and nights! The key step was to convince people to let us pilot our project while assuring parents there would be no moonlight diving off the crow's nest. A series of successful excursions soon overcame concerns and original objections. We were even allowed to take off our life jackets!

The role of the classroom teacher is to act as facilitator and generate a high level of interest in the unit of study. The teacher should introduce the program using motivational materials, both print and non-print, and arrange to provide follow-up materials (videos, archival documents, computing resources, guest speakers, and books). Children need to be prepared not only attitudinally for the program but also with suitable clothing and equipment for the outing. The teachers must open, and maintain, close communication with the site interpreters.

The role of the site interpreters is to bring the magic and drama of the historical simulations to life. The interpreters create the atmosphere in which students are caught up in their roles as people living in historical settings. Interpreters are also the expert sources of information, providing specific site-related knowledge and insights which teachers may not reasonably have.

Communication is vital to the success of the programs. There must be pre-trip discussions between the classroom teacher and the site interpreters to clarify mutual expectations in logistics and instruction. When both parties recognize each other's enthusiasm and commitment, there is a high probability for success.

Support Documents

Once designed and tested, each program is outlined in a support document which describes the program's activities and the required preparations and procedures to use when arranging a visit. *History Comes Alive* currently contains five programs.

"Fort Henry: An Educational Experience" outlines the range of experiential visits to Fort Henry, lasting from a few hours to an overnight stay. The Fort Henry program now provides experiences of life in a 19th-century fort suited to ages from kindergarten to adult.

"The Rideau Canal: An Educational Outing" outlines the comparative studies available along the 100-mile-long waterway and canal system joining Lake Ontario to the Ottawa River to the north. Students experience the daily life of workers along the canal system and at locks built in the early 1800s. Both day trips and overnight visits are possible.

"The Marine Museum of the Great Lakes: Shipbuilding in Kingston" focuses on the early shipbuilding and transportation activity in the area. The Museum itself is a rich collection of marine artifacts and archaeological research. A decommissioned Coast Guard vessel, moored at the Museum, provides a realistic site to experience life on board a working Great Lakes ship. Overnight stays on the ship and the associated hands-on learning highlight this unit of study and make it adaptable to various age and grade levels.

"Historic Kingston: Walking Through our Past" encourages students to walk through the city of King's Town as though it were the early 1800s. Excursions vary in duration but they are all detailed, with self-guiding features designed to support individual interests and curiosity. Stops at major points of interests must be arranged in advance.

"Our Historic Waterfront by Ship or Sail" outlines the options to explore the historic waterfront with its mix of military and commercial activity, ancient and modern. Students choose between boarding a sail training ship or a replica paddle steamer. Costumed interpreters and crew help provide a touch of realism with information about the significance of the vessels and the waterfront in the students' heritage.

Sample Programs

Each of the five programs in the set has a different character, but they have common features. Careful preparation is required. Students often wear some aspect of period costume; they live out several aspects of life in the setting being studied. Where possible, they sleep at least one night within the historical context. The heritage experience is extended in subsequent classroom work, which may include writing journals, extracting information from related historical documents, works of art and drama, cooking period food from authentic recipes, and preparing a celebration of the unit of study for parents and friends.

These common elements will be illustrated by examples from the Fort Henry and Rideau Canal programs.

The Fort Henry Experience

The central feature of the Fort Henry experience is playing the role of a recruit in a British regiment of the mid-19th century. Students wear uniform tunics and caps and perform recruit drills of the period while surrounded by the sights, sounds, smells, and mystique of the great stone fort. All of this is under the watchful eye and noisy guidance of the recruit Corporal—for many students, as for military recruits anywhere, it is their worst nightmare. They also meet kindliness and concern as a second costumed interpreter, the Corporal's assistant, gives students helpful advice and suggestions just in time to be ready for the next inspection. The students literally step into learning the meticulous attention to detail of the life and daily struggles of the 19th-century British soldier. "What do you mean no walkmans, no video games, no hair dryers, or no makeup! Why would we want to go to some place like this?" sums up the initial reaction of a Grade 8 student.

Students sleep in barrack rooms on replica cast-iron cots and take their meals in the mess of the period. The ceremonial events of garrison life, such as flag lowering and raising, with proper musketry salutes, are carefully followed. The evening is a more relaxed time for storytelling and experiencing a lesson in the fort's school room.

Most students today have never experienced strict discipline such as that of a British regiment 150 years ago. For the duration of their visit, the students, as regimental recruits, are taught this discipline. For giggling, yawning, or not answering with the proper, "Yes, Corporal!", they receive extra sentry duty, the task of polishing cannons, or run laps around the parade square. This makes a lasting impression on all young recruits.

The Rideau Canal Experience

The Rideau Canal was an engineering marvel of its day. It still operates as a waterway joining Lake Ontario and the St. Lawrence River to the Ottawa River, some 200 miles to the north. Historically, it was a strategic device to link the safer inland Canadian capital with the vulnerable but economically valuable trade routes along the uneasy border with the United States of America. Building the canal was an epic undertaking for which large numbers of surveyors, masons, and labourers had to be obtained. Communities, which now hold some 150 years of canal history, sprang up as many of those people took their reward in the form of land grants along the waterway.

In this program, students play the parts of canal workers. Students may also examine and research four lockstations along the Canal, acting as mapmakers and Royal Engineers in a comparative study. Local residents in a village along the canal accommodate the young workers in their Community Hall. Community members within our partnership supply authentic period meals to the students after a tiring day of researching the Canal. They then bunk down on the Hall floor for a well-deserved rest.

The Celebration

The Celebration is the finale to a unit study in *History Comes Alive*. Parents, relatives, and others, like media invitees or agency personnel, gather with the students at the historical site. Students dress up in period costumes to describe their experiences in an evening of fun and demonstration of the joy of learning. Students display their curriculum work: written journals, diaries, and research papers. Creative murals and descriptive artwork line the walls, and technological and family-studies projects they created in shops and workrooms are displayed on the tables. Food of the day, which was prepared by the students, is enjoyed by all. Proud parents and guests listen attentively as educated students retell their experiences, all with remarkable retention of facts and descriptive recollection of the time period of study.

One of the personal and professional joys for the teacher in the celebration is to witness the public demonstration of students' accomplishments. It is the reward for the expenditure of energy and risk in leaving the safety of textbook and classroom.

Discussion

Responses of Participants

Through role playing life in earlier times, students suspend disbelief and quickly gain a sense of authenticity.

> I felt I returned to the past as I put on the artillery uniform. As the sergeant-major bellowed "Steady UP!" at me, a reality of having been transformed into the past truly sank in. I was a recruit of 1867. (Grade 8 student journal)

> For me the highlight was the way in which the soldiers at the Fort were able to suspend our disbelief, by sheer force of personality and unflinching attention to their roles, and allow us to get an authentic feel for what it was like to step from civilian life into the discipline of Her Majesty's army circa 1867. (Education professor)

Of special vivid recollection for students, adults included, is the use of the outhouses over earth pits as toilets. They record very descriptively their experiences of the "little ol' building out back":

> The curses of nature were truly felt. Cold toilet seats, humongous spiders and their webs, the smell, the noises at night make one realize true fear and a hurried trip to the outhouse. (Student teacher)

The popularity of "Fort Henry: An Educational Experience" far surpassed original expectations as over 1,400 students have annually discovered this part of their heritage. The numbers of participants in the other programs are rising as more educators become aware of the opportunities for out-of-classroom learning. Students not only learned, but also discovered the joy of learning. The diversity of activities in the programs works to challenge students at all levels of capabilities. This includes provisions for special-needs students to access all facets of the programs. Gaining knowledge through hands-on experiences lets students who learn in a different way shine in group situations.

Teachers note an improved climate in the classroom and a trend for students to be more responsible. There is a higher level of discussion among students, and observable gains in retention. Teachers participating in the programs praise the opportunities for building life skills, with improved problem solving and cooperation as important accomplishments.

> Even the sawdust on the floor needed to be swept up and beds aligned. Our group, as a matter of survival from the Private's wrath, quickly bonded and worked cooperatively as a team. (University student)

Opportunities to sketch, sing, and incorporate drama into their understanding while in historical settings allowed creative growth and expression while replacing formal lectures and testing within the classroom. Teachers watch with delight as real learning is experienced. The students truly are the players as each drama unfolds.

> The students relate to reliving their past as actors in a play, and working together is the best method of learning. We all had to place ourselves into the time warp. (Grade 8 teacher)

Learning doesn't stop when the role playing ends and the bus rolls back to school. Follow-up discussions, related role playing at school, assignments, and library research encourage expansion and extension of the experience. Learning stimulated by live experience spans across subject and grade boundaries. When students sleeping deep inside Fort Henry learn that moisture dripping on the walls was rainfall from years ago working its way through the cracks in the fortification, it becomes a future geology lesson.

> Facts stay in your mind a lot longer if you experience them first and you enjoy it much more too. I'd go back again soon. (Grade 8 student journal)

Students are intrigued by the story of a soldier's widow bursting into tears when asked by the Sergeant for her hand in marriage while leaving the cemetery. The Sergeant quickly apologizes for his untimely proposal. The widow explains her tears are not for her dead husband but for the fact that she accepted a Private's proposal at the graveside. Discovering that wives of soldiers who died on duty had 30 days to pick a new mate from the ranks of unmarried soldiers or leave the Fort generates lively discussion of social customs, then and now.

> It's better than staying cooped up in a boring classroom. You don't have as much fun learning from books and you sure don't remember as much. (Grade 8 student journal)

Keeping the Programs Alive

Innovations in education, especially ones that take the students out of school, are vulnerable to collapse. There are two issues. One is keeping the program fresh, innovative, and responsive to changing community needs; the other is to sustain and renew the partnerships with various government and private groups that make the programs possible.

History Comes Alive is not sitting on its laurels because, to survive, programs must be updated and reviewed constantly. New resource materials, reports of teaching methods, and plans actually used from teachers who have participated in activities strengthen and renew the overall package. Writing for new curriculum units which also involve overnight stays is a continual process. New resource materials are routinely produced while improving older materials with motivating pre- and post-visit activities.

The programs thrive. There are rapidly growing numbers of participants. One cooperating agency, Parks Canada, is becoming a leader in the development of experiential education. Parks personnel are working with representatives of school boards and other agencies to create a 100-mile-long heritage classroom along an historic trade and colonization route. Parks Canada granted a sabbatical to one of their educational interpreters to set this plan in motion, to strengthen the existing partnerships already in place, and to recruit new participants. Support from other central authorities gives hope that further developments are possible in the future.

Meetings between representatives of our formed partnerships and teachers who use the programs also helps ensure the continued success of *History Comes Alive*. These meetings are revealing in two ways: first, teachers make remarkably strong statements about how the class climate changed for the better after participating in one of the programs. Teachers report noticing greater overall retention, as well as more cooperative and helpful students after their visits. Such positive reports are encouraging for agency and community representatives. Second, the very fact that nonschool agencies would participate in such meetings to exchange feedback and perceptions demonstrates serious reflection and desire to ensure and sustain high quality. Commitment is found in practice as well as in rhetoric.

In-service training and development for the programs is critical. It was important to communicate first with those who have the authority to make school decisions on curriculum and field trips. I presented *History Comes Alive* initially to senior administrators and, once having received their support, met with school principals and curriculum resource teachers who oversee excursion planning and organization. Having resource packages for each program available for all interested teachers provides written follow-up material.

Teacher in-service is accomplished by circulating information about existing and emerging programs to teachers. Program excerpts, teacher and student reports, and highlights from individual visits are published and circulated. There are workshops and poster sessions sponsored by individual schools, school boards, and other interested organizations. Careful pre-service work and well-refined support documents enable teachers to make thorough pre-visit preparation with their classes. That preparation makes them partners in a learning enterprise that virtually guarantees success.

Applications in Other Places

Not every school district is as fortunate in having fortifications, historic waterways, or residences of their nation's founders readily accessible. Nevertheless, heritage is present wherever we live and it is the challenge of educators, working through partnerships, to develop experiential learning programs to bring the local heritage to life. Initially, as I did, one must examine which facilities, whether historic sites or other unique situational learning opportunities, would be potential, hands-on learning sites. Those already present with interpretive personnel or educational facilitators are obviously likely choices.

One must be careful to ensure that the facilities chosen as sites will allow for expansion and in-depth experiences to meet curriculum needs. A benefit to the heritage site is an increased market. Already *History Comes Alive* activities have expanded to include stays by youth groups like Scouts, tourist groups, senior travelling groups, staffs from neighbouring school boards, and business groups.

The words of one participant convey the enriching benefits of this type of experience:

> *History Comes Alive* provides students with a post-modern, first-hand experience—a memory of a memory of the past. The cobwebs covering my earlier studies [of history] were being dusted off by an innovative approach to education. (Student teacher)

I believe that valid learning experiences will create long lasting impressions. I enjoy watching children and adults alike participate as they experience an engrossing event. Such programs do enhance learning and provide many cherished memories, both academic and personal. Our past, our present, and their implications for our future can be experienced and each individual's quest for knowledge enhanced to allow them to develop to their potential. Educational experiences such as these are the many important minutes in time that will last for years.

Chapter 5

COMMUNITY INVOLVEMENT IN EDUCATION

Bill Patterson and Bert Horwood

Bill Patterson was educated with a BSA from the University of Guelph in 1961. He taught Sciences and headed the Science Department at Mackenzie High School, Deep River, Ontario, for most of his career. For 20 years he was one of the leaders of Trekkers, a highly successful outdoor program. In 1990, Bill began a multicredit, integrated program, called TAM-ARACK, in which students make full use of community facilities and people.

Bert Horwood, as editor, is introduced elsewhere. Bert had taught with Bill in Deep River and they collaborated subsequently in several research projects.

This chapter explores the interface between the school and the community. The relationship works both ways. The community entering the school and the school moving into the community enrich both the kind and number of experiences for students. There are tensions in that interface but, as the authors show, communities can supply great support for experiential education. Teachers will need to give up some control, but there is no need for them to give up influence.

Introduction

Up until the late 19th century, except for a few private schools, educating children was a family and community function. Children learned from their parents, their extended families, and frequently from neighbours. The community exerted an enormous influence on children, both in terms of what they learned and what values they developed. Children were not only responsible to their parents, but also to the community which insisted on appropriate behaviour. Unacceptable behaviour led to community feedback which often resulted in conduct being modified. Children had regular, close contact with adults and were called on to do important work in the home or community; they made a contribution to their society. Community involvement in education is not new. In fact, it has been the rule as long as there have been human communities.

As schools staffed with specialized, professional teachers evolved, there was an increasing separation of education from the community. Professional teachers became society's official educators and schools were built as the official place of education. With increasing separation, the importance of the parents and the community became less, and education as a business began. As we moved through the 20th century, and larger numbers of students stayed in school for longer periods of time, the isolation from the community became greater. While school buildings may be frequently used by community groups, few people in the community, including parents, really know what is going on when school is in session. They feel they have little real influence. They are right. Public dissatisfaction with the educational system and the hankering back to imagined good old days is almost certainly a result of this ignorance. At the same time, teachers and the education business march on to a curriculum drummer that has little to do with the local community or the real world.

The official curriculum of schools is mostly designed by people who have spent their lives within the world of schools. This makes the curriculum reflect its own values and contain little of community influence. The energies of students are driven into this isolated curriculum, and as a consequence, they are removed from making the contributions to family and community life which had been usual through most of human history. The growing isolation of school and community was fed by compulsory education laws and even more powerfully by the social stigma attached to young persons who dropped out to make their own ways in the world. To the extent that this separation of community and education is complete, both students and communities lose out on important aspects of learning. Perhaps this is what Oscar Wilde meant when he remarked that, while schooling may be admirable, nothing worth knowing can really be taught.

Society, in the age of the technical expert, has generally left education up to the professionals. The result, in spite of routine criticism, has been the evolution of a public conviction that *real, important* education is something that occurs only in official learning places, like schools, colleges, and universities, under the tutelage of professional educators (National Commission, 1983). The general acceptance of this perception is expressed in help-wanted advertisements. Job applicants must be high school or college graduates or hold university degrees as evidence of schooling. Relevant experience may be valued but the seal of approval from the official education place is centrally important.

Through the last quarter (approximately) of the 20th century, there has been a significant interest in involving the community more actively with the school, and vice versa. Cooperative education (known as internships in some jurisdictions), where students work at jobs in the community as part of their schooling, is a good example. The formation of committees of parents to look at specific aspects of school life and work is another trend which reverses isolation. While these are important actions, there are many other potential ways in which a positive, informed interaction between education and the community can be reestablished. Such interactions will make the schools more completely an integral part of the communities they ought to serve. They will also bring community people into active participation with children rather then being nothing other than remote sources of funding through taxation.

It is not our intention to advocate a return to communities without schools and professional teachers. Rather, the purpose of this chapter is to describe ways in which a typical high school has increased its interactions with its own community. Those interactions have two dimensions. One is to bring community members into the school and into partnership within school programs. The other is to bring the school into the community and into partnership with community events and activities. This chapter itself is an example of a third kind of interaction in which a high school teacher and a university professor collaborate. There are mutual benefits for all parties and the processes described can be adapted to fit many different situations.

The school which provides all of our examples (with one exception) had about 550 students at the time of writing, down from a peak 1,110 students ten years earlier. It is the only secondary school serving its town and surrounding area. Part of a scattered County system of schools with headquarters some 40 km away, the school offers a largely traditional mix of academic and vocational courses, plus a normal range of extracurricular activities. The description which follows is based on the actions of a single teacher or small groups of teachers as they do their work. As such, it represents a grass-roots development of increased community involvement rather than an implementation of school or County policy.

Bringing the Community into the School

The People in the Community as a Resource

The citizens in the community represent a deep well of resources that is rarely tapped, especially by secondary schools. These people possess a host of skills, great knowledge, wisdom, and broad experience. They are at a variety of stages in their lives and offer perspectives related to their ages, a vivid contrast with the narrower spectrum of ages and stages with which most secondary students spend their days.

Based on interactions in our community, most of these people are willing to share their experiences with students. Indeed, they are eager to do so. Unfortunately, schools tend to give the impression that such help is not wanted. And this may well be the case, as a community visitor or community placement might not deal with matter related to the curriculum. To the extent that the curriculum, and its expression in textbooks, is the driving force in schools, this should not come as a surprise.

Community people can, at the most basic level, be sources of information for the school. A physician discusses sexually transmitted diseases, an artist leads a watercolour workshop, a garage owner tells stories about auto repairs as a career, or a geneticist visits a senior biology class. These people from outside the school are seen by students as a part of the real world and are perceived by them, as a result, to be reliable. Visits to community facilities like industries, shops, hospitals, and courts are equally useful and unique experiences which provide students more information about their world than can possibly be revealed in school. The generator hall in a hydroelectric dam is a very different thing in reality than is its textbook or film portrayal. You have to be there.

Every community includes people who have exceptional skills in traditional crafts and who are willing to instruct others. Such people teach students elementary skills in a traditional craft in a traditional way. At the same time, students develop an appreciation of the traditions involved (Steele, 1989). An illustration of this type of community involvement occurred in our high school when one of the teachers learned that a member of the community made Native-style, canoe pack baskets from black ash logs, using traditional hand tools. The craftsman cut fresh logs and brought them to the school. For the next two days, students stripped bark, pounded the logs with sledge hammers, peeled off thin strips of the ash wood, and wove the strips into large baskets. All of this required hard work, care, and cooperation. Throughout those days, the students talked with the craftsman and used his tools. At the end, each student had made a basket, gained pride in his or her work, learned to appreciate the craft of black-ash weaving, and acquired, through direct experience, a better understanding of life in the days of hand tools. Students also experienced the quality of "complete process" (Horwood, 1994) as they worked the original materials to the finished product. Equally important, they had made friends with the craftsman and experienced his love for working with wood.

Retiring at earlier ages and with enormous specialized skills, retirees offer opportunities for productive collaboration with schools. Our experience in another high school, where a Foreign Service retiree gave lessons in a language not otherwise available, suggested that a similar opportunity could be developed in our school. Here, retirees with computer skills are organized to help students with some of the excellent computer simulations available on environmental and global issues. Such involvement takes advantage of available technology which a busy teacher is not able to put into place. The retirees become direct instructors and leaders, the teacher facilitates and organizes, and the students execute the computer simulations. This type of cooperation between schools and communities has almost unlimited potential.

Community Assistance with Transportation

As the economic squeeze is put on education, schools have less money to spend on transportation. There are two possible responses to this situation. The easy one is to simply cut back travel. Unfortunately, this solution further reduces the contact between students and the community and makes the isolation worse. The second, more creative and difficult response is to actively seek alternative travel arrangements helped by people in the community.

One way to achieve this is for individual teachers to involve community members as active participants in all aspects of projects, including those requiring extra travel. Community helpers may participate to varying degrees in the projects, but one certain result is that travel can occur, often at little or no cost to the school. In one experiential program in our school, students travel approximately 1,000 km to access three different wilderness trips during the semester. The parents meet as a group with the teacher once a month as part of their involvement with the program. At this meeting, the activities of the past month are reviewed and plans for the next month are discussed. Planning includes parental participation in transportation for the next outings. Other residents from the community also help to staff the program and they may provide transportation as well. The end result is that parents and other community people not only support the program with their presence but also provide caring transportation at virtually no cost. This service is essential for the operation of the program.

This example may not be feasible in places where education is governed by law suits, and may not be needed where school districts have a generous supply of busses, vans, and trailers. The point is to illustrate the kind of community response that is possible to a chronic need in an experiential program.

Community Attitudes Toward Schools

A continual theme in the popular media since the 1980s is carping criticism of the educational system and its standards. Fingers are always ready to point to the schools, districts, and nations whose scores are below average. The criticism is almost always associated with calls to return to rigorous standards of examination and heavy emphasis on reading, writing, and arithmetic.

In our experience, much of this criticism is based on ignorance of what actually goes on in schools. Judgments about what adolescents are like are made at a distance, either from remote standardized test scores, or from images of teenagers in malls, on T.V. screens, and from newspapers. When adults do not live with school-age children, they have very little direct contact with the young.

In our school, where as many as 10%-15% of the school population is made up of adults, or where adults are involved in helping with programs, a different attitude exists. These adults combine their normal roles in the community with roles as stakeholders in the school. They have much better information about the school, and have it from direct observation and experience. It is commonplace in our school to hear adults make statements like, "I wish I had had an opportunity like that when I was in school." This kind of statement reflects a much more positive attitude than one which wants the school to return to an imaginary, no-nonsense past.

The result is that there develops in the community a body of taxpayers who are accurately informed and strongly supportive. These people become politically active, lobbying the County School Board and urging support for good programs even if it may mean increased taxes. People are willing to pay for value for the children of the community, but first they must be convinced that value is there. It is impossible to overestimate the influence exerted by informed community people acting as an advocacy group. The fact is that active involvement of the community in a school will convert the majority of taxpayers from critics (a problem) to allies (a solution). However, for this to happen, teachers and school administrations must act on the potential and not hide behind school walls. It is also necessary that community involvement go far beyond the tokenism that has plagued the Parent Teacher Association movement. In this account, community members who participate in our school programs have a real voice and a real job to do.

Community Staff for Trips

School programs with large experiential components are usually stretched when it comes to supervision in the field. School policy, common sense, safety, and simple management factors clearly indicate that one teacher with 20 students on a wilderness outing, for example, is an impossible situation. Somehow, more supervising staff members must be found.

Most communities include men and women skilled in and enthusiastic for outdoor travel. They are invariably willing and able to help when invited. Parents of students currently in the school are especially keen, but help is easily found among those whose families have outgrown school as well as those who have never had any connection with the school. In our community, the teacher was able to develop a list of such people from parent interviews, discussions with youth leaders such as Scouts and Guides, contact with outdoor groups, and local news stories.

Once possible helpers are identified, it is important to invite them to a meeting to discuss the proposed trips, the trip goals and philosophy, mutual interests, needs, and expectations. Not everyone will be able to take part. But from the willing and able, it is possible to build a powerful support team.

Our community team has helped staff major wilderness trips for several years. On one remote canoe trip (8 days, 150 km) with 16 students, the following support team was in place:

> the teacher and program leader,
>
> a student-teacher intern,

a retired mechanical engineer with extensive arctic canoe experience,

a retired technologist and Scout leader,

a retired Math and Science teacher from the leader's school,

a former English teacher,

a forestry technician and naturalist,

a forester with special expertise in fire-fighting technology,

an engineer, parent of one of the students, and

a professor of experiential education.

The ages of these people ranged from 69 to 25; three were women.

Clearly, the group of adults is impressive and large. It might be argued that the trip was overly supervised. We would agree except that it was the students who requested that particular people be included in addition to the original staff of six. As well as providing the supervision needed for safety and high quality, the adults from the community brought a dimension that the teenagers lack in school: friendly, non-authoritarian contact with adults who are perceived as being part of the real world beyond the world of school.

The long-term advantage of having a staff group like the one described is that the school has nine more strong advocates with direct experience of the educational processes in the program. The 69-year-old man, who had not had much contact with teenagers for many years, was tremendously impressed with the students. He summed up by saying, "They were cooperative, friendly, hard working, and easy to get along with. They made me feel a part of the group."

Bringing the School into the Community

The emphasis so far has been on bringing the community into the school. In this section, we look at examples where the school moves into the community. Two cases show that what starts out to be a simple exercise in fund raising becomes a mutually beneficial exchange of service and learning between students and community members. The third case shows how work-experience can be fitted into a particular subject curriculum. The example is in Biology, but could well be in any subject which matched industrial or commercial opportunities in the community.

Beyond Fund Raising

In 1970, our school began an extracurricular, outdoor adventure program. School funds were not available and expenses promised to be high. The staff saw both the need for fund raising and the need for students to do the work involved. Self-reliance and personal responsibility were important elements in the philosophy of the program. The idea of a Work Day to coincide with spring cleanup time was put into operation.

For two weeks prior to the selected Saturday, ads were placed in the local paper and in store windows. People with work to be done, such as window washing, yard raking, wood piling, or gardening, were asked to call the school and book student workers for the time required on Work Day. Students were assigned to specific jobs in pairs. People paid what they felt the job was worth, usually averaging well over minimum wage. As time passed, there was sufficient demand to add a second Work Day in October. In the '70s, each Work Day would generate $1,000 to $1,500.

In the beginning, Work Days had something of the air of a high school car wash in that people accepted useful work but could have managed without it. The day was an organizational burden for teachers and something of a combined labour and lark for the students. Over the 25 years that Work Days have been operating, significant changes and trends have appeared. Some citizens have had student workers every Work Day for 20 years. They are now seniors and have come to depend on students to do the essential spring and fall work in house and yard. The significance of the students' work has shifted from token help for fund-raising purposes to provision of an essential service in the community.

The reality of that service was revealed by the steady increase in job requests even as student enrollment declined. It became evident that one Saturday in the spring and fall were not enough to meet the demand. Therefore, Work Days are now spread over two, two-week intervals. There is still local advertising, but orders for help are now assigned differently. Groups of about four students are assigned four to six jobs, depending on the demand. The students are responsible to get in touch with their employers and organize themselves to do the work at suitable times. It works well.

What started out as a simple fund-raising event has become an annual spring and fall institution in the community. Many people, some of them elderly, are dependent on the service and also enjoy having contact with the students. Fund raising is still an important element, but so is the public service component. At the same time, although it is not part of the structure of the Work Days, students learn that they are productive and important contributors to community life. They also learn about the lives of others in their community, especially seniors.

An integrated curriculum project in our school required additional fund raising for major outdoor expeditions. Coincidentally, a relative of one of the teachers told his friend, a nationally known folk singer, of the newly approved program. As a result of this conversation, the singer offered to perform a benefit concert in the school auditorium. The offer was accepted and the students were mobilized to organize advertising, ticket sales, a refreshment booth, the auditorium sound system, and decorations. The results were a fine concert in a small town, by a performer who would not normally have booked there, a fine service to the town by students who attended to the detailed arrangements, an opportunity to learn something about the behind-the-scenes work of a professional musician, and a profit to the program of about $1,500.

This case illustrates not only serendipity and opportunism, but also the value in perceiving fund raising as an important vehicle to make students important contributors to community life.

Subject-Specific Work Experience

Many schools have a variety of work experience or internship programs. The usual placement could last for as little as a month and as much as a semester, and could have relatively weak connections to course work. Here, we describe a pattern of work experience that takes less time and is an integral part of a particular course of study.

The teacher had been in the school about seven years and had been employed during two summers at a local industry's research lab. This provided a basis of acquaintance and friendship to support the program. Industrial researchers with some expertise in biology were asked to have senior students studying University-entrance, biology work in their labs for two to five days on a specific research project. The criteria of the project were that it would be something a student could do (given instruction), and that it would be of interest to the student and of use to the scientist. All the scientists were excited about the idea and it became a matter of routine administrative procedures to make firm arrangements, getting approval of both school and industry management.

The scientists provided a list of projects they would like to have done in the available time. Students worked in pairs and negotiated their work days directly with the scientist. A day in the industrial lab was worked in the same way by students as by any other worker: they rode the busses to and from the plant, had the usual breaks, and were subject to the usual industrial discipline (ID badges, and the like). Students were required to prepare whatever report the scientist required. There was no additional report required for school although, as students finished the biology research project, they were asked to tell their classmates about both the science and the work experience aspects of their project. Each time the program operates, the teacher meets with the scientists to review it. Because the patience and willingness of the scientists does have limits, and so does the number of suitable projects, this program is operated only once every two to three years.

But are the research projects of real value, or merely indulgent make-work? The projects have varied, but are consistently rated as very good to excellent. In one outstanding example, students replicated the famous Urrey-Miller experiment on the origin of organic molecules necessary for life. The students successfully synthesized and identified 15 different amino acids. Here, again, the sustained enthusiasm of scientists to have students participating in an aspect of community life shows the useful contribution that students make. There is a mutuality in this kind of curriculum-driven community interaction.

Discussion

Community involvement in education raises two critical questions. First, because there is a potential for loss of professional control of education, what happens when things go wrong, either with community volunteers working with students, or when students are out in the community? Second, how does a teacher learn to involve the community effectively and responsibly?

There is a potential for unhappy incidents to occur when students and community volunteers interact. One example stands out, partly because it is the only one of its kind in our experience and partly because it illustrates the unexpected nature of such problems. A retired volunteer (male) and a young female student-teaching intern, both staff members on a long canoe trip, engaged in a noisy, angry shouting match. It did not augur well for an effective, safe staff on the trip. It turned out that there were long-standing disagreements between members of their families, and these were compounded by gender sensitivities that defied resolution. Fortunately, the staff was large enough that duties could be performed without those two needing to work together, or even to be in very close proximity.

The potential for that kind of disruption, based in history outside the program, must be recognized and accepted. Another kind of potential disruption is that volunteers have no professional obligation to follow through on offers to help. Volunteers are as free to opt out as they are to opt in. In our experience, we have never been let down by volunteers from the community. When one person's participation changes, an alternate is always found. This is a powerful reason for having a large list of collaborators and helpers who are kept abreast of ongoing programs and events.

The most serious implication of community involvement is the consequence of having people learn what is happening in the school. Suppose they don't like what they see? The kind of community involvement we are describing opens the world of school to community members and invites them to participate. For their participation to be informed and significant, for instance, to go beyond tokenism, community members must develop commitment to the curriculum. That means that their views must be heard, respected, and, wherever possible, included in the program.

This is a radical notion. To the extent that schools are opened to the community and community participants are given effective voices, it becomes impossible for teachers and administrators to use textbooks, course outlines, government mandates, and tradition as defences when practices are challenged. If a school seeks allies in the community, it must be prepared to join in a reexamination of its curriculum, teaching methods, and administrative arrangements. The school must be willing to go further and act on the community values expressed in that reexamination. Only then can the benefits we describe be obtained.

This view of community involvement changes the pattern of accountability in the school. It adds an axis of community accountability to those already existing. In our experience, this has been a benefit, rather than a pain, to all concerned. But it has the potential for awkward questions to be asked and difficult requests to be made, and to generate a sudden, unexpected need for defensiveness on the part of teachers.

In our school, some simple operating procedures helped to ensure that community involvement was supportive rather than interfering. First, it is essential to hear and respect suggestions from community members. It is important for teachers to be very confident in the soundness of the program for which they are seeking help, and to be firm and clear about goals and the kind of help needed. Expectations and roles for community helpers must be spelled out clearly. When adjustments are made to use suggestions and requests from volunteers, the changes must be specific, reasoned, and widely supported. Early meetings with community helpers are critical in setting the stage. The meetings should be brief, well organized, interesting, and only as frequent as required for the specific program. In our experience, meetings for a nonspecific agenda, lengthy meetings, and overly frequent meetings merely invite disagreement.

How and where do teachers learn to work with community members in the sorts of ways described here? In our school, community involvement has grown to be an important and visible aspect of school work, yet learning its dynamics is notably lacking from teacher education. In our case, learning how to involve the community effectively was a matter of long, slow evolution. It takes time to develop knowledge of community resources and to establish trust and good will to activate them. A stable teaching staff, most of whom live in the community, is able to develop accumulative, positive community relations. Time, patience, and sustained interaction taught both teachers and community members a set of skills and procedures for which there is, as yet, no training manual.

The interactions between school and community described here have the effect of restoring the central place of community in the experience of children which existed before the trend to confine education to places called school. There are many benefits which accrue to both the school and the community. Learning, understanding, and increased self-worth are the benefits to the young. Ownership, pride, and commitment grow in community members as they participate in school work. The school, as an organization, gains in resources of personnel, funding, and political support. Wherever teachers are willing to take on a new axis of accountability, community involvement with schools is bound to enhance learning.

References

Horwood, B. (1994). Integration and experience in the secondary curriculum. *McGill Journal of Education, 29*(1), 89-102.

National Commission on Excellence in Education. (1983). A nation at risk. The imperative educational reform. Washington, DC: US Office of Education.

Steele, T. A. (1989). Harvesting the riches of experiential learning in the far north. *Journal of Experiential Education, 12*(1), 16-18.

Chapter 6

GENDER AND ENGAGEMENT IN A JOBSITE CLASSROOM

Karne Kozolanka

Karne Kozolanka is a journeyman carpenter turned teacher. He was educated in his trades through apprenticeship, at Acadia University, and later with an MEd from Queen's University. Karne has published several articles on the nature of experience in technological education. He teaches at the Faculty of Education, University of Regina.

In this chapter, Karne draws on his study of students on a building-trades course to explore the interacting ideas of engagement, gender identity, and experience. He pays particular attention to the voices of 4 women in a class of 20 men as he grapples with the tensions between utilitarian education on the one hand and education for personal development on the other. In doing these things, he connects us to the relevant literature and shows where much more work needs to be done, both in understanding practice and in developing theory.

The house is two stories high with a roof that slopes in four directions. It is partially covered from the bottom up with shingles and figures wearing yellow hard hats. The roof over the wrap-around porch is almost completely shingled and the figures there are bent over on their knees. Two sides of the house angle away at the corner and are in the process of being covered as well—with siding instead of shingles. One side is flanked with scaffolds on which are stacked long bundles of siding. Here, too, the siding is creeping up the wall, the grey vinyl contrasting sharply with the rough texture of gold-coloured waferboard. Behind a rusty Honda Civic, still partially loaded with tools and cords, are three students leaning over an aluminum bending-and-cutting machine. Two of them are holding a long, wide piece of aluminum and the third is pulling down on the handle. On the far side, a mid-morning delivery from the lumber yard has just dumped a load of lumber onto the mushy ground. One student is already handing 2x4s in through the basement window, as two others are looking over the invoice with the driver of the truck. The scene is like an ant colony—everyone bustling about, intent on one task or another.

It's a jobsite, but it's a classroom too. Just as every jobsite has its workers, this classroom has students. In fact, at the beginning of the semester, there wasn't even a class "room"—only a hole in the ground. To a passer-by, it would seem to be a site with a lot of workers—much more than the usual number. Looking closer, one would also see that the workers aren't all male either; there are at least four females visible....

Scenes like this are becoming more typical in mainstream secondary schooling. This particular building-trades program is representative of a worldwide trend in education to provide experiences which reflect the realities of life in the world beyond school (Gibbons, 1974, 1976, 1984; Horwood, 1987, 1993; Ontario, 1989a, 1989b, 1993; Wigginton, 1985). Technological Studies has long proven to be fertile ground for the establishment of such experiential programs. Experiential education and the teaching of technological subjects have similar roots, for example, in apprenticeships, internships, and cooperative education.

One such program was studied by Horwood (1994) in which students used a theme of cultural journalism to explore and publish accounts about their community. Two of the students, Emily Doubt and Gillian Ramsey (1991), expressed how it was for them:

> A lot of learning went on throughout the semester although the approach was quite different from the school we've been used to. The things we learned could not have come out of a textbook; we had practical experience and learned by doing things, not just by listening to an explanation. We learned valuable lessons from our mistakes, from everything we said and did, and from everyone we came into contact with. That's what life is all about. We went out into the world for half a year and we lived. (p. 25)

My interest in these programs stems from my own background as a marginally engaged secondary student and my subsequent awareness of the potential for these new programs to interest, motivate, and, ultimately, engage students. I was interested in finding out what qualities were present that allowed students, in their words, to "learn valuable lessons." When the opportunity arose, I took part in a house-building program which integrated several high school technological subjects with English. Students granted me interviews and allowed me access to their journals, written as part of their English credit. Their quotations are meant to represent a much larger body of similar material. All names, of course, have been changed and the texts used with permission.

Although an earlier account (Kozolanka, 1993) demonstrates that both the women and men were engaged at different levels in numerous and varied activities, this discussion focuses more specifically on engagement as it relates to the development of one's gender identity. Closely related to the experiences of these adolescent and adult women are issues that impact the engagement patterns of men as well. I begin with a discussion of engagement followed by an interpretation of the lived experiences of male and female students on the jobsite as they relate to gender issues. I then re-frame these interpretations in a critique informed by critical pedagogy, and finally, discuss some implications for practice.

Engagement

Engagement is a difficult term to define. While the Oxford dictionary (Allen, 1990) provides some assistance and a logical starting point, it seems that the term can have confusing meanings. For example, a student who has come into battle with the school system and is in constant trouble could be as intimately engaged as an honours student. The same could hold true for one who is just taking part. Engagement can, it seems, be at either end of a scale which could range from open hostility to friendly collaboration.

Engagement can also be understood in terms of what Csikszentmihalyi (1975) calls the experience of "flow," in which people are participating in activities they find intrinsically enjoyable and "outside the parameters of worry and boredom" (p. 35). Literature from experiential education also provides some help in defining what engagement in school is about. Proudman (1992) describes experiential education as a set of relationships. Gibbons (1976) and James (1968) each outline a vision of student experiences at different relational levels. Where Proudman identifies the axes of relationship as individual to self, to the teacher, and to the learning environment, Gibbons reaches further and identifies the personal, interpersonal, and impersonal levels. James, however, describes three modes of active engagement with the environment—enquiry, dialogue, and making—which can also be understood as relational terms. Enquiry represents formal investigation; dialogue depicts a kind of curious and speculative wondering; making is creative, productive activity which is the culmination of enquiry and dialogue. It is these relational descriptions that help to formulate a definition of engagement which, simply stated, is *being emotionally involved within the substance of an activity*, where emotional involvement suggests some kind of intimate contact with others and phenomena. This intimate contact would result in some kind of social or technical artifact: for example, new understanding represented in some concrete manner.

Lived Experiences in the Program

Being female and coming to school in this secondary, technological-studies program was a different experience from that of the males in the program. Nevertheless, in general, the females worked with the males doing similar tasks. There were some exceptions; for example, females did not spend a lot of time doing the high work on the roof. But neither did all of the males. While the stories of each of the 4 females (among 20 males) in the program are different and unique, general threads emerged from their experiences that corroborate some of the literature in feminist theory. Of the four, the two adults kept extensive journals on a regular basis. The two adolescent women wrote less, but still a substantial amount more than their male classmates. All four helped to shed some light on what life was like as a female working and studying in the program. What emerged were three themes. The journals of the females reflected a primary concern and attention to interpersonal relationships. The two other themes were self-esteem, and sexism and harassment. Relationship interests permeated their journal entries and conversations with me:

> The whole day went really well. It seemed like everyone partici-pated in something. . . . I felt really proud when we put up the part-ing wall. I almost felt like crying. It was a very happy moment for me. (Susan journal 1, p. 20)

> I feel this type of environment and types of activities let a person be themselves. My first opinions of some specific people has really changed . . . yesterday, I had really negative feelings about taking the course. Tracy knew everybody—I often felt left out. (Aimee journal 1, p. 1)

The engagement of the females in this program can be measured in part by the degree that the program allowed the women to experi-ence and express relational needs. According to Gilligan (1982), women have different developmental needs than men. I'm wonder-ing if this particular program met the relational needs of the women enrolled:

As Freud and Piaget call our attention to the differences in children's feelings and thought, enabling us to respond to children with greater care and respect, so a recognition of the differences in women's experiences and understanding expands our vision of maturity and points to the contextual nature of developmental truths. (Gilligan, 1982, p. 174)

Journalling, interviews, and observations of the women revealed a concern for the manner in which the job was being done, who was getting along with whom, and how they felt about their contributions and sense of place in the class. Of course, their concerns were not limited to relational issues alone (for example, they were also committed to finishing the house by the end of the semester), but relationships played a central part in their experiences. A number of examples emerged—more frequent and intense use of journalling, females defining their roles in terms of their relationships with others, and how the women perceived themselves as persons capable of making positive contributions to the class.

The second theme was self-esteem. This was also linked to relational issues. The two mature women in the program expressed surprise and delight a number of times when told in one way or another that their work was appreciated by others:

When I was deciding whether or not I wanted to take this program, I was really afraid that I wouldn't fit in or the group would have their own little cliques. Thanks Brian for letting me in. Paul, thanks to you too for telling Dan I was the best nailer. (Susan journal 1, pp. 1–10)

The board that I had been working on was leaning up against the wall and Dave picked it up and handed it up to the guys on the roof. Michel said, "Who cut that?" And someone said, "Helen did." Then someone else said, "Well if Helen did it I bet it's all right, so let's just put it in." So they did and it fit! None of them knew I was listening from down below. One part of me said, "Oh, they're being sarcastic," and the other said, "Maybe I'm not that bad after all." (Helen journal 1, p. 39)

What the others on the site thought about their skills really mattered to the females. If these things did matter to the males, for some reason they did not write or talk openly about them. Another distinct difference between the genders was the females' inclination to internalize problems. At one point early in the semester, Aimee was quite frustrated when she thought she was not being taken seriously by the teachers in the assignment of tasks. In the following excerpt, we see how she questions her ability to make decisions, her patience, and her skill level:

> Once again I was questioning myself as to what I'm doing out in the freezing cold at 8 a.m. building a house!!!??? This morning such as every other morning was horrible. I seem to have no patience. I always seem to be stuck doing menial tasks. (Aimee journal 1, p. 15)

None of the males reflected a similar process of self-doubt. They seemed to project uncertainty and problems onto someone or something else. In their exploration of women's ways of knowing, Belenky, Clinchy, Goldberger, and Tarule (1986) report that "Some women were so consumed with self-doubt that they found it difficult to believe a teacher's praise, especially when the teacher was a man" (p. 197). Journal entries and interviews with the females of this program show a tendency for them to think of themselves as lacking in capabilities and not worth much. This is important because a person who feels that she is of less value than males, for instance, would not be likely to challenge the status quo in a mixed group. It is possible that she would be perceived as a radical, challenging existing social orders. Aimee took a long time to tell the teachers that she was not happy delegated to menial work. When she did, it was indirectly through her journal. Helen's first reaction to the comments by her male co-workers was to think that they were being sarcastic. Helen was street smart and wise in the give and take of the jobsite, yet despite her life experience and older age, she often questioned her role on the site:

> So it seems every job I get lately has been what I'd consider a thinking job and I have had to do it myself, which is beginning to annoy me. Sometimes I get so frustrated I want to just walk away from it. I'm sure if I was working with someone else I could at least bounce ideas off them to get their impact. I'm also wondering if everyone

has said to Dan that they don't want to work with me. Maybe I'm just being paranoid. (Helen journal 1, p. 32)

Even though Helen wondered if her self-doubts were paranoia, she was not able to see that she was clever and the teachers recognised her ability to handle "thinking" jobs.

The third theme was sexism and harassment. These could be both subtle and overt. Often it was in the form of what is called "good-natured fun":

Wednesday September 23rd, freezing cold, everyone kept saying, "Oh she'll last another week," or "I give her a couple of days." It really bothered me. I guess I'm not a morning person, I don't think I did a thing all morning. (Aimee journal 1, p. 11)

Comments like these can be particularly demeaning. After identifying her feelings of being bothered, Aimee went on in the next sentence to internalize the experience, writing that she was "not a morning person." Could it be that in a somewhat hostile environment, Aimee attributed the reasons for difficulty with the new language and skills to some kind of personal deficiency? Is expressing a deficiency like this, a product of harassment? It seems that in these situations, the women tended to internalize factors that the males in the class would not have internalized. Helen's first reaction to overheard complimentary remarks, Aimee's quiet frustration, and Helen's speculation on her paranoia are examples of women's responses to perceived harassment. Here is another example of a woman feeling silenced:

He didn't like to be challenged by a different approach. . . . I found [the way he spoke to me] to be offensive and I wasn't as experienced as him or because I'm just a "dumb woman" doing a job I have no business doing. Both ways annoyed me. One problem we had was the blue chalkline on the floor, it was very faint and he kept saying it doesn't matter, we can measure five-and-a-half inches from the edge all the way along. Well, I didn't think that was the correct way and I kept saying we have to get it on the blue line. As it turned out, Dan came over at the end and confirmed what I had been saying. He didn't acknowledge that I had been right all day. . . . I wanted to confront him but I let it go. I really wanted to say, "I told you so, so why wouldn't you listen to me?" (Helen journal 1, p. 9)

It's possible that if Helen was a male she might have been accorded more respect for her views. For example, one of the mature male students was regularly given leadership roles despite a record of numerous mistakes. On occasion, Susan was given responsibility, possibly because of her quiet achievement and commitment to learning. However, despite her being the best in the class, at one point she wrote, "I guess I need to get a little more aggressive and push my way in. Nancy (roommate) said about two weeks ago that I shouldn't let the guys who think they know everything just push through and do everything" (Susan journal 2, p. 9). And yet when she would get pushy, she was not listened to. It's a common dilemma for women, according to Caplan (1989), who describes two sets of labels provided by society: "the seductive–submissive–admiring–compliant kind and the powerful–dominant–bitchy–cold–castrating kind. Who can imagine wanting to be classified either way?" (p. 126). Sometimes these dilemmas were quite frustrating:

When Dan started explaining the starter strip, someone picked it up and held it up to the wall. They held it up backwards. I said, "I think it goes the other way." They turned it right around so that it was upside down. (Nailing strip at the bottom.) I said, "No, just turn it around." It ended up being placed the way I thought was right so I said, "That's right." Dan said "How do you know this?" I said, "I'm pretty sure that's the way the siding guy showed us. Michel agreed. Lenny said, "Turn it around, it goes the other way." They did, and Dan said "How do you know this?" Lenny said "Because I've done it for years." So, they nailed it in that way . . . Jimmy marked the wall for the chalk line and we snapped it. Something didn't look right. It was only up one inch instead of one-and-a-half inches, so we had to do it again. After this, we put the starter strip on the same way as they did earlier. Minutes later, Peter one of the graduates from last year showed up. We started to put siding on but it didn't seem to want to hold. Pete had worked for the siding company last summer and he said, "The starter strip is on backwards." I was not a happy camper . . . It was kind of a frustrating day. Dan wanted me to be in charge of the siding crew which included Johnny, Michel,

Theo and Dean. I couldn't seem to get them working. No one wanted to look for a ladder or hold up an end of the building paper so I could nail it. I'd just get going on something and would need an extra hand and I'd turn around to ask for help and there would be no one there. I think I spent more time looking for help than I did actually working. Not my kind of day. (Susan journal 2, p. 34)

Susan's frustration was common to those placed in leadership roles. Both of the student teachers (males) assigned to the program expressed similar feelings. However, it is possible that despite Susan's competence and achievement in the program, she had less credibility because she was a woman. I was unable to corroborate this with statements from the male students involved. When I asked them about the incident their responses were noncommittal. They may have been embarrassed.

These findings have some impact on how the form and content of curriculum should be redesigned to accommodate the learning perspectives and needs of women. A number of questions arise. Will effective teaching environments for females differ from those of males? Should the evaluation process be different for males and females? Can we learn from the reflections of these women and build more opportunities for communication, within the group and between teachers and students? Is it possible that the males may be suffering from misunderstanding and misinterpretation but are unable to express their feelings? Before addressing these and other questions, we now turn to the experiences of the males which have some relevance for the engagement of females in this program.

Males in the program were involved in a culture that valued most highly the ability to do the job. Personal regard within the class was determined largely by perception of ability. The work at the site was very task-oriented, for example, work that related to group functioning, feelings of accomplishment, and resolving conflict was addressed primarily in the context of getting the job done:

Everyone is trying to get the job done, we didn't quit until the job was done. (Field notes, p. 12)

We worked like steers and didn't quit until the job was done right, it was a good day. (Field notes, p. 27)

I asked both teachers and students if the students in the program could be grouped in any way. Both teachers and all but one of the male students first described the subgroupings in terms of their ability to do the job:

> So there's a group of "doing it types," they work hard but don't press the edges . . . and then there's the group that are putting out, sort of finding what is sufficient to put out . . . and there's the "doers," they're pushing all the time. (Lewis interview, pp. 1–57)

The one exception mentioned friendships as a primary classifying feature. However, he subsequently referred to ability in his descriptions. By contrast, two women spoke of the subgroups primarily in relational terms. One saw them as "leaders and followers" or "Lenny's boys"; the other as "liking what they are doing" and "annoying or bossy" (Field notes, pp. 16, 36).

A common ritual among the lunch and break groupings was telling sexist jokes. If the males were not hanging out in one of the vehicles, then conversation at a break might typically centre around jokes, automobiles, smoking, hunting, or drinking exploits:

> And Lenny's the leader, he's 44 and they look up to him, like, they use him as a role model even though they think at times he's a little bit stupid. But still, they go drinking together. (Helen interview, pp. 1–16)

> At lunch the guys are gathered in a rough circle, handing around cards from a parlour game. Laughter comes across as someone tells a joke. People are smiling as they put on their aprons and hardhats. (Field notes, p. 62)

In the preface of his book on male initiation and the role of the mentor, Robert Bly (1990) is critical of standard North American rituals of socialization:

> We are living at an important and fruitful moment now, for it is clear to men that the images of adult manhood given by the popular culture are worn out; a man can no longer depend on them. By the time a man is thirty-five he knows that the images of the right man, the tough man, the true man which he received in high school do not

work in life. Male initiation . . . defective mythologies that ignore masculine depth of feeling, assign men a place in the sky instead of earth, teach obedience to the wrong powers, work to keep men boys, and entangle both men and women in systems of industrial domination that exclude both matriarchy and patriarchy. (p. ix)

My impression of the teachers was that they wanted to involve their students at deeper levels than those described by Bly. They certainly advocated a collaborative spirit. However, getting the job done was associated with doing well, and if it came to a choice between spending time exploring depth of feeling such as in journalling or discussions, the choice would fall on the side of doing the work. One particular conversation I had with a student teacher who had completed a practice-teaching placement was an example of how getting the job done was paramount:

I felt really frustrated twice with two students, but the frustration wasn't necessarily because of them. It was because I . . . didn't know how I was being evaluated or even if I was. I got there as a student teacher and I didn't know whether they were going to—how they were looking at me—on the amount of work that I got done? So the amount of work that I got done was directly proportional to the way that the students performed, right? Or whether I just got the point across and I could speak to them or get the instructions across so they could understand—which, also if I did that properly . . . the efficiency of the whole group would be better too. Like, they got more work done and it was all based on that. (Bud interview, pp. 1– 145)

Getting the job done, toughing out the weather, not quitting, hanging out, and acting like "men" were the rites and images adopted and played out each day. They served to enhance a common male view of coming of age that tends to devalue the qualities that Bly refers to. There was an almost unconscious downgrading of these qualities; for example, journalling was not popular and was seen as something that was imposed. Journals were explained as an opportunity for students to express feelings and reflect on their experiences. It was a major part of their Communications English credit, but little or no time was allotted for reflection and completion of journals during class time. In a direct manner, it modelled that reflection was less important than the work of building. This is not to say that reflection necessarily needs to be done in a formal manner such as journalling or group discussions. Horwood (1992) has shown how informal storytelling can be a valuable form of reflection. "To learn from an experience, a person must interpret it in some way. To relate an event as a story is to construe the event and to put it into some reasonable context that makes sense in the light of the person's other experiences" (1992, p. 20).

Stories told at a break or lunch time tended to follow a predominantly male perspective. This perspective tended to devalue any stories that females were inclined to recount. When the females did contribute, they were inclined to tell stories associated with the subjects males commonly discussed. For example, one of the adolescent women would often be involved in listening to and telling sexist jokes. With the exception of formal exercises such as journalling, the females did not have a forum for expressing their relational needs. The emphasis on getting the job done rather than on other appropriate relational experiences such as journalling, discussions, and informal storytelling could be seen as an impediment to the more complete engagement of the female students and quite possibly of the males as well.

What can we say about engagement as it relates to the development of gender identities? Were these women emotionally involved within the substance of the activity? To the extent that engagement means being embroiled in personal and interpersonal relationships, or to the extent that engagement comes with enquiry, dialogue, and making, these women were fully engaged. But the gender quality of their engagement is what concerns us here. In their own words, these women reveal what it is like to live their lives in an environment underscored by sexism, double standards, stereotyped roles, and prejudice ingrained in the structures, routines, and relationships of daily schooling. What, then, can schools (and teachers) do?

Reconstructing a Critical Curriculum

There are two camps with opposing strategies. The first addresses the need to develop identity separately (Gilligan, 1982; Belenky et al., 1986) and is based on research that attributes capacities such as increased self-esteem and career satisfaction to schooling males and females separately. This view includes my own speculations about the benefits of having a class exclusively made up of women build a house: The opposing view is represented by those who demonstrate how issues of developing positive gender identities are incumbent on programs which involve both sexes:

> Girls and boys, men and women, live in a web of reciprocal and interactive relations. Boys and men are so important a reference group for girls and women that they are unable to change without bringing the other sex with them. In sociological terms, boys/men have both power and influence. Girls/women cannot change by themselves, and in practice they do not want to. (Stevenson, 1990, p. 23)

Research supports either view—that both separate and integrated schooling have value in developing positive gender identities in women. The key factor, however, seems to be a critical evaluation of curriculum, about the nature of what is being studied, regardless of the structural characteristics of a program. For our purposes, the means for transforming relationships between girls and boys and men and women would include concern for the involvement and development of boys. It follows, then, that men need to take on leadership roles in anti-sexist work with boys. Work with boys and men would also assist in reducing some of the contradictions inherent in focusing one's energies on girls and women alone. One example is the hidden stigma that Edwards (1993) writes of when programs are focused exclusively on quality-of-life strategies for adolescent women:

> . . . which is as dangerous as ignoring self-esteem completely. The former risks transmitting a message to young women that they are (yet again) deficient and in need of repair while allowing society to focus on girls themselves as the locus of the problem rather than taking responsibility for the social context which devalues them. Yet to ignore self-esteem is to deny the fundamentals of empowerment. As with most strategies, balance is everything. (p. 25)

So, such male leadership could involve boys and adolescent men in becoming successful at feminine-attributed qualities such as caring, sensitivity, and the expression of other feelings. But in this program it seemed that to do so was to diminish one's status. By way of illustration, I remember a comment made by one adolescent male in response to a query about his lack of willingness to discuss or reflect on his relationships with others in the program: "Uh, I don't need no journal to build a house," he replied (Field notes, p. 64). It seems that to this male there was nothing to be gained from efforts not normally associated with building a house, or being a male. Steinem describes this as a "polarization of feminine and masculine," where playing out what she calls "totalitarian gender roles" (1993, p. 257) becomes familiar to the point of being recognised as one's nature. This is particularly debilitating in contexts such as this program because where there is a definite division of labour—of who does what and how value is determined for what is done—this entrenches the notion that so-called masculine qualities have more value.

One can speculate on how difficult it is to involve males in roles that challenge common views of what it takes to become a man. I am reminded of one student's difficulty in dealing with an ongoing problem she was experiencing:

> I'm really having a dilemma with [my son] Jimmy. He is bored in his daycare. He has been there for two-and-a-half years. When he started again in September I really didn't give it any thought, but it's the same teachers, same toys, same room, and all of his friends, well most anyway, have moved on. Well, he hates going there and I can understand why. He loves school in the afternoon but the morning daycare he hates. I'm having a hard time justifying why he is there, just so I can learn carpentry. While I was going to school last year I promised things would slow down, but really they haven't. (Helen journal 1, pp. 1–47)

It really does represent a dilemma for Helen; on the one hand she is questioning her worthiness as a mom in farming out her child so she can just learn carpentry, and on the other hand there is the unspoken consequence of leaving the program—risking the stigma of becoming a quitter, an important consideration for a woman attempting to break into a nontraditional occupation. How can teachers begin to provide the leadership Stevenson (1993) suggests when she says that in sociological terms, boys and men have both power and influence?

One possibility emerges from Kaufman's (1993) critique of Robert Bly's (1990) conception of masculinity as a core biological reality and/or one developed through roles. Kaufman suggests that "the dominant forms of masculinity exist, not as timeless archetypes, but as power relationships with women, children, other men and our surrounding world" (p. 267). In other words, it may be erroneous to think that the development of one's gender or way of behaving in the world is based on some essential male or female quality perceived to exist at one's emotional core. This individualistic conception of learning and development is a view which ignores a social and cultural construction of masculinity which is based, according to Kaufman, in a patriarchal society. Kaufman is really pushing for a critical view of the commonplace, taken-for-granted practices and dominant modes of thinking that permeate society and classroom cultures.

In returning for a moment to Helen's dilemma, one could reconstruct such an experience within the context of this program by connecting her problem to issues of power and role definition. The first thing that comes to my mind is to suggest a means for looking after her child at the jobsite with her classmates as caregivers. This would certainly fit the popular notion that involvement in childcare activity would help to connect boys and men to the emotional intensity of care for infants and young children. Kaufman feels that such work is important for boys and men in reconnecting with a maleness which has been set aside.

Simon and Dippo (1992) are also helpful in formulating an understanding of what can be done to engage young people in the process of questioning their future identities and possibilities. They call schools sites of cultural politics where value in terms of identity and worth are formed. Like Kaufman, Simon and Dippo say that there is a need to transform individualistic conceptions of learning by challenging the wisdom of experience—to challenge the prevailing wisdom that experience is the best teacher. Their contention is that work experience similar to the one studied here is often "taken for granted as complete or self-contained and is ignored in the classroom in favour of general employability skills" (1992, p. 123). They call for teachers to acknowledge work experience as a legitimate aspect of schooling at the same time as challenging its form and content. They identify four primary ways in which work experience can be understood. These versions of experience are relevant because they help us to understand how to reconstruct the practice of work study programs as they relate to the development of gender identities.

According to Simon and Dippo, "the emphasis any given program places on one or more of these notions of experience has different implications for thinking through the ways in which the practice of work education should be accomplished" (p. 124). Simon and Dippo believe that the emphasis placed on these ways of experience will determine the nature of cultural politics in a program.

1. *Experience is information and techniques one acquires by participating in new and different situations.* These situations are valued because they are about learning what to do and how to do it, and are usually consistent with what the teacher expects the work experience to provide. For example, Helen's description of learning how to hammer nails fits with common assumptions about the development of procedural knowledge—that it is a process of puzzling out how to do something.

> So I do notice that the guys can nail about three times faster than I. I don't think strength has anything to do with it. I think it's when I'm starting to nail I don't whack it as hard as them because I'm afraid of hitting my thumb or finger. I think that would annoy me for the whole day. I think it's like skiing, that once you fall, you begin to lose the fear of falling and can go on with your skiing, the same with hammering . . . I'm feeling more comfortable with the saw as well. (Helen journal 1, p. 10)

While this particular experience may be congruent with school knowledge, others were not. For example, in the narrative outlined earlier where Susan is assigned a leadership task in the application of the siding, we see that, despite her obvious competence, her leadership goes unrecognised. Situations like this are fertile ground for teachers and students to explore the social relationships of the worksite. Susan was unable to do this—outside of her journal in a passing comment on how her day went. There was a tacit assumption here that if she is deemed to be competent and is assigned a leadership role, then the male students will be able to handle it. In this instance, working with the males of the program might help by challenging the conservatism inherent in allowing experience to speak for itself. For allowing experience to speak for itself without some kind of critical reflection is simply just job training and sexist training at that.

2. *Experience is a personal characteristic that one has as a result of participating in real work.* The emphasis in this program on getting the job done was, in the main, a reflection of one of the qualities associated with the engagement of the students in this program—real world experience. Real world experience was valued by the students above all else as a means of preparing them for acceptance in the job marketplace. This includes such capacities as work habits, dispositions, perspectives, and other qualities one would attribute to work experience. Such authentic experiences are perceived to be assets by the students and prospective employers; authenticity is a main selling feature of work study programs within schools and colleges. Simon and Dippo refer to this as a "commodification of self," where the work experience is perceived to equip graduates with the skills necessary to survive in the world of work (i.e., to turn one's self into a commodity). But commodification of self presents problems for the development of gender identities. For when the self is commodified, are not students encouraged to fill capacities that fit prevailing social forms? For example, making a fuss about not being listened to because you are a woman will not usually get one a job, whereas knowing how to do the job might.

A critical reconstruction of the curriculum of experience in this respect calls for radical shifts in the realities of the world of work. Such shifts could not reduce the ability of students to do the job, but rather would add the capacity for more interactive and more happily engaged workers. This is very difficult, even dangerous, for schools to attempt because it means nothing less than changing prevailing social norms.

3. *Experience is a challenging situation that is to be endured or undergone.* Impelling students into rites of passage that involve opportunities for growth associated with the challenges (perceived or otherwise) of the world is a tenet of experiential learning. The basic idea is that one is made stronger by experiences that test one's character. Aimee tells of her experience:

> It's hell, it's like you know, the worst. But when you're done, you're so proud of it you want to go back again . . . it feels the same with the house, I know in the long run I'm going to be really, really proud and glad I did it...I mean there have been points, like you know, working in the mud or in the rain or snow—it's just like you wish you could give up but you know, like—I COULDN'T—give up. I don't want to, I'd be afraid of what the others thought of me and . . . it's kind of like if you stop on a portage and you say "I'm not going any further" you know you've still got to do it. You might as well work your hardest, you're going to end up finishing it. Just do the best you can. Suffer through and it'll get better. (Aimee interview, pp. 1–85)

Now, in reading Aimee's words, one could also surmise that she has developed certain qualities—a positive attitude for example, one that indicates her willingness to participate and learn. But Simon and Dippo suggest that such quality can be construed as "a particular practical congruence between a specific set of student capacities and the existing requirements of an already-established social form" (1992, p. 128). In other words, the perception of having a so-called "good attitude" or to be engaged in a certain manner (or with certain people) is evidence that one possesses certain qualities. For young women and men forming their gender identities, this is particularly important as there is considerable pressure to conform to that which is already known. The same holds true for Susan's experience as a leader—males don't listen to females whether they're right or wrong. She may then form the view that she has to grin and bear it in order to make it through.

Here the choice can be problematic for participants. Aimee can choose to stay with the portage and grow and feel good after—or Susan may grin and bear it. Both risk sustaining potentially inequitable and disrespectful relationships within existing social norms about the roles of women. But although the choice needs to be clearly that of the student, teachers and curriculum need to anticipate, acknowledge, and respond to such dilemmas. Anticipation, or examining the potential for development in an experience, is common in experiential education—why not include discussions of the dilemma of sticking with a difficult and fundamentally flawed situation? Why not discuss how one might conceptualize and negotiate issues of identity formation within challenging, endurance situations? The key here, of course, is for practitioners to frame challenges in a way that would maximize the transformative potential of experience.

4. *Experience is the knowledge and understanding one accomplishes or develops in the way in which one makes sense of a situation or set of events.* Simon and Dippo see the relationships that people form "as an understanding that is constructed as a particular interpretation of a specific engagement with material and people over time" (1992, p. 128). This version of experience is dependent both on what participants bring to the situation in terms of predispositions, ideas, and assumptions, and on the context and

reflective opportunities that programs may offer. Helen's account of misuse of the chalkline on the floor is a case in point. She found the reaction of the males to her different approach to be offensive. In the end, although she wanted to confront one particular male about his sexist attitude, she decided "to let it go" (Helen journal 1, p. 9). This was an opportunity for her to confront the ideas, terms, procedures, relations, and her feelings—and in doing so, to make sense of their presence in the workplace. However, she had already learned the uselessness of confrontation, and the teachers were not modelling anything that told her how it might be different. A critical pedagogy of work education, according to Simon and Dippo, would mean that such situations would be examined in order to establish whether "existing forms encourage expanded capacities or whether they deny, disable, distort, dilute these capacities" (p. 123). It would mean that no experience would be celebrated uncritically.

These four views of experience can be summarized and under-stood in a broader fashion through the field of cultural psychology—the study of contextual behaviour of psychological processes. Cole (1990) understands that what makes humans different from other species is that we are able to modify our environment through the production of artifacts, and that these artifacts are the means by which humans are able to reproduce and transform subsequent generations. Now, artifacts are constituted of both technical and social relations—for example, the development of a procedural skill such as building a house is a technical relation. Technical relations are embedded in social relations which are the symbolic understandings that accompany productive activity. In other words, the two mutually modify one another, not unlike theory and practice relationships. The first two views of experience formulated by Simon and Dippo, those of experience as infor-mation and techniques and as the acquisition of personal character-istics used here, are examples of technical relations. The latter two, endurance of challenging situations and knowledge and under-standing, can be understood as social relations or the conceptual side of practical production. This secondary, technological-studies program was based on the notion that the authentic experience of building a house would be an appropriate rite of passage for the development of these adolescent and adult men and women. Simon, Dippo, and Schenke (1991) contend that the development of proficiency and a sense of competence is valuable to the extent that where

> work education programs focus exclusively on the technical relations of production, they deny students the opportunity to develop insights into the social relations within which technique is embedded. (p. 132)

The currents identified here represent tensions found in schools: an emphasis on education for work training on the one hand, and education for personal development on the other. This tension is played out in the context of an emphasis on work preparation at the expense of development of gender identities which question the legitimacy of prevailing social roles. The main point is that researchers are only just beginning to observe and listen to the narratives of teachers and what they have to say about their teaching. This study is part of that process, but more importantly, it has also given voice to students. Their voices are important because, like teachers, students not only have significant (and sometimes cryptic) stories to tell but these stories represent departure points from which researchers and, more importantly, teachers can engage in the development of a critical praxis.

References

Allen, R. E. (Ed.). (1990). *The concise Oxford dictionary of current English* (8th ed.). Oxford: Clarendon Press.

Belenky, M., Clinchy, B., Goldberger, N., & Tarule, J. (1986). *Women's ways of knowing: The development of self, voice and mind.* New York: Basic Books.

Bly, R. (1990). *Iron John: A book about men.* Don Mills: Addison Wesley.

Caplan, P. J. (1989). *Don't blame mother: Mending the mother-daughter relationship.* New York: Harper & Row.

Csikszentmihalyi, M. (1975). *Beyond boredom and anxiety.* San Francisco: Jossey-Bass.

Cole, M. (1990). Cultural psychology: A once and future discipline? In J. Berman (Ed.), *Cross-cultural perspectives,* Nebraska symposium on motivation, 1989. Lincoln, NE: University of Nebraska Press.

Doubt, E., & Ramsey, G. (1991). In the world for half a year: A student's view of TAMARACK — A new approach to learning. *Pathways, The Ontario Journal of Outdoor Education, 3*(6), 24–25.

Edwards, P. (1990). *Self-esteem and adolescent women.* (The A Capella Papers). Ottawa: Canadian Teacher's Federation.

Gibbons, M. (1974). Walkabout: Searching for the right passage from childhood and school. *Phi Delta Kappan, 55*(9), 256–271.

Gibbons, M. (1976). *The new secondary education.* Bloomington, IN: Phi Delta Kappa.

Gibbons, M. (1984). Walkabout ten years later: Searching for a renewed vision of education. *Phi Delta Kappan, 65*(9), 236–248.

Gilligan, C. (1982). *In a different voice: Psychological theory and women's development.* Cambridge: Harvard University Press.

Horwood, B. (1987). *Experiential education in high school: Life in the walkabout program.* Boulder, CO: Association for Experiential Education.

Horwood, B. (1992). The goat portage: Student's stories and learning from canoe trips. *CAHPER Journal.* Winter 1992, 18–22.

Horwood, B. (1994). Integration and experience in the secondary curriculum. *McGill Journal of Education, 29*(1), 89–102.

Horwood, B. (1994). Outdoor education and curricular integration. In L. H. McAvoy, L. A. Stringer, & A. Ewert (Eds.), *Coalition for education in the outdoors second research symposium proceedings* (pp. 14-21). Cortland, NY: Coalition for Education in the Outdoors.

James, C. (1968). *Young lives at stake: A reappraisal of secondary schools.* London: Collins.

Kaufman, M. (1993). *Cracking the armour: Power, pain and the lives of men.* Toronto: Penguin.

Kozolanka, K. (1993). *Beyond integrated curriculum: Student voice and the nature of student engagement.* Unpublished master's thesis, Queen's University, Kingston, Ontario.

Ontario Ministry of Education. (1989a). *The action plan: Restructuring the educational system.* Toronto: Queen's Printer.

Ontario Ministry of Education. (1989b). *Technological studies: The way ahead.* Working paper. Toronto: Queen's Printer.

Ontario Ministry of Education. (1993). *The common curriculum.* Working document. Toronto: Queen's Printer.

Proudman, B. (1992). What is experiential education?: Experiential education as emotionally-engaged learning. *Journal of Experiential Education, 15*(2), 19–23.

Simon, R., & Dippo, D. (1992). What schools can do: Designing programs for work education that challenge the wisdom of experience. In R. I. Simon (Ed.), *Teaching against the grain* (pp. 121–136). New York: Bergin & Garvey.

Simon, R., Dippo, D., & Schenke, A. (1991). *Learning work: A critical pedagogy of work education.* Toronto: OISE Press.

Steinem, G. (1993). *Revolution from within.* Toronto: Little, Brown.

Stevenson, J. (1990). The quality of education and school life. (The A Capella Papers). Ottawa: Canadian Teacher's Federation.

Wigginton, E. (1985). *Sometimes a shining moment.* Garden City: Anchor.

Chapter 7

AT THE HEART OF EDUCATION: PORTFOLIOS AS A LEARNING TOOL

Rick Gordon and Thomas Julius

This chapter takes the form of a conversation between a Grade 3 teacher and a teacher educator. Rick Gordon, who speaks first, has a BA from Stanford University, an MA from the University of Minnesota, and is completing a PhD at the University of Colorado. He is a world traveler, especially leading youth groups in Asian and European adventures. Tom Julius, who has the last word, gained his BA from Tufts University and his MEd from Antioch New England Graduate School. Tom has worked as an educator for more than fourteen years, nine of those spent learning from third graders in Keene, New Hampshire.

This chapter is important because the central value of portfolios in assessment is shown to be applicable across a large grade range. The characteristics of a tool with such universal application shed light on how the curriculum is experienced and reveal connections to other powerful experiential methods, such as those described in the chapters by Gail Simmons and Rena Upitis. The chapter retains the give and take of a conversation, but it has been rewritten to eliminate aspects of speech which do not read well, and to insert literature references, which hardly anyone that we know uses in even the most professional of dialogues.

Introduction

For many educators calling themselves "experiential," "progressive," or "student-centered," there is long-held tension in their practice. The direction for their teaching is clear—to actively engage students at the center of the learning process. Unfortunately, assessing the results of this learning has proven more problematic. Examinations fail to adequately capture the learning we seek for our students; nor are they consistent with the learning processes we value. In striving to touch hearts and minds while contributing to intellectual and emotional growth, richer and more personal forms of assessment are needed.

Confronting this dilemma, we have discovered that portfolios offer a profound solution to our needs. Whether with elementary students or college-level, pre-service teachers, portfolios touch the heart of education—inspiring students to demonstrate their growth while contributing to their continued learning. Rather than causing a break with other educational experiences, portfolios have become central to the learning process for our students, serving as a powerful tool to engage people of diverse ages, as we relate in this discussion of our work in two very different settings.

Coming from opposite ends of the educational spectrum, we thought it would be valuable to explore the issues of portfolios together—engaging in a conversation regarding their advantages and challenges, and where they fit into the learning process for our students. Through this discussion, we came to new understandings and insights into our own thinking. We hope these reflections will inspire fresh insights for other teachers and encourage similar conversations with teachers across grades and subjects.

Rick: As a teacher of pre-service teachers, I have used portfolios in lieu of a final exam in an effort to have students comprehensively reflect on, and synthesize, their learning in my courses. Counting as half their grade, the portfolio and its half-hour presentation to several classmates and me, is a serious undertaking. While students are expected to include selections from required work in class, such as research and reflection papers, the breadth of other materials which constitute their portfolio grows ever more interesting as the personal nature of each student's way of knowing shines through. Adding personal mementos like knitting projects, poetry, or rosary beads, my students have constructed meaning for themselves as teachers-to-be, relating experiences from our course to experiences in their lives to create their understandings which are simultaneously a touchstone and a jumping-off point for further growth (Gordon, 1994).

Tom: Like many educators, I have struggled to reconcile my knowledge of the complexity of child development with the bureaucratic, institutional imperatives of modern public schools. At the Jonathan M. Daniels Elementary School in Keene, New Hampshire, we have instituted an alternative to letter-graded report cards and conventional parent-teacher conferences that traditionally begin at third grade in our school district. Our reporting process includes two family conferences, in which students present their portfolios to their family and teacher, and two report cards, each consisting of a narrative and a skills checklist.

When we piloted this alternative evaluation system, we were looking for methods that would dispel the need to quantify, categorize, and distill a student's school experience to fit on a three-inch-square, self-adhesive record card, affixed on a file folder and forgotten. We wanted to release teachers, students, and families from the constraint of measuring a student's learning solely through the testing of rehearsed performances. We wanted to develop alternatives to letter-graded report cards. We discovered that what we were really engaged in was creating a culture of evaluation (Julius, 1993).

Advantages of Portfolios

Our conversation began by looking at why we chose to use portfolios. What we discovered was that portfolios were not just an assessment tool but, more importantly, were a powerful learning tool. Central to their value was the concept of authenticity—being "real," they were defined by quality standards not merely determined by the teacher, but inherent in facing a real audience with personally meaningful work. This idea of audience helped us better understand what distinguishes portfolios from other forms of assessment and what makes them work effectively for students.

T: At the elementary level, kids are accustomed to school being parceled into subject areas. Portfolios can make the whole curriculum come together in an integrated way. The essential importance of portfolios is that they are created for an audience. When you're doing important work, it always has an audience. When you're doing work for a grade, the only audience is the teacher. With portfolios you have the potential for the audience to be much broader. It could be your peers in the classroom, your teacher, other kids in the school, your family, even the much larger community outside the school. I think there is a sense of importance to performance that isn't there when you're doing work just for yourself.

R: In a sense, you're saying that it's more authentic. Performance is more authentic than presenting a paper to your teacher, because in life you perform in front of others and, in doing that performance, the quality should increase.

T: For me, in order for a piece to be authentic, you need three things: a product, a performance of some kind, and reflection. Who your audience is going to be puts the parameters on what this piece is like. You have what you produce, who you're going to produce it for, and your reflection on it.

R: I'm trying to relate this to the college experience. I have somewhat different reasons for doing portfolios. My problem is that, by the time I get people in college, they know how to perform for an audience, a teacher particularly. I'm seeking to get them to think more about their own learning and motivation and how to be self-responsible, self-directed learners. I'm trying to get the students to switch from thinking of the audience as being their teacher to the audience being real life, either their peers or the outside community— to get away from performing for the teacher audience or some objective criteria out there and to think more about, "What am I really learning here in the real world sense?"

These concepts of audience and authenticity link the two different ages.

T: When you think about traditional portfolios being a big folder that artists carry around, you're talking about a portfolio as something that is useful not only for oneself but that also says who you are to an outside audience. I think that's true for elementary students as well as adult learners.

R: How does that relate to the rest of your teaching philosophy? Has it changed the way you teach or is it just assessment?

T: Portfolios really match the way I teach. I moved to portfolios because I was looking for some form of evaluation that was in concert with the way I was teaching. I would say that portfolios haven't changed the way I teach; they've made me look at what I'm already teaching in different ways. It makes me look for ways to reach different kinds of learners, so that the portfolios aren't just filled with paper-and-pencil tasks. Instead, there's a broad range of examples of learning within the portfolio.

R: That's been the greatest thing for college students, and this might be an advantage with their age, as their repertoire of skills is so much greater than most younger kids. With portfolios, I hoped they would include a representation of their work beyond simply assigned written work. That's been the most exciting thing for me. I was trying to address multiple intelligences (Gardner, 1991) and allow people with other strengths to bring them in. By college, what they know how to do is write papers or take multiple-choice tests. But I was surprised that some students brought in stuff that was so interesting. For example, one woman brought all these objects that had meaning to her. This tiny bag of beads from a self-defense course, a Dr. Scuss book, a drawing from a student she tutored. . . . Through all these objects, she explained how these experiences made her better understand her role as a teacher. Another guy brought in a computer and had done a hypercard kind of program that was very interactive. The point was that he wanted his teaching to be very interactive and this allowed us to be involved. By college, too often we tend to confine people to the written word.

T: Was having their peers be their audience somewhat new for them?

R: I think so. For them, their peers were familiar. They had done a lot of work with them in class and they felt relatively safe. I think that allowed them to do more risky things some times, to be more personally exposed than they might be otherwise. The reason I included peers was that I felt that their fellow students learned from being there. It was the reinforcement of hearing someone else's learning and then you discussing your own. Rather than the final being that end-point of learning, where students think, "This is it, I finished, I can forget it," students leave the portfolio presentations either with some new insights or with reinforcement for what they were thinking.

T: What do you imagine them doing with it? Clearly they carried some learning with them beyond that. For instance, one of the things that I hope happens for my third graders is that they save the work. The portfolio goes home with them, and 20 years from now they're going to be able to look back, reflect on themselves and what they were learning back then, and think about who they are now. Do you see that happening at all?

R: I've heard people say they did portfolios as teacher ed. students and it's the only thing they kept. So I think maybe they do. I think this brings up a different issue. In the teacher training program I worked in, what I did was so different from the rest of the program. There was no agreement on how the department as a whole evaluated. If portfolios were to be used throughout the program, then I think students would build a record of their understanding of themselves as teachers and learners. They would then develop and take this with them and it could be central to their teaching. They might look at it and think, "Wow, I've come a long way. I may be having a tough time, but look where I was four or ten years ago." I think if we had final portfolios as the exit from the teacher ed. program, where they brought in all their stuff, you might find some really powerful things. Likewise, I think it's a question for K-12 to look how portfolios fit across ages and subject areas.

Starting Out and the Implications for Practice

Beginning with portfolios requires both teachers and students to explore new concepts for standards of quality. Portfolio participants need to reflect on what constitutes quality work which, sadly, is too rarely considered in traditional educational settings. The exercise of determining these standards, often through a process of submitting work for review and comments, is a valuable learning tool in itself. Through this process, both teachers and students become more responsible for their learning and the outcomes they value.

T: When I started with portfolios several years ago, it was the first time that the students had ever been asked to reflect on their work in any kind of organized way. We had to teach them the language that they needed. When we asked them to select a piece of work, we had to teach them what "select" meant. We had to teach them from ground zero. Recently, we have the first and second grades in the entire school district using portfolios for evaluation as well as reporting. We're excited to be getting kids in the third grade who have experience and practice with the language of portfolios. Now they have an image in their mind of what a portfolio is. It's a huge advantage for us.

R: It's funny that you said starting at ground zero, because I felt like that with college students. Sometimes I think it's worse with college students because they're so entrenched in not being asked to make choices. When I ask what standards we should use to evaluate, they don't want to deal with it. They have been so immune to having to consider that question over the last 18 years that they don't even want to discuss it. It would be interesting to see your kids in college.

　　I think that's what schools should be about—the refinement of people's sense of quality. They learn that quality is something that we strive toward and that they themselves determine the standards of quality to a large degree. And that's the standard to which they should be held. That's where integrity comes in—that you live up to your standards. Not the traditional structure where students more and more must accept outside imposition rather than expanding their abilities to be decision makers and choosers in life.

T: I think portfolios really assist students in producing and recognizing what William Glasser (1990) calls quality work. One of the reasons is that portfolios lend themselves to sharing one's work with others. Having a sense of producing quality work is one of the things that we try to get across to kids, as well as learning the essential skills that they need for third grade, practising self-evaluation and becoming reflective learners. It sounds like that's pretty similar to the college level.

R: Of course, the primary goals are for people to develop skills and content knowledge—I think that's ostensibly still the role of schools—but also, what Dewey (1938) calls collateral learning in terms of collaboration and sharing. Students learn that not only is it okay to share with your peers, but that's where quality develops. Individually, you're probably going to produce weaker work than you will with others. Another lesson is that it's okay for kids to produce work that's very different from others: to learn that quality is something that runs across different styles and that it might look very different for this ESL kid, this visual learner. They're each going to present different pictures perhaps, but they can all be strong in their own way.

T: Collateral learning brings up the question of how to establish common standards for the group at the same time that you are enabling opportunities for individuality. Portfolios are a beautiful vehicle for that. You may have the teacher setting criteria for particular tasks, but the students, via their portfolios, present the way they approach the tasks as individuals. The standard remains the same. I have started to experiment presenting models from which students can generate standards—projects from last year, examples of pieces of writing that we talk about in terms of quality. From those models we create some standards as to what writing would need to have in order to be a good piece of writing. The standards become a collaborative effort.

This also gets back to the question of audience. Our primary audience is reporting to families, so we never say to the children, "Select your best piece"; we say, "Select a piece of work that you want to present, something that is meaningful to you." Inevitably, they select work that shows the range and depth of their abilities. One of the things parents worry about is, "If all I ever see is my kid's best work, how do I know what they need to improve on?"

R: Portfolios don't lend themselves to sorting, which I see as a benefit. I see the role of schools to help all students succeed to the greatest degree they can. When I think of portfolios, it's as a teaching and learning tool, not as an assessment tool. When I used a final exam, I thought that I was establishing a floor beneath which these kids couldn't sink. I had a final exam to assure a minimum level of understanding. I found that with portfolios, when I said to students, "Figure out what you want to include," the floor was never the problem. I realized that my final exam was both the ceiling and the floor at the same time. No one could come up with things outside the final exam. They could answer the questions, but they couldn't bring in these things from their outside class experiences. They didn't fit. I realized that we create these parameters that confine students more often than not. When we take away the parameters, students can excel far beyond what we often think they can do.

T: As an educator, I'm much more interested in learning than I am in teaching. Unfortunately, that's not always true with people in education.

R: I would agree; schools should be about learning. That's why we like portfolios—they are a learning tool and they happen to work well with assessment. But their fundamental purpose, like that of schools, is learning. Instead of wasting time preparing for and taking final exams, I felt like students were actually doing more learning. Especially in college where you only have 20 classes with a group of students. I hate to waste 10% of my classes on grading people. I'd rather spend 100% on student learning.

T: When you have letter-grades, people stop looking at the actual piece of work and start looking at the grade. Eliminating the grades has forced our audience, our families, to pay much more attention to the work students are doing. We are very up front with parents. We tell them, "You will no longer be able to ask your children when they come home with their report card, 'Wadjaget?' This system of evaluation is going to require you to look at your daughters' and sons' work and talk to them about it in ways that some of you may not have done before."

R: In college, we must submit grades. Portfolios really improve the quality of students' work, so on one hand it wasn't a big issue, grading. Again, I'm trying to make the students succeed, not fail, and this allows them to show their strengths. I also enjoyed the process and the feedback from their peers, who very much try to be positive. The last comments I make to the students, in the context of grading the portfolios, are ones that can lead to further growth and not be just a final assessment. That gives me an opportunity to compliment their progress and push them to think about issues.

T: One of the things that's been striking for me, at family conferences where students present their portfolios, is that dads come much more frequently than when it's a parent-teacher conference. When is it that fathers usually come to school anyway? They come to sports events, a play . . . some kind of a performance. When students are presenting their portfolios, it's a performance; dads are more inclined to come because they have a role. There is a way for them to participate, as opposed to a conventional parent-teacher conference where a parent's role is not as well defined, or it may be to go in and defend the child against the savage educational system.

R: The performance idea reminds me of the question: "Why do kids get letter jackets for sports, and awards for concerts and plays, while academics don't get any rewards except grades, and that's not the same?" I never intended to use portfolios as ways of individually recognizing students, but it certainly plays more into the concept of the way, socially, we look at what gets rewarded in society. Accomplishment and performances get rewarded. I think portfolios play into the way our society looks at rewarding people, in a way that makes it worthwhile.

T: And look at what behaviors portfolios are rewarding. They encourage critical thinking, decision making, organization, reflection, and presentation, as well as content knowledge. These are practical, necessary life skills for literate people.

Interestingly, I have found that students who are less skilled at conventional school behavior, like fill-in-the-blank tests, are some of the most adept portfolio presenters. The students who are very good at sitting quietly and parroting back the right answer often become flustered when asked to perform for a portfolio presentation.

R: I think the perception at the college level is that portfolio presentations are stressful, anxiety-ridden, unsettling—lots of negative feelings before them, and that's good. On the whole, this reflects that people are being challenged to think in ways they haven't been asked to before and that inspires them. What is stressful for them is to think about what they have learned and not just answer what the teacher is going to ask on a multiple-choice test. It's more in the heart than just in the head and that's hard on people. Afterward, they say the portfolio was the most effective part of the class, commenting, "I learned that I still need to process more," or, "It gave me things to think about afterwards. I realized how much I learned because I couldn't fit it all in." To me those are very positive things to be realizing.

T: That makes me think about kids having to go from the collecting process to the selecting process with their portfolios. That can be a very difficult point because some kids want to put it all in. Agonizing over choices indicates to me that they find value in doing portfolios. There's something about saying, "I've got all this stuff and this is the one piece I'm going to select and put out there for others to view." Something about that speaks much more to the heart.

R: Portfolios emphasize students as decision makers—throughout life, you need to make choices. This is part of the real life skills that kids say school doesn't address. This is one of those skills that is so inherent in life—making selections of quality and learning to live with those choices, and maybe change them and reflect. I think that lesson is something that is very valuable.

T: It doesn't matter who you are or how much you've achieved academically . . . those skills of decision making, self-evaluation, and reflection are the kinds of skills that are essential whether you're going to drop out in the tenth grade or go on for a doctorate.

Challenges of Portfolios: Rethinking Time and Control

Although their advantages are overwhelming, portfolios certainly provide challenges. The most common concern is the time they require, although in the context of student learning, we would argue this time is well spent. The other primary issue for some educators is the need to relinquish some of their control in order to empower students at the center of the learning process. For experiential educators, this is a natural fit. For more traditional teachers, this step is more difficult, but can potentially be a powerful impetus for rethinking one's relationship with students. Witnessing students' growth through portfolios has been the most gratifying experience in our work. Only when we make students free to demonstrate their learning are their, and our, accomplishments truly evident.

R: There's got to be some things about portfolios that are not great. Can you think of any? Time certainly is one for me; these do take up time. The process is valuable, so the time is well spent, but it does change the use of time in a course from strictly transmitting information to developing a group that can make decisions and construct meaning from issues. It's not like a test where I can say, "I'm giving an exam on Friday and I determine what's on it." Portfolios take a lot of time with your class determining what should be included, how they're evaluated, what are standards of quality. These are valuable skills to learn, but they do take up time which may have been used for other things in the past.

T: That may be true at the college level, but for a long time in early childhood education, we have been focused on process as well as product. Portfolios match the way we teach in early childhood education. High school teachers who are more confined to a content area may feel that they lose time. However, I think that the time you lose from teaching content you gain back in students reflecting on their work. While they are selecting work for their portfolios, they are reflecting on the content of the course in a different way than when they were trying to produce it. I would argue you aren't losing any content.

R: I agree. Being in those presentations is a million times more gratifying to me than grading exams. To hear students discuss their learning makes me feel like I've contributed to something positive. That, to me, is a great benefit. With tests you never know. It could be a person just studies for the test and forgets it a minute later. Again, it comes back to the heart being in it. Hearing people speak from their heart means more than seeing what they write from their head.

T: One of the most moving experiences I've had as a teacher is watching my students present their portfolios at family conferences. Recently, one of my students presented her portfolio to a group of six adults: her biological mom and dad, her step-dad, myself, a student teacher, and our school's reading specialist. There we were, six adults, listening to the child, encouraging, helping the student to reflect on her work and set some personal goals. This is the kind of thing that rarely happens in schools, and that you never have the opportunity for in a regular class day.

R: Do you confront this issue of giving up control—trusting kids to come up with standards—or do your parameters take care of that?

T: Since we don't ask students to select best work, we end up receiving work that comes from the heart as much as from the head, so students select work that is representative of their skills. This allows me to demonstrate, to the student as well as to the family, the student's skill level and ways in which he or she is improving. Everyone can look at it; it's a concrete example. It actually gives me more control in the sense that I'm looking for demonstrations of improvement in authentic work and not in a test that is abstracted from student's work.

R: This issue of losing control goes back to fitting assessment with your teaching philosophy. Part of my teaching philosophy is to give students more control over their own learning. I think for third graders as much as for college students, it's a skill they need to learn. They might not have learned it yet by third grade, and by college it may have been taught out of them. I learned it was disingenuous when I told my students I would give them responsibility and then pulled the rug out from under them by having a final exam at the end of the course. It contradicted what I was saying all along. This idea of consistency in our practice is critical; our philosophy of teaching must fit with our methods of assessment and our focus on learning and growth. That should be part of courses throughout what we do, and shouldn't change the last day of class when we surprise them with some sort of teacher-directed test to make sure they got just what we wanted. Students have to believe in what we're saying, and we need to provide models of integrity, and I think that's what we're saying.

T: This is an interesting point and one I'm beginning to wrestle with this year. If we really believe in models of integrity, then shouldn't we also be modeling, doing ourselves what we're asking students to do? This year will be the first time in four years of working with portfolios that I'm going to keep a portfolio of my own which I will share with my students. I'm going to be modeling the use of a portfolio as a way of reflecting about myself. As a teacher, I'm going to use the same criteria I expect of them.

R: I want my pre-service teachers to be reflective practitioners. I try to get them to start reflecting on their thinking on teaching and, hopefully, they'll continue this throughout their careers. Certainly that's the model of a professional in teaching—someone who reflects on and is conscious of their practice.

T: Howard Gardner (1991) talks about schools needing to become more like apprenticeships. I like the idea that as teachers, we have students apprenticed to us. We're not only conveying a body of knowledge, we're teaching a way of learning. Apprentices of old were required to show examples of their work on the way to achieving levels of mastery. Today, in much the same way, portfolios have the potential to demonstrate learning in powerful ways.

Conclusion

As teachers, we are tempted to go beyond a conversation about the merits of portfolios and to enter the realm of suggesting ways for implementing them. There are many reasonable, practical guides to getting started with portfolios at the elementary, second-ary, or college level. We have noted a few in our List of Resources. In practice, however, the power of portfolios lies as much in the act of creation as in the resulting product. This is as true for the teacher as it is for the student.

While imminently more messy than pre-digested guidelines, matching the portfolio process to the way you teach by engaging students in the process of developing standards, collecting and selecting from their authentic work, and making presentations to an audience is where the experience will flourish. It is through this col-laborative process that students are empowered to make decisions, set personal goals, and develop self-evaluation. This experience of personal and social construction is the vehicle that brings meaning and value to learning. We encourage teachers to explore the possi-bilities of portfolios with their students and, together, to reach out to the heart of learning.

In addition to their benefits for students, portfolios are a way for teachers to develop professional community. Lave and Wegner (1991) discuss communities of practice and argue that we need to develop common languages in those communities. Portfolios can serve as a means for teachers to collect and reflect on their own work, lesson plans, and creative curriculum, as well as on work their students have done. Portfolios give us a picture of profession-als who are growing and learning about their work. They also give guideposts to look back and see where we've been, what we've accomplished, and what we've learned.

Moreover, portfolios support the idea of collegiality, teaming, and integrated studies. We need to have more authentic links between disciplines. No teacher wants to make artificial links between disciplines. We need to have teachers talking to each other in schools about what they are trying to achieve in their educational settings. What are those common themes, skills, and abilities we want kids to be learning across the disciplines? Those shared objec-tives do exist; we want kids to be critical thinkers, problem solvers, able to articulate ideas using numbers and words. That runs across content areas. For portfolios at the end of the year, or for gradua-tion, students can bring together all their work to show they have those skills of critical thinking, problem solving, and working with others. This would start making those ties and breaking down the artificial barriers we so long created between subjects where the focus is almost entirely on content acquisition and too little on application and use.

References

Dewey, J. (1938). *Experience and education.* New York: Collier.

Gardner, H. (1991). *The unschooled mind.* New York: Basic Books.

Glasser, W. (1990). *The quality school: Managing students without coercion.* New York: Harper & Row.

Gordon, R. (1994). Keeping students at the center: Portfolio assessment at the college level. *The Journal of Experiential Education, 17*(1), 23-27.

Julius, T. (1993). Creating a culture of evaluation. *Democracy & education, 7*(4), 11-23.

Lave, J., & Wegner, E. (1991). *Situated learning.* Cambridge, England: Cambridge University Press.

List of Resources

Batzle, J. (1992). *Portfolio assessment and evaluation.* Cypress, CA: Creative Teaching Press.

Graves, D. H., & Sunstein, B. S. (1992). *Portfolio portraits.* Portsmouth, NH: Heineman.

Grosvener, L. (1993). *Student portfolios.* (Teacher-to-Teacher Series.) Washington, DC: National Education Association Library.

Tierney, R. J. (1991). *Portfolio assessment in the reading-writing classroom.* Norwood, MA: Christopher-Gordon.

Chapter 8

PRACTICE AND PERSPECTIVE: TWO VIEWS OF EXPERIENTIAL EDUCATION

Ed Raiola

Ed Raiola earned his BA in Philosophy at California State University at Chico, an MEd in Outdoor Education from the University of Northern Colorado, and a PhD from Union Graduate School. Between rounds of study, Ed developed and tested his interests as a VISTA volunteer and as a teacher at Unity College. Now a committed educator teaching at Warren Wilson College, he uses outdoor recreation and environmental studies as vehicles to train other educators. His special interest is to investigate the respective roles that intention, attention, and intuition play in wise outdoor leadership.

This chapter breaks new ground in experiential education by describing the contributions of two thinkers who have not previously been recognized as heroes of experiential education. Ed Raiola courageously leads us into the down-to-earth understandings of Earl Kelley and challenges us with the ethereal and mystical insights of Jiddu Krishnamurti. In doing this, he places them into the pantheon of experiential educators along with people like Thomas Dewey, William James, Kurt Hahn, and Charity James.

Foreword

What if we said that in order for learning to take place, students must learn in accordance with their own purpose (or needs) and experiences? What if schools emphasized opportunities for students to talk and listen, read, write, do, and reflect as they approached course content? What if we all agreed that 1) learning is by nature an active endeavor, and 2) that different people learn in different ways? How would schools look and what methods would we use to teach?

If knowing about the world, and about life, consisted only of assimilating a body of static, concrete information, learning by rote might be the most efficient model for educating anybody about anything. What we know about teaching and learning seems to contradict those notions. To illustrate, let's summarize what is known about teaching and learning.

- People come to classes with their own perceptual frameworks firmly intact, rather than as "empty vessels" to be filled with knowledge (Erickson, 1984, p. 55).

- People learn in different ways (Kolb, 1984; Briggs-Meyers, 1980).

- Learning is a dynamic process that involves teacher and student as co-inquirers (Tiberius, 1986).

- Learning does not happen by just absorbing content (taking lots of notes and memorizing for exams), but by critically analyzing, discussing, and using content in meaningful ways (Hutchings, 1990).

- Lecturing has severe limitations as a predominant teaching strategy:

  - In the first ten minutes of lecture, students retain 70% of the information; in the last ten minutes, 20% (McKeachie, 1986).

  - While teachers are lecturing, students are not attending to what is being said 40% of the time (Pollio, 1984).

- Students lose their initial interest, and attention levels continue to drop, as a lecture proceeds (Verner & Dickinson, 1967).

- Four months after taking an introductory psychology course, students knew only 8% more than a control group who had never taken the course (Rickard, Rogers, Ellis, & Beidleman, 1988).

For many people, knowing about the world, and about life, has apparently been enriched by translation through the individual's perceptual frames (talking and listening, reading, writing, doing, and reflecting), yielding a deeper, broader world view than might be possible without such translation.

In my search to improve my teaching and learning, I began a journey to learn from the rich history of progressive thinking and writing about experience and education. I was especially touched by the ideas and practices of two relatively "unknown" practitioners: the philosopher-educators, Earl C. Kelley and Jiddu Krishnamurti, surveyed in this paper. They both address the role of experience in learning, which is especially relevant to those of us who have struggled as teachers, experimenting and trying to expand our repertoire of teaching approaches, sometimes successfully, sometimes not. Kelley's concepts emanate from a Western mechanistic tradition, but Krishnamurti's evolve from a more synergistic Eastern world view.

Earl C. Kelley

One of the less-recognized contributors to the field of experiential education is Earl C. Kelley. Dr. Kelley's rich career included work as a public school science teacher, a secondary school administrator, an instructor, and, finally, a distinguished professor of education at Eastern Michigan University. His writings include *Education for What is Real* (1947), *The Workshop Way of Learning* (1951), *Education and the Nature of Man* (1952), and *In Defense of Youth* (1962). In order to understand Kelley's model of the experiential learning process, we must first examine some of his basic beliefs about the nature of learning and perception.

Kelley (1947) suggests that many of the ills of our educational system and its product (people) come from two major areas: "(1) That we present knowledge as absolute and existing before learning can begin, instead of something to be lived; (2) that we disregard and often work counter to the learner's purpose or needs" (p. 72). For Kelley, learning must begin before knowledge can exist; learning is not a matter of acquisition and acceptance, but is a result of process and is subject to continuous modification. Learning is made possible through memory and is uniquely held and uniquely used. To Kelley, knowledge is what we know, subjective in nature and unique to each learner.

Kelley's second point is that the educational system disregards and, therefore, impedes the learner's purpose. From his perspective, the traditional classroom has two important factors: the teacher and the subject matter. The student gets his or her purpose from the teacher and then learns, perhaps, the subject matter presented by the teacher. The subject matter remains a given, and most of the modification necessary to bring the student and subject matter together takes place on the part of the student. If the student can find suitable meaning within the framework of the subject matter, that is considered optimal, but if not, then the student must be coerced. While we may not think of grades as a form of coercion, the threat posed by this judgment upon each student's worth, according to the criteria set by the teacher, is not at all subtle.

What Kelley and Rasey (1952) proposed is that students learn, without coercion, in accordance with their own purposes (or needs) and experiences. Therefore, we must look to a modification of the role and usefulness of the subject matter, the role of the teacher, and the learning environment. In order for learning (seen as a continuous dynamic throughout life) to take place, the learner must have the purpose and experience to receive whatever is available in any particular situation. Kelley and Rasey believe that one cannot teach anything until the learner is ready to learn it:

> When the organism lacks experience and purpose to receive, it lacks readiness. Now we can see more clearly how crucial to education the matter of readiness is. The force of this idea is much greater when we realize that readiness is basic to the nature of the percep-

tual process, and lack of readiness is not a matter of unwillingness to learn. (p. 34)

They go on to say that if the energy spent by teachers (as well as learners) in defying this factor of readiness could be turned to constructive uses, enormous progress in growth could be made and readiness itself could in many cases be acquired. For example, we educators could put a high premium on active, experiential learning for elementary- and middle-school-age students who are at a developmental point where they interact with and learn from their environment kinesthetically. Honoring and addressing students' readiness to learn through their entire sensory apparatus, instead of such a strong emphasis being placed on sitting in a classroom, passively giving back what has been handed out, might transform the majority of behavior problems we find in schools.

For Kelley and Rasey (1952), an individual's experiential learning process begins with perception and purpose, moves to experience, and then proceeds to thought and value, which results in knowledge or learning. Perception is the person's line to his or her externality; it is an interpretation made by the learner that comes into consciousness, originating within the learner and not from without. Purpose, as Kelley uses it, means a conscious or unconscious urge to satisfy a perceived need. "Purpose is a driving force which gives expression for, or points a path to, the expenditure of the energy which we constitute" (p. 55). Purpose is both conscious and unconscious. Conscious purpose is that which comes into our awareness; unconscious purpose is the biological "driving force of tissue purpose that shows the path through which energy may be spent with compliance and satisfaction. It is the force through which the plant, the animal, the human being become more perfectly that which it already is" (p. 55).

Purpose not only influences what can come into awareness and become part of one's constructs about reality, it also points the path along which the energy that makes up the total person can be spent. The learning that can take place as an individual interacts with his or her environment and the way in which the accumulation of power and knowledge can be used depends upon the person's purpose.

Kelley and Rasey (1952) state that "experience is the process of undergoing, the contact with the concrete, the working out of the project circumstances" (p. 38). Humans are bundles of experiences, in flux and in process, continually being modified. We acquire knowledge through experience. In the learning process it is not the event alone which constitutes an experience, but the interaction between the event and the experiencing person. "Knowledge . . . is a product or residue of the perception-experience process. . . . It is a result of process, and is subject to continuous modification as process goes forward in a changing world" (p. 71).

Since we have the ability to remember, there is a memory of experience. Something is left after the experience is over. Kelley describes what remains as knowledge, ever subjective in nature and unique to each learner. Although in many of my courses I begin with very carefully designed, specific learning objectives that I hope the students will be able to achieve or demonstrate, I usually find that, by the end of the course, the lessons learned are as many and varied as the students themselves, sometimes having nothing whatsoever to do with the education objectives that I had planned.

The final step in Kelley's process is that of thought and attribution of value. After we have had an experience, we think about it, make some generalizations, and may apply our knowledge to new situations. We may come up with new perceptions or new purpose. We may evaluate the effect of the experience upon us, making value judgments. A young, outdoor-leadership student might start leading a new group feeling quite pleased with the plan she's devised for their activities, only to find that the group is thoroughly bored with what she has arranged. She may go through stages of frustration and reevaluation of herself and the work before she realizes that other people have different values than hers.

Thus, this thinking phase of Kelley's mode involves the organization and integration of experience. For Kelley, we are all accumulated experience; we perceive what we have the experience and purpose to perceive, and take our perceptions with us, so that our future perceptions are shaped by them. Kelley's (1947) view of this interrelationship between the individual, with all of his/her history, and the environment, is "growth in its widest meaning; growth which enables the whole organism to become more competent to cope with life" (p.72)—it is education.

Jiddu Krishnamurti

Attempting to crystallize the extraordinary life and singular teaching of Krishnamurti is like trying to grasp a child's blown bubble: as soon as you think you have hold of it, you discover that your hand is empty. Since the essence of his life work was to question the attachments which we ordinary humans have created for our own reassurances about "how the world is," describing his confoundingly simple teachings is a paradoxical task. Beliefs, disciplines of a prescribed sort, methods of achieving anything (and, indeed, most all of the "anythings" we think we should achieve), and teachers as sources of knowledge are all cleanly dismantled by Krishnamurti as distractions from the real brilliance of self that evolves from the quiet mind. Paradoxically, to put words and images to this man's thought is, in his view, to partially obscure it.

In 1910, at the age of about 14, Krishnamurti became the protégé of the leaders of the Theosophical Society, C. W. Leadbeater and Annie Besant, who saw him as candidate for the next corporeal vehicle of the "World Teacher" or "Christ-energy," according to their belief in the hierarchy of spiritual matters guiding the evolution of humankind on earth. They all but kidnapped him from his widowed Brahmin father, and took him, with his younger brother, to England to be trained, in accordance with the clairvoyantly received wishes of the Master. Krishnamurti was carefully fed, exercised, and taught the disciplines of meditation under the auspices of the Theosophists.

After several years of this not-at-all-uncomfortable life, Krishnamurti began to have intense spiritual experiences of his own and to talk about them with others. Around 1929, there developed a schism of sorts between him and the established power-figures of the Theosophical Society when he began to teach that:

> Truth is a pathless land, and you cannot approach it by any path whatsoever, by any religion, by any sect. If an organization be created for this purpose, it becomes a crutch, a weakness, a bondage,

and must cripple the individual, and prevent him from growing, from establishing his uniqueness, which lies in his discovery for himself of that absolute, unconditioned Truth. (Lutyens, 1983, p.15)

Krishnamurti continued to expand his enigmatic teaching, now long dissociated from the Theosophists, through a loosely structured Foundation which has focused on providing forums for his talks and publishing his books, as well as through a few Krishnamurti schools in Europe, India, and the United States. The volumes that particularly address the topics of education, knowledge, and learning are: *Education and the Significance of Life* (1953), *Think on These Things* (1964), and *Krishnamurti on Education* (1974).

From his perspective, education is much more than a matter of accumulating information and knowledge. The function of education and learning is to create human beings who are integrated and, therefore, intelligent. We need to remember that, for this man, the categorization process by which we attempt to establish reality as a series of facts is not learning, but is rather a distortion of learning.

Krishnamurti speaks of mind functions as operating upon different levels. The "intellect," in his terms, is the function of the rational mind, that which collects information and technical skills for living in the world on a day-to-day basis: driving the car, remembering your phone number, balancing your checkbook. "Intelligence," however, is not the ability to accumulate information, in Krishnamurti's terms; it is, rather, the transcendent mind, that which can perceive the wholeness of something in a more spiritual sense. For Krishnamurti, the function of education is to create learners who are integrated and intelligent. Intelligence goes beyond information. "Intelligence is the capacity to perceive the essential, the *what is* [italics added]; and to awaken this capacity in oneself and in others" (Krishnamurti, 1953, p. 14). This aspect of mind is not at all involved with the residue of facts: on the contrary, one must quiet the internal voices that endlessly catalogue our beliefs about reality in order to experience through intelligence.

"Knowledge" is that body of data that comprises our rational picture of the world and how to live in it, and, while Krishnamurti recognizes its usefulness, he cautions us about education systems that focus too exclusively on the building-up of knowledge at the expense of cultivating the larger mind, or intelligence. It is this cultivation, a freeing from the limits of knowledge, that he considers true "Learning." Learning, an active and immediate experience of the self in relationship to whatever else is in the moment, ". . . is never an additive process. . . . Learning ceases when there is only accumulation of knowledge. There is only learning when there is no accumulation at all" (Krishnamurti, 1974, pp. 101-102).

This semantic entanglement serves to remind us that as soon as we begin to describe and classify any internal experience, we have ceased to be fully in that experience and have stepped back to observe ourselves. It is this sort of solidifying that language attempts, in an effort to hold the object still enough for another's scrutiny. Krishnamurti would have us consider the possibility that learning involves only the action, the energy, the awareness of the experience, without translating into fact, which "becomes an anchorage which holds your mind and prevents it from going further. In the process of inquiry the mind sheds from day to day . . . so that it is always fresh and uncontaminated by yesterday's experience" (Krishnamurti, 1964, p. 195). Yet there seems to be a possible compromise, wherein learning through doing, integratively, creates a balance between the sublime and the mundane: "It is this experiencing that will put capacity and technique in the right place" (Krishnamurti, 1953, p. 17). Accordingly, in practical discussion of the role of education, Krishnamurti emphasizes the importance of developing the learner's ability to discover where and when knowledge and technical skills are necessary, and where they are irrelevant and even harmful. For Krishnamurti, the highest function of education is to bring about an integrated learner who is capable of dealing with all aspects of life. This presupposes an education environment that not only recognizes the "intelligence" it offers students, but also helps to nurture it. "Education in its truest sense is the understanding of oneself, for it is within each one of us that the whole of existence is gathered" (Krishnamurti, 1953, p. 21).

Afterword

Each of these authors offers a rich perspective on education and the learning process. Although they have varied and divergent beliefs about the nature and purpose of education, each agrees that experience is somehow central to the learning process.

Education, as learning in doing, involves a unique and special relationship between the event and the experiencing person(s). Kelly and Krishnamurti both recognize that it is the way in which the individual interacts with his or her experience, and the meanings gleaned by that individual, that form the learning process.

They differ most dramatically in their assumptions (or lack of them) about the nature of reality and the character of the individual's relationship to it. Earl Kelley's thinking is grounded and shaped by a mechanistic world view. He assumes that reality is different for each of us, both through our individualized perceptions of whatever is out there and also by virtue of our unique purposes as individuals, which shape our perceptions. Kelley argues that, for each person, any given object will be experienced in a way that is somewhat, or even radically, different. Therefore, although as an educator I may assume some consensus about "what the ocean is like," I cannot anticipate the effects of a marine biology expedition on any two individuals.

Krishnamurti almost ruthlessly dismantles everything except pure awareness; his sense of reality is far removed from Kelley's. He speaks of experience on the spiritual (not religious) level, rather as a synonym for aliveness. The physical world and its effects are, for Krishnamurti, a temporarily necessary distraction (since we live in bodies) from a higher truth. Education, then, becomes any method for clearing the essential vision of the learner, freeing her or him from the cobwebs of limiting beliefs about self and life. To provide an experience for another in the ways that Kelley might propose would, for Krishnamurti, be to obscure that person's process. Each of us must seek our own clarity, and the journey of that seeking is education.

My own search and practice has continually informed me about the art and science of teaching. Kelley's writings emphasize the science of experiential learning while Krishnamurti embraces the art or spirit of education. I adhere to Krishnamurti's notion that education should seek to help the leaner to become free of limiting beliefs of self and life and become a whole or integrated person.

I have learned that I must take some responsibility to impel and provide opportunities for people to get excited or motivated to learn. I have found that I must be prepared and create a framework around what we will be learning together (Kelley's notion of providing purpose and experience to help create readiness in the learner). I must also listen to the people I work with because they do indeed know what they want to learn.

The puzzle that keeps coming back to me as an educator is that I believe that there are certain knowledge bases that my students should be exposed to or demonstrate competence in. These can range from knowing the history and philosophy of experiential education to demonstrating how to plan, lead, and facilitate initiative games. My presupposition about what constitutes "minimum competencies" does indeed come in conflict with the notion of learner-directed education. So I bounce back and forth between my need to ensure that students are minimally competent to letting them choose what they want to learn about.

Both Kelley and Krishnamurti have helped to inform me in my ongoing exploration and questioning of education and how best to engage in that process. In a sense, one can think of these educators as colors in a spectrum, not contradicting each other so much as shading, subtly or abruptly, into one another. Kelley, with his metaphysical (or quantum physical) theories about perception and reality, shakes our perhaps inflexible beliefs, loosening us up for Krishnamurti, the radical, who challenges everything we think, urging us to open our minds to greater possibilities.

These educators have helped me to remember to ask myself what's worth teaching and knowing and what is the best way to get that to happen.

References

Briggs-Myers, I. (1980). *Gifts differing.* Palo Alto, CA: Consulting Psychologist Press.

Erickson, S. C. (1984). *The essence of good teaching: Helping students learn and remember what they learn.* San Francisco: Jossey-Bass.

Hutchings, P. (1990, June 30). *Assessment and the way it works.* Closing plenary address, Fifth American Association of Higher Education Conference on Assessment, Washington, DC.

Kelley, E. C. (1947). *Education for what is real.* New York: Harper Bros.

Kelley, E. C. (1951). *The workshop way of learning.* New York: Harper Bros.

Kelley, E. C. (1962). *In defense of youth.* Englewood Cliffs, NJ: Prentice Hall.

Kelley, E. C., & Rasey, M. (1952). *Education and the nature of man.* New York: Harper Bros.

Kolb, D. A. (1984). *Experiential learning: Experience as a source of learning and development.* Englewood Cliffs, NJ: Prentice Hall.

Krishnamurti, J. (1953). *Education and the significance of life.* San Francisco: Harper Bros.

Krishnamurti, J. (1964). *Think on these things.* New York: Harper & Row.

Krishnamurti, J. (1974). *Krishnamurti on education.* New York: Harper & Row.

Lutyens, M. (1983). *Krishnamurti: The years of fulfilment.* New York: Avon.

McKeachie, W. J. (1986). *Teaching tips: A guidebook for the beginning college teacher* (8th ed.). Lexington, MA: Heath.

Pollio, H. R. (1984). *What students think about and do in college lecture classes.* Teaching-Learning Issues No. 53. Knoxville, TN: Learning Research Center, University of Tennessee.

Rickard, H., Rogers, R., Ellis, N., & Beidleman, W. (1988). Some retention, but not enough. *Teaching of Psychology, 15,* 151-152.

Tiberius, R. G. (1986). Metaphors underlying the improvement of teaching and learning. *British Journal of Education Technology, 17*(2), 144-156.

Verner, C., & Dickinson, G. (1967). The lecture: An analysis and review of research. *Adult Education, 17*(2), 85-90.

Chapter 9

FIELD TRIPS:
MAXIMIZING THE EXPERIENCE

Deborah A. Millan

Deb Millan was educated at Queen's University in Kingston, Ontario, where she earned BA, BEd, and MEd degrees. She has taught elementary grades and specialized in the fine art of organizing field trips. Deb helped design the school tours offered by the Vanden Hoek Farm, Wolfe Island, Ontario. The farm program includes tone-setting in an old, rural, one-room school, hands-on work with agricultural problems at activity stations, storytelling and conversations with old-timers, and classroom follow-up.

Deb's chapter is an account of what she learned from her experiences in leading field trips as part of the regular curriculum. The value of the chapter lies in the highly practical distillation of that experience being made available for others. The chapter is also important because Deb enthusiastically shows that out-of-school work is accessible and worthwhile for every classroom teacher.

Introduction

During my teaching career I've led field trips for students from grades Kindergarten through Grade 8. The children have come from urban, rural, and inner-city schools, and class profiles have included a full range of economic status and academic ability. I have led day trips involving as many as 150 intermediate students, and overnight excursions of up to four days' duration involving 30 students. Regardless of my grade assignment or the environment in which I found myself teaching, field trips have been an integral part of the program I deliver because I believe that field trips are a valuable vehicle through which classroom studies can become meaningful to students, regardless of their academic abilities.

Studies have shown that field-based instruction positively affects the understanding and retention of knowledge of concepts presented (Lisowski & Disinger, 1991; Moles, 1988). Field trips can be motivational for the seemingly disinterested learner. They permit the classroom teacher a new environment in which to observe his or her charges. O'Toole (1981) refers to the "opening up" phenomenon exhibited by students who scarcely speak in class, yet become positively animated learners while on field trips. Learning should be fun, and field trips can add both excitement and an element of fun to a program in a novel way. Pinero (1985) indicates that planned field trips can be both fun and instructional. The value of field trips as an instructional strategy is both broad and legitimate.

What makes a good field trip? Certainly all those involved in the education of students, except perhaps the students themselves, expect a field trip to be educationally significant and suitable (DuVall & Krepel, 1975). The focus for each stakeholder is likely to be slightly different. From the perspective of someone in a supervisory officer's role, a good field trip may be one that meets the school district's policies (Zirkel & Gluckman, 1983). From the principal's perspective, a field trip may be considered successful if it doesn't disrupt the regular programming in his or her school, or put stress on staff not participating in the field trip. If the field trip is free of accidents and disruptive behaviour, and promotes good public relations in the community, it is likely to be viewed in a positive light. From the students' perspective, a good field trip might be one on which they are able to see and do something new, spend time with their friends, eat, and spend money. Parents and guardians may be concerned about the cost, duration, distance from home, and safety.

The purpose of this chapter is to describe the factors which contribute to the success of a field trip, from the perspective of a classroom teacher. Under the umbrella of policy guidelines, classroom teachers maintain a wide degree of latitude with which they may influence both the organization and content of a field trip. The method here will be to examine the literature and to reflect on personal experience in an effort to illuminate factors, beyond those that typically make up field trip policies, that enable some field study situations to be more successful than others. This chapter does not offer a step-by-step guide to planning field trips. Instead, it presents a palette of ideas and experiences, concluding with a list of guiding principles. Two sets of factors are considered: one set relates to the facilitation of the trip, and the other set addresses the actual content of the trip. Facilitation of the trip refers to all the things the teacher, or trip leader, can do in advance to ensure a successful excursion. The content aspect focuses on what the students actually do while they are involved in the out-of-classroom learning experience.

Facilitating Field Trips

There are five considerations in facilitating field trips: local politics, logistics, linkage to the curriculum, timing, and accessibility. Of these five considerations, four are readily recognized and discussed in the literature. The exception is local politics.

The Political Element of Field Trips

By organizing a field trip, the teacher initiates connections among the school, the parents, and the community being visited. When dealing with people, some thoughtful anticipation of their responses can eliminate difficulties. In this chapter, the politics of field trips refers to how to approach and engage the cooperation of the people affected by the trip being planned.

Unlike normal classroom work, teachers on field trips are open to public observation and comment. This is not a bad thing if the trip is well planned and educationally suitable, and the students are behaving in socially acceptable ways. The political preparation for a field trip can do much to alleviate potential public relations difficulties, and it begins with a teacher's greatest ally, the principal.

It is critical that the field trip leader has the support of his or her administration. Although the principal has to give approval for the trip, it is worthwhile to do more than secure the minimum approval needed. For example, most principals will be glad to read an outline of the planned activities and discuss the trip informally. By making sure the principal knows the plan details, and appreciates the connection between the trip and classroom work, potential difficulties, such as a telephone call from a concerned parent, can be dealt with knowledgeably.

The permission slip that goes home to parents must state more than the date, time, and cost of the field trip. It must provide the parents with a brief description of the plan, show them how the trip supports what is being studied in the classroom, and, if at all possible, invite their participation. This note must be sent out well in advance (three weeks minimum) and include the school telephone number. In this way, parents are able make their own plans and provide feedback. For field trips involving an overnight stay, or some sort of risk, an informational parent's meeting is warranted. (For a fuller treatment of parental involvement, see Chapter 5 by Bill Patterson and Bert Horwood.)

Unfortunately, there may be students in the class whose behaviour is a concern. When determining a child's participation on a field trip, two philosophies emerge. One extreme is to picture field trips as a privilege, or a reward for good behaviour. In this case, a student's right to attend a field trip is linked to his or her behaviour. If the individual is disruptive in class, he or she does not go on the trip. David Hawke (1991) supports this picture: "If students haven't earned the privilege of an outing, then leave them behind. It can be done, it has been done, and the rest of the class benefits because of it" (p.17).

The other way is to picture field trips as a central feature of education to which each student is entitled as much as to classroom instruction. In this case, every effort must be made to ensure that all students have the field trip experience. However, this does not mean that the trip leader should throw away all standards for appropriate behaviour and safety, and never leave a student at school while the rest of the class goes away. Communicating expectations clearly to students, parents, and administrators is essential. These standards must be reasonable and, in some cases, reflect the special needs of individual students. For example, one student may not function well in a group format. Inviting the parent, or other suitable adult, for the specific purpose of working with that student is one way to ensure that even the most difficult student has the field trip experience. If field trips are seen as an obligation for the student rather than a privilege, then the teacher takes on a special program and supervisory burden which must involve the entire class and may require additional adults to accompany the trip. After addressing those needs, if a child's attendance still poses a safety threat, the child should not be permitted on the trip. Detailed arrangements for the child's programming and supervision at school must then be made. None of that should prejudice the child's participation in future out-of-school work.

In larger schools where there are several classes in each grade, an added consideration when initiating field trips is the reaction of teachers of the same grade. If one teacher's class goes on more field trips than others, students are usually quick to complain of unfairness. Parents may question the discrepancy as well. Planning meetings of teachers in the same grade cluster allow teachers to let others know of their field trip plans. By exchanging field trip intentions, colleagues are forewarned and have the opportunity to respond appropriately.

When teachers share similar approaches to teaching and plan objectives together, shared field trips can be rewarding because dialogue among colleagues tends to enhance the program. On the other hand, a teacher may try to join trips organized by others without having common goals. In some cases, their involvement in the trip will not have a great effect on the ability of other classes to have a successful outing. For example, trips to view a performance may be taken by several classes at once because viewing is the primary task of the students, and large numbers can be seated at one time. I organized a trip to a large city for 135 students to see a famous musical. Each teacher was responsible for preparing his or her students and there was no collaboration among teachers regarding such preparation. The students, parents, and teachers were happy and felt that the experience had been a rewarding one.

Trips that require readiness and are action-based are not suited to last-minute, tag-along students or teachers. Their attendance tends to be disruptive to the success of the field trip. Hawke (1991) refers to these students as bus fillers who have no idea why they are there, where they are, or what to expect. It is unwise to make a trip less expensive by filling a bus. Those extra, unprepared people are a safety risk and could ruin the hard work students have done in preparing for the experience. Successful trips are led by teachers who have a genuine interest and some expertise in the destination. Teachers who tag along are less likely to inspire or prepare their students, and if that work is done by the organizing teacher, the critical classroom connection will be lost.

Some of these political considerations can be put into context by examining two excursions that helped me learn how to work with people in field trip planning.

I was placed in a school late in September and told by my principal that I was responsible for taking thirty-five Grade 8 students on an overnight camping excursion in two weeks' time. My better judgment told me that I didn't have time to adequately prepare the students, let alone build the type of rapport needed to work with this age group. The overnight camping trip was a tradition at the school, and I was expected to carry it on.

Having a modest amount of experience in the outdoors, I immediately began pre-trip lessons, including supplying the students with a list of easily obtained gear. I requested that no personal tape players or battery-operated items be brought along so that we could enjoy the outdoor setting without distraction. I also presented the students with suggested menu plans for the meal they were to prepare. To my amazement, the students, who had more tenure in the school than I did, raced to the principal's office, complaining of my unfair treatment and my plans to ruin their excursion. The other two

Grade 8 classes had already had their overnight trip, and hadn't faced any of the guidelines that I had put to my new class. I stubbornly persisted and told the students that I would check their packs if necessary to ensure that junk food and radios were not brought along. This time, it was the parents of the students who protested to the principal's office my unreasonable restrictions and intent to invade the privacy of their offspring.

My principal of two weeks backed me all the way in front of parents and students alike, and privately suggested that I not search any packs.

Despite feeling uncomfortable with the preparations and the tone of the class, the trip proceeded. My objectives for that field trip—introducing the students to low-impact camping, menu-planning, and heightening the use of their senses while in the outdoors—were not realized. The students' objective of partying until they were too tired to move was heartily met. The trip also had a great effect in strengthening class unity!

Had I been a little more politically astute, the trip could have been more successful and the objectives I set could have been reached. I was fortunate that the principal gave me the support that I needed. Communication to establish shared values among teaching staff, administration, parents, and children is extremely important.

I didn't recognize that the students had previously been given a major stake in the nature of the field trip. While it is the responsibility of the teacher to determine the trip's objectives, input from the students can give them a sense of ownership and contribute to the success of the trip. Chandler (1989) noted, "Teachers should decide the purposes and benefits of specific field trips, of course, but students should have some say about them too. That way, classroom assignments can be designed to help students concentrate on the intended benefits and to think about what they should watch for on the outing" (p. 30). The objectives for a field trip must match the needs of the class.

Although this particular field trip had already been initiated before I arrived, a second letter from me to the parents, outlining an overview of the event and describing how the guidelines I established would help promote what was happening in the classroom, would have gone a long way to eliminate the difficulties that arose.

That same year, the school's traditional, end-of-year field trip to Montreal was prepared by the other two Grade 8 teachers. After the September fiasco, and having little influence with fellow staff members, I followed the path of least resistance during the one brief planning session that took place. The one-day outing was to include unsupervised shopping in downtown Montreal, a hike up the three hundred or so steps of Mt. Royal, a stop at St. Joseph's Oratory, a walking tour of Old Montreal and several more churches, an unsupervised supper, a subway ride, and, finally, a Montreal Expos baseball game.

The day of the field trip was extremely hot and humid. The hike up the steps of Mt. Royal was debilitating and, in some cases, humiliating for students who were overweight or who suffered from asthma. Parent supervisors had difficulty with this task, and fit students raced ahead, unsupervised. Aside from the remote possibility of flagging down a passing taxi, there was no alternative but to climb the mountain. Our students held a variety of religious beliefs, and three Catholic churches were featured on the trip for no apparent reason. Essentially, the day's "educational" activities provided an excuse for being in Montreal to watch a ball game. These types of trips no longer gain approval from most administrators.

Both the camping trip and the Montreal experience have influenced my approach to dealing with staff members when considering field trips. Hawke (1991) notes that there are some real problems aligning the attitudes of students, teachers, principals, and site staff. I agree. Because of my experiences with field trips, I do not usually participate in excursions that I haven't organized. By being the organizer, I can control the learning outcomes, the choice of location, the activities planned, and the standard of student behaviour. Without control over these factors, the success of a field trip is in jeopardy.

When planning field trips, I try to think about the people who are going to be affected. By putting myself in their shoes, and by thinking of potential concerns before they arise, I can gain the much-needed support for my endeavours. For me, this has been an effective way to deal with the politics of field trips.

The Pre-Trip Visit

The second major consideration when acting as a facilitator for a field trip is whether to visit the destination prior to the excursion. If a teacher is taking students to a new site for the first time, a pre-trip visit is advisable for two reasons. First, the pre-trip visit will allow the leader to examine and explore the facilities and make any logistical adjustments. Secondly, the pre-trip visit allows the trip leader to assess more accurately the educational potential of the site.

Gemake (1980) says that the pre-trip visit is a way to broaden the experience of the students. To prepare the students for the trip, the teacher must have a comprehensive understanding of what the site has to offer. Chandler (1985) suggests that "every proposed field trip should be screened in advance by sending an appropriate teacher on the trip without the students to determine its suitability and value" (p. 30). Hawkc (1991) also values a pre-trip visit. He cites this as a time to meet with site staff and make arrangements for students with special needs, such as wheelchair access.

On the Montreal trip, I was unfamiliar with the setting and had had no opportunity to visit the site prior to the trip. I was particularly concerned about the subway. Imagine 150 students, who have never before been on mass transit, individually buying tickets in a second language, making change, and trying to stay with their group leader in order that the entire group could board the train together! Did I fail to mention that a transfer was also required? Of course, it was pandemonium! Indeed, the situation was dangerous as several students lacked the proper respect for the warning lines painted on the floor of the subway station. The facts that group tickets could be purchased and that certain stations at peak hours were extremely crowded, were small bits of information that could have been learned in advance.

There are times when pre-trip visits are not essential. A pre-trip to a theatrical performance is not really necessary because the trip leader can question the performing box office personnel as to the suitability of a program, or rely on reviews, long in advance of booking tickets. Information packages that accompany promotional material for a variety of sites can range from mediocre to outstanding. A telephone conversation with the appropriate site staff can supplement the literature and take the place of a pre-trip visit. This is especially worthwhile if the site is some distance away.

A useful source of good information is other teachers. If a pre-trip visit is not possible, a colleague who has already taken a class to the site may be able to provide useful information. Teachers' individual interests and areas of expertise often affect the success of their field trips. Some level of expertise is required. Caras (1977) suggests that "one of the most common mistakes educators make is to underestimate the amount of expertise required in the field" (p. 50). There is also a difference between having a skill or high level of expertise and being able to share it with a class of students. For example, a highly skilled paddler may not necessarily be skilled in teaching others or leading canoe trips.

Linking the Field Trip to the Curriculum

Connecting field trips to the curriculum is emphasized in the literature. Brehm (1969) identifies this connection as an overriding value. Chandler (1985) concludes that elementary school teachers see field trips as an integral part of their curriculum. Gemake's (1975) first step in preparing for a field trip is to "survey the curriculum guidelines and decide upon the concepts which can be best developed through a field trip. Choose a field trip which will provide activities of direct observation to supplement classroom learning" (p. 24).

A field trip that does not have a legitimate link to the curriculum is hard to justify educationally. In the past, going to large cities to watch a baseball game or to attend a theme park could be the sole purpose of a field trip. As these trips became harder to justify and the flow of students stopped, some major entertainment centres began promoting "educational" programs, such as science days and backstage tours. Apparently these sites realized that, without some claim to academic merit, approval for student trips to their site would be reduced.

When planning a field trip, make certain it is really worth taking. Trips don't have to be expensive or far from home to be successful. Indeed, Falk and Balling (1982) concluded that teachers should strive to take students on outings that provide a varying amount of novelty, depending on the age and experience of the students. New settings and the task of getting there sometimes overwhelms students, and the desired learning outcomes are not met because there is simply too much for the students to take in. A familiar site within the community may be a reasonable and effective alternate.

Whether a field trip is within the community or goes beyond it, is expensive or inexpensive, is a one-day venture or one of several days, it must have direct value and importance to the curriculum.

Timing the Field Trip

The fourth aspect to consider when organizing a field trip is its actual timing in relation to the curriculum. Should the trip be at the beginning, middle, or end of a particular unit of study?

Some argue that field trips should be the starting point for a unit of study (Sesow & McGowan, 1984); others call for them at the end of the unit. Sesow and McGowan largely base their claim, that field trips should be initiated as the beginning of a unit of study, on Jean Piaget's observations on cognitive development that "seem to support a progression from concrete activities to more abstract experiences for students" (p. 69). Experiential learning theory also suggests that firsthand experience must come early in the learning process.

Olcott (1987) differs in his approach and arms his students with knowledge prior to the excursion so that, when they are on the trip, they may attain a high level of thinking, such as problem solving. He notes that many features of a site, such as guides and displays, are under-used if students are unprepared.

To be successful, the timing of the field trip lies on a time line somewhere between pre-trip and post-trip learning. A field trip is somewhat like a book: it requires an introduction and purpose, and would seem pointless if it didn't have an appropriate conclusion. Both Gemake (1980) and Olcott (1987) stress the idea of building background and pre-teaching before visiting a site. Berliner and Pinero (1985) conclude that "failure to require classroom follow-up devalues the trip's instructional purpose" (p. 15). No doubt it is in the classroom, following the trip, that experiences can be relived and examined, ideas and observations shared, and unanswered questions researched. The timing of the field trip also depends on the objectives that the teacher hopes to achieve, and on the ability and experience of the students. Whether early or late in an instructional sequence, teachers and students should exploit the particular advantages of that sequence.

Field Trip Accessibility

Three types of accessibility must be considered: intellectual, physical, and financial. It is the teacher's responsibility to meet the needs of all students, providing individualized programming if necessary, whether inside or outside the classroom. When contacting the field trip site, it is essential to find out what the students will be expected to do and, if necessary, to inform the site staff of any special needs students have.

The whole idea behind a field trip is to get out into the world and move away from abstract configurations. O'Toole (1981) refers to students with learning disabilities, or other physical and emotional handicaps, "opening up" as readily as the average student in response to their experiences at Colonial Williamsburg. "Because the museum experience is such a direct physical experience, one that has *things* rather than *words* at its core, it is equally accessible to every class member who has been mainstreamed. It works powerfully and well for everyone" (p. 64).

Physical accessibility for all students is essential. Every member of the class is valuable and has the right to participate in the activities of the class. Field trips are no exception. There is no doubt that students with physical challenges require additional attention so that they can participate as fully as they are able in all school activities. Parents and guardians of these individuals are a great source of information and support. A classroom teacher should not be hesitant in conferring with them when concerns regarding field trips arise.

Whether written or unwritten, many schools have a policy that no student should miss a field trip because he or she cannot afford it (Zakariya, 1985). The teacher's knowledge of students' finances is often relied on to identify individuals who require financial assistance. Unfortunately, relying on such knowledge for supporting these students does not guarantee that those in need receive help. Teachers, although perhaps having the best opportunity to judge the situation, sometimes lack a thorough understanding of the financial situation in the student's home. Pride, and the fear of ridicule by peers, can also cause a needy student to turn down a private offer of assistance.

One alternative to addressing this problem is a plan that includes all students in fund raising in order to offset the cost of the trip. A second strategy is to ensure that all students and parents are informed of the nature of the trip, and its cost, well in advance of the trip date. Having this information allows parents and students the opportunity to plan for the costs involved.

Sometimes, for no apparent reason, a student decides not to attend a field trip. On the surface, it appears that the student has simply decided not to go. It takes time to find out the real reason; perhaps he or she feels uncomfortable or uncertain about the proposed activities. Often, talking to the student, answering his or her questions, and providing reassurance, is all that is needed to secure the individual's participation in the field trip. Occasionally, a conversation with a child's parent solves the mystery. Sometimes athletic or cultural factors are at work, and program adjustments will make inclusion possible. For example, some cultures require young, unmarried women to have continual adult supervision. Providing this to the parents' satisfaction makes attendance possible.

The Content Component of Field Trips

How the student's time is occupied while on the field trip is critical to its success. All the background learning and pre-teaching that occurs in the classroom before the class sets foot outside the door can be wasted if a connection between what the students know, what they hope to learn, and what they are about to do, isn't made in a fashion that is meaningful to them. Four factors that enhance this meaning on a field trip are active learning in real-life settings, incidental learning, the human factor, and the use of stories.

Active Learning in Real-Life Settings

There is great support for activity-based learning situations. Field trips that engage the students both mentally and physically are likely to be more successful than ones where guides or teachers perform for passive students (Berliner, 1985.). Active participation in a novel setting was found by MacKenzie and White (1982) to lead to new learning, to reinforce what had already been learned in school, and to aid greatly in the retention of information.

It is important to treat the actual activity the students are involved in while on the trip as just one aspect of learning. The field trip represents the "challenging action" stage in Joplin's (1985) model of experiential education. The challenging action is preceded by preparation ("focus") and followed by some form of reflection ("debrief"), all the while nurtured by support and feedback. Reflecting on the significance of field trip events is essential to enable the student to internalize new meaning.

In my own experience, I have found field trips most successful when students are able to actively participate at the site. On a visit to an archaeological dig, my Grade 7 students grew restless as the guide relied heavily on a static display to present historical detail. Their level of attentiveness and questioning blossomed when they were given tools, participated in the dig, and eventually cleaned and catalogued actual artifacts.

Gibbons and Hopkins (1985) present a scale of experientiality that enables educators to judge the experiential quality of a given program. "The degree of experience increases as the participant becomes more responsible for the experience that occurs, and more responsible for mastering the activity involved to the fullest extent possible" (p. 98). Gibbons and Hopkins illustrate their point by comparing a field trip to a farm, to the sustained challenge faced by a 4-H Club member who plants, cultivates, and markets crops. It is apparent that the more experiential the activity, that is, the closer it is to reality, the more significant and lasting the activity's effect is on the individual. This was the case in the archaeology experience of my class.

Although what the students did at the site wasn't exactly the way in which an archaeologist would have conducted his or her work, it was a close approximation. It could be called an on-site simulation. The artifacts and tools were real, but for safety reasons and a lack of expertise on the part of the students, caustic chemicals and sophisticated computer programs were not used in the cleaning and recording of the artifacts.

O'Toole (1981) describes a simulated archaeological dig at Colonial Williamsburg and identifies two areas of learning that can be facilitated through such activity, skills, and values. "Participation in such an inquiry can both teach and allow the application of a range of cognitive skill every social studies teacher aspires to develop in his or her student from classification, and measurement, to dating historical reconstruction and interpretation" (p. 64). He continues, "Comprehension of the value of another culture as well as a growing appreciation of the importance of preserving old things and, perhaps, commitment to further study can also flow from experience with objects and object analysis" (p. 64). I observed these characteristics in my students as well.

Incidental Learning and Dealing with the Unexpected

Joplin (1985) claims that all learning is experiential. She states that "not all of it [learning] is deliberately planned or takes place through an educational institution or setting" (p. 117). The awareness of incidental learning is valuable for a teacher with limited tripping experience in order to be open to the possibility and potential of this characteristic of field trips. It is a characteristic that is sometimes beyond the control of the teacher.

Opportunities arise spontaneously, and the trip leader must be able to adapt readily to the situation and recognize the value of the moment. Chandler (1985) observes "the unexpected is the spawning ground for creativity" (p. 30) and supports the idea of capturing an unexpected opportunity and integrating it into the field trip plans. Gemake (1980) is more regimented and advises the trip leader to "stick to the purpose of the trip" (p. 25).

On a trip involving a ferry crossing, I permitted the students to get off the bus once it was safe to do so. I asked them to observe the shoreline as we departed the dock. The ferry ride was a novel aspect of the trip and I anticipated that they would explore the vessel.

What I didn't count on was that they would request permission from the captain to have a look around the wheelhouse. Before I knew it, all 34 students were lined up, waiting their turn to enter the wheelhouse with three or four of their classmates. They had a great view of the shoreline and a chance to chat with crew members. For some students, this unplanned learning opportunity was the highlight of the excursion.

Incidental learning is sometimes obvious as in the example above, but more often it is subtle, occurring on an individual basis. The work a student does after returning from a trip often reveals some insight into experiences that had unplanned influence.

The Human Factor

A trip that involves resource people at the site has a human factor that can influence the content of a field trip. This human factor is largely out of the control of the trip leader except through experience with the site and return visits. If you take a trip and are fortunate to have a guide who handles children well and is knowledgeable and personable, make a note to request that person for future visits. If possible, build a rapport with site staff prior to your visit.

I once took a class of Grades 3 and 4 students to a military historical site. One of the students had an uncle who was working there as a costumed guide. I invited the uncle to come into the school to meet the students prior to our visit, and he did so—not in uniform, but in his ordinary dress. He told the class about his job, his training, and his costume.

When we arrived for our tour, the children were full of anticipation as they tried to pick out which costumed guide was Trevor's uncle. Throughout the day, the students followed their guide about, eagerly asking questions. They had a clear understanding that his military manner with fellow interpreters was part of his performance, and that the person they had met in the classroom and were comfortable with, was still there to guide them. They felt very much at ease with him.

These children had made a connection with an individual who enabled them to become engaged in the environment they were experiencing. Because they had met their guide in a setting familiar to them—their own classroom—they were to some extent more prepared to interact with him in a new setting. Having a guide who was familiar to them helped them get beyond the "novel field trip effect" that Falk and Balling (1982) refer to. Their ability to assimilate much of what they had experienced was revealed in the art work they completed in the days following the trip.

The Role of Stories

Another side of the human factor on field trips is that of story. Most sites have associated with them characters either living or dead, fictional or nonfictional. I have observed that children appear to digest, internalize, and make sense of a site more readily through a story than through other methods. When students participate in the human element of a site in a storytelling situation, or from literature, the site becomes more real to them. As Leonard (1990) indicates, "A good story, well told, is an experience that opens us to new perception, emotion and behaviour" (p. 12). She further suggests that listeners may "develop knowledge and moral character" (p. 12) from listening to a story. Stories can add meaning to experience.

Olcott (1987) identifies the use of the written word, that of both the historian and novelist, and primary sources of historical evidence, as being valuable tools in enhancing the success of an excursion. He describes a field trip to Gettysburg where the students discover a site described in a popular Civil War novel and read the passage while standing in the exact spot where the characters were located. He tells us that "one class upon reading the selection became so excited that they spontaneously let out a cheer and chased imaginary Rebels down Little Round Top all the way to Devil's Den" (Olcott, 1987, p. 492). Further, he used a collection of old photographs and had the students duplicate poses from original scenes. These types of activities enable the students to gain deeper insight and engagement.

I have had similar positive experiences using the written word as a catalyst for learning when on field trips. I took a class of Grades 5 and 6 students to visit a restored heritage house. The pre-trip literature noted that a children's novel was set in that house. I read the novel to my students; when we arrived at the house, they were full of comments before we even entered through the front door. "This is what I thought it would look like!" "Do they have any of her things?" "Can we find the window she looked out?" "Hey! There aren't any willow trees!" "Is this open on weekends?" Their questions and comments were ably dealt with by the costumed interpretive staff who were impressed with the level of the students' enthusiasm and obvious appreciation of the site. Finally, when it was time to board the bus, I noted that several of my more "difficult-to-motivate" students were nowhere to be seen; a quick search found them at the rear of the house, arguing over how the novel pertained to the actual site.

In this case, the students were able to make a link with the site they were visiting because of a story we had shared prior to the outing. Visiting the site motivated them because they had characters and a plot in mind. Prior to the trip, they formed an idea of what they thought the site would be like. They went on the trip looking for things that were relevant to them and were quick to point out any discrepancies they observed. They were able to develop an appreciation for the author's license to write a fictional story that had an actual setting.

The ability of stories to contribute to the success of a field trip is supported both by personal observation and by the literature. Why they influence the success of the field trip is less clear. Perhaps a story, well told, meets individuals at their own intellectual levels. Students can relate to characters in stories because they can use their own lives as a basis for comparison. Knowledge needed to gain an appreciation of a site is easier to comprehend if it is woven into the context of a story. Costumed interpretive staff and living storytellers are found at many historic sites as testimony to the effectiveness of the use of characterization to enable students of all ages to gain a better understanding of the site they are visiting. I have found that stories contribute to the success of a field trip and, when planning for a trip, I take the time and make the effort to seek them out.

Conclusion

There is obviously overlap between facilitation components and content components when examining the make-up of a successful field trip. How can one discuss the logistical aspects of a field trip without considering the stakeholder? How can one plan the activities of a field trip without considering the resources available? Furthermore, individual teachers will bring their own experiences, interests, and teaching styles to the table when planning a field trip. Therefore, the ideas presented here are meant to be starting blocks for a solid foundation rather than a recipe to be followed to the letter. Heath's (1985) comment applies:

> I am dismayed by teachers who ask me how I teach, believing that my specific teaching methods will necessarily help them. We do not empower others by offering them our techniques; we empower them by helping them internalize principles of broad generality that provide guidelines to them for creating their own techniques. (p. 111)

What follows is a summary of broad guidelines developed in this chapter.

1. When initiating field trips, addressing the concerns of all those affected in a politically astute manner can eliminate barriers to a successful trip.

2. Reconnaissance trips can improve knowledge of the site and thus facilitate the trip in terms of both logistical and curriculum considerations.

3. Field trips must be linked to curriculum.

4. Field trips must fall somewhere between focusing activities and reflective activities. The timing of trips is dependent on the particular course of study and on the previous experiences and ability of the class.

5. Field trips must be accessible to all students, regardless of their physical, intellectual, or financial profile.

6. Field trips are successful if students are actively engaged, both mentally and physically, at the site.

7. The closer to reality an experience is, the greater the benefit derived.

8. Incidental learning can be rewarding and is often an unexpected bonus of field trips. When the unexpected occurs, it is only prudent to give priority to safety.

9. The human resources available at a field trip site can contribute greatly to the success of a trip. It is worthwhile to cultivate a good rapport with these individuals.

10. Oral and written stories, fictional or nonfictional, contribute meaning to field trip experience in a manner particularly accessible to learners.

References

Berliner, D., & Pinero, U. (1985). The field trip: Frill or essential? *Instructor, 94*(4), 14–15.

Brehm, S. A. (1969). *A teacher's handbook for study outside the classroom.* Columbus, OH: Charles E. Merrill.

Caras, R. (1977). Putting the *field* back into the field trip. *Instructor, 86*(8), 50.

Chandler, T. A. (1985). These policy tips make the most of field trips. *The American School Board Journal, 172*(6), 30–33.

DuVall, C., & Krepel, W. (1975). School board policies related to field trips. *Education, 95*(4), 331–333.

Falk, J., & Balling, J. (1983). The field trip milieu: Learning and behaviour as a function of contextual events. *The Journal of Educational Research, 76*(1), 22–28.

Gemake, J. (1980). Making the most of a class science trip. *Education, 101*(1), 24–26.

Gibbons, M., & Hopkins, D. (1985). How experiential is your experience based program? In J. Kraft & M. Sakofs (Eds.), *Theory of experiential education* (pp. 97-102). Boulder, CO: Association for Experiential Education.

Hawke, D. (1991) Field trips and how to get the most out of them. *Pathways, 3*(2), 16–17.

Heath, D. N. (1985). Teaching for adult effectiveness. In J. Kraft & M. Sakofs (Eds.), *Theory of experiential education* (pp. 108–113). Boulder, CO: Association for Experiential Education.

Joplin, L. (1985). On defining experiential education. In J. Kraft & M. Sakofs (Eds.), *Theory of experiential education* (pp. 117–120). Boulder, CO: Association for Experiential Education.

Leonard, L. (1990). Storytelling as experiential education. *The Journal of Experiential Education, 13*(2), 12–17.

Lisowski, M., & Disinger, J. (1991). The effect of field-based instruction on student understandings of ecological concepts. *The Journal of Environmental Education, 23*(1), 19–23.

MacKenzie, A. A., & White, R. T. (1982). Field work in geography and long-term memory structures. *American Educational Research Journal, 19*(4), 623-632.

Moles, J. (1988). The classroom and the field: A necessary unity. *The Journal of Experiential Education, 11*(2), 14–20.

Olcott, M. (1987). A field trip to Gettysburg: A model experience. *The History Teacher, 20*(4), 487–496.

O'Toole, D. (1981). Field trips are basic. *Social Education, 45*(1), 63–65.

Sesow, W., & McGowan, T. (1984). Take the field trip first. *Social Studies, 75*(2), 68–70.

Zakariya, S. (1985). Here's more field trip advice. *The American School Board Journal, 172*(6), 30.

Zirkel, P., & Gluckman, I. (1983, March). What is "adequate supervision" on school trips? *NASSP Bulletin,* 112–114.

Chapter 10

THE INFLUENCE OF EXPEDITIONARY LEARNING IN OUTWARD BOUND AND COLLEGE

Rogene McKiernan

Rogene McKiernan is the instructor and coordinator of the Environmental Conservation Outdoor Education Expedition of Western Illinois University. She holds an MS from the same institution in Recreation and Park Management and a BA from Graceland College in Religion. Rogene is also an instructor for Voyageur Outward Bound School and for the Wilderness Education Association. Her experiences teaching in these settings continue to drive her desire to find more effective ways to educate university students.

In her chapter, Rogene tells the story of the unexpected influence of Expeditionary Learning in two settings for which it was not designed. In the first, Outward Bound training sessions for Expeditionary Learning teachers from a school system rebound and force the instructors to reexamine their own practice. In the second, Rogene, with the help of students, tells the story of Expeditionary Learning introduced as a principle vehicle for instruction in a university program. These stories are important because they illustrate the intrinsic power and adaptability of experiential models like Expeditionary Learning. The stories are also significant because they reveal the difficulties which must be overcome by students and teachers when methods of instruction change.

Introduction

Expeditionary Learning grew out of a proposal for change in the educational system. At the request of President Bush in 1992, a fund-raising group, The New American Schools Development Corporation, made available $40 million for ideas and plans "to create an unconventional school on a conventional budget" (New Designs, 1992). Outward Bound USA, working in conjunction with Harvard University, presented a proposal for Expeditionary Learning. Of the 600 proposals submitted, 11 were chosen, including the one by Outward Bound. In this way, Expeditionary Learning Outward Bound: A New American Schools Development Corporation "Break the Mold" Design came into being. Selected schools across the United States were chosen to begin implementation. Teacher education and training included a wilderness expedition with various Outward Bound Schools. Minnesota's Voyageur Outward Bound School (VOBS) provided several such teacher-training courses within the educational community of Dubuque, Iowa.

I was a VOBS staff member in that training work, and in this article I use that vantage point to describe two unexpected effects of work with Expeditionary Learning. Training teachers on wilderness expeditions forced VOBS instructors to reexamine the relationships between Outward Bound and Expeditionary Learning principles, and also to reconsider the nature of their work as instructors. Those relationships will be described. My experience of Expeditionary Learning was so powerful that I decided to use its principles in a college course I also teach. That experience and students' reactions to it form the second part of this chapter.

Expeditionary Learning—An Overview

Expeditionary Learning postulates that:

True learning is an expedition into the unknown. Expeditionary learning organizes students' education into purposeful expeditions of inquiry, discovery and action. Expeditions are journeys undertaken by tightly organized groups for a specific purpose, often in the accompaniment of an expert guide. Though they may vary in length, they have a beginning, a middle and an end. They immerse people right from the start, travel light, and go somewhere. Expedition members must depend upon one another to fulfil their mission because they are travelling through uncharted territory to new destinations. They must prepare for the journey, develop goals in order that their actions have clear, recognizable consequences, and celebrate their achievements. Expeditionary Learning utilizes personal experience and intellectual growth to promote self-discovery and knowledge. (VOBS, 1993, p. 1)

Expeditionary Learning specifies Ten Design Principles to be used in planning:

The Primacy of Self-Discovery	Collaboration and Competition
The Having of Wonderful Ideas	Diversity and Inclusion
The Responsibility for Learning	The Natural World
Intimacy and Caring	Solitude and Reflection
Success and Failure	Service and Compassion

(VOBS, 1993, p. 1)

These principles are implemented by teachers who become guides or facilitators. As lifelong learners themselves, they are responsible for helping create learning opportunities by clarifying and focusing student efforts, celebrating ideas and accomplishments, helping design relevant and appropriate evaluations, and developing their own Expeditionary Learning curriculums. They are not the primary source of information or knowledge for their students, but a valuable support for information and educational processes.

The structure of student-centered learning is based on the above design principles and three basic assumptions: all students can learn, success breeds success, and parents and communities are part of the process that enhances student learning (VOBS, 1993). Expeditionary Learning provides choices which are structurally and developmentally appropriate for the ages of the pupils and their educational experience. In this framework, students can be highly involved in designing their own content, determining how to learn the desired material, and assessing their progress.

Expeditionary Learning and Outward Bound

Comparing Outward Bound Practice with Expeditionary Learning

The VOBS instructors wanted to determine the extent to which the Expeditionary Learning Design Principles were already reflected in Outward Bound practice, identifying which ones were basic to our process and which were not used well. This knowledge would help us find points of transference for the Dubuque educators who were already acquainted with the principles. Members of the VOBS Expeditionary Learning team focused on this task. The following is a summary of their work and related discussions by other VOBS staff members.

As expected, there was a good fit between the Outward Bound Process and the Expeditionary Learning Design Principles. Seven principles match Outward Bound practice closely. These will be outlined briefly. The remaining three, which fit less well and which provoked the most learning for us, will be discussed in more detail.

The primacy of self-discovery is achieved by placing students in situations in which they encounter aspects of themselves and others that they don't normally face. This includes any activity that challenges perceived limits and boundaries. We help create the setting where students can face and overcome fear, learning that they can do more than they think they can. We then call attention to what is taking place and being discovered, validating the discovery by the students.

The responsibility for learning is accomplished at VOBS by starting all courses with goal setting, and clarifying what students want to accomplish. We check during the course to see how they are progressing. Our style is to give skills training, share our knowledge, and pull back from the responsibility of directing specifics, thus granting students free space to take responsibility for their learning.

Success and failure, as a design principle in Expeditionary Learning, are described:

> All students must be assured a fair measure of success in learning in order to nurture the confidence and capacity to take risks and rise to increasingly difficult challenges. But it is also important to experience failure, to overcome negative inclinations, to prevail against adversity and to learn to turn disabilities into opportunities. (VOBS, 1993, p. 2)

Outward Bound operates out of the concept that choices have consequences and that we have to accept responsibility for both. We are conscious of consequences and manage them purposefully. Most of the activities on courses provide situations for success because students use newly learned skills in their decision making, and find taking risks rewarding. Neither Expeditionary Learning nor Outward Bound have clear definitions of "failure" or "mistakes." Outward Bound students certainly do experience mistakes, burned noodles for example, but what constitutes failure is difficult to determine because the consequences of error are invariably turned into positive learning.

Collaboration and competition are another polar pair constituting a design principle. Collaboration is one of Outward Bound's core operating values. It is exemplified by the frequently stated adage at course start: "You're in this together; you need to support each other to bring your *group* through the course!—you need each other." Outward Bound and Expeditionary Learning both emphasize competition with one's personal best, and against one's own perceived limitations and prejudices.

Intimacy and caring are fostered by Expeditionary Learning by using small groups where trust, sustained caring, and mutual respect can develop under the guidance of a caring adult (VOBS, 1993). Outward Bound operates in the same ways, developing mutual support. Caring, in this sense, is an area of high compatibility with Expeditionary Learning expectations. Intimacy is more difficult to achieve unless the concept is one simply of close proximity. School groups in Expeditionary Learning have greater opportunities for intimacy because of being together for longer periods of time.

The natural world is critical to Outward Bound because the outdoors and wilderness heightens disequilibrium and a sense of separation from everyday life. This stimulates feelings of connectedness, and a healing of the inner spirit. Outward Bound needs to broaden its environmental education components to help students understand, as well as feel, their connection with the natural world.

Solitude and reflection are found in Outward Bound in the forms of solos and quiet time during wilderness travel. Reflection is supported by posing questions to consider, giving instruction in how to give and take feedback, holding frequent group debriefs, and writing journals.

The remaining three Design Principles from Expeditionary Learning fit Outward Bound practice less well. Two of them are difficult to adjust, as will be shown. But the third stimulated a significant change in our instruction.

Diversity and inclusivity are required by Expeditionary Learning.

Encourage students to investigate, value and draw upon their own histories, talents and resources together with those of other communities and cultures. Keep the schools and learning groups heterogeneous. (VOBS, 1993, p. 2)

Outward Bound is good at fostering divergent thinking in problem-solving situations, at making sure people are included physically in group activities, and at monitoring inclusion in group discussions. But with the exception of special populations in dedicated courses, Outward Bound serves fairly homogeneous groups. The range of cultural diversity is small and, consequently, it is difficult for Outward Bound to demonstrate this principle in action.

Service and compassion as described by Expeditionary Learning are equally difficult to demonstrate fully in Outward Bound. The Design Principle states that, "We are crew, not passengers, and are strengthened by acts of consequential service to others" (VOBS, 1993). Compassion is a corner stone of Outward Bound, from the small things like baking apple turnovers for students after solo, to spending hours helping students to work through personal problems. Service is something we work hard at doing, yet we struggle with finding ways of extending service beyond the wilderness experience.

The having of wonderful ideas is the Design Principle which had led us to examine our practices and make adjustments. The principle is based on the work of Eleanor Duckworth (1987).

> Teach so as to build on . . . curiosity about the world by creating learning situations that provide matter to think about, time to experiment, and time to make sense of what is observed. Foster a community where students' and adults' ideas are respected. (VOBS, 1993, p. 2)

Outward Bound expeditions do provide time to experiment and reflect on experience, but we felt, as we examined our instructional practice, that we do not teach from this principle. We generally present "a way" to do something when teaching a skill like setting up a tent. We don't often develop opportunities for students to experiment with the dynamics of a situation, then reflect on the outcomes, determine what their next step could be, and try again. Implementing the principle of having wonderful ideas became an area of experimentation and excitement for us as we designed several field components to implement this principle.

For example, paddling is normally taught by explanation and demonstration. Students then copy our example, practice, receive feedback, and work toward proficiency. We decided instead to structure the sequence based on student discovery first, with instructor information given in response to students' experiences. Students were instructed to figure out how their actions with the paddle moved the canoe. To do this, they would play with their paddles, moving the canoes with every stroke they could imagine, while they observed what was happening. They were encouraged to be creative in their exploration and were expected to articulate the result of their actions on their canoe's movement in the water. Students then came back together as a larger group to share what had occurred, to exchange wonderful ideas about making a canoe move. In the large group, questions were asked in such a way as to validate new information gained. Students entered the canoes again to try more things, perhaps something another student had reported to produce desirable results. Discovering why the canoe behaved the way it did led to being able to move the canoe in a desired direction. Instructors became a resource for additional knowledge and a source of assurance that the learning would help students become good paddlers.

VOBS Staff Prepares
to Train Expeditionary Learning Teachers

Members of VOBS Community Education staff had anticipated the unique opportunities present in the training expeditions for Dubuque school personnel. They had deliberately pooled senior instructors to work all three Expeditionary Learning training courses and provided time before the first course and also between courses to design curriculum out of a shared vision. These two components, senior staff and planning time, plus working with intact groups from the same community over a period of three months, were novel for Outward Bound instructors. Instructors usually work with different partners for each course, disallowing continued collaboration on curriculum development. Outward Bound course groups are generally made up of strangers who come together only for that wilderness experience; they do not come with a common history, return to work with each other, or live in the same communities. Generally, Outward Bound instructors do not have a new curriculum focus to develop, implement, reflect upon, and try again with the same population who are also exploring their own educational process.

During the spring months prior to the courses, the designated VOBS instructors received literature on Expeditionary Learning. Only one of the instructors had any previous knowledge of the project. We were somewhat skeptical of a new educational fad. Materials compiled into a manual by VOBS, although interesting, gave little direction. Much of the open, honest questioning of our learning process was possible because, as senior instructors, we felt confident to operate a sound, educational Outward Bound course. We were excited about looking at what we do from another viewpoint. We were trying to use our comparison of Outward Bound practice and the Design Principles to express our practice in the language of those principles. Basically, we became learners experiencing disequilibrium, scrambling to make sense of all the data, knowledge, and new demands in the light of our own past experiences. We were setting out on our own Expeditionary Learning journey.

VOBS Staff Reflect on the Preparation

A cooperative environment was present in our planning, despite disagreement, confused communication, and the struggle to be open to different ideas. But our environment was deliberately focused on solving problems and structuring a learning experience that would meet the needs of the Dubuque educators. Unique challenges for us were understanding the ten Design Principles of Expeditionary Learning, being open and honest about our weaknesses in light of the principles, developing new language, being transparent, and altering our course components to reflect teachers' concerns and feedback when appropriate.

The desire to offer the teachers more than a wilderness Outward Bound course and the need to find common language were the driving forces for our course preparation. Many models of education were considered for their potential to enhance transference of Outward Bound practice into language familiar to educators in the mainstream. We found that Nadler and Luckner (1992) introduced one framework that made sense to the teachers and reflected our own journey during the summer courses.

> The student experiences a state of disequilibrium by being placed in a novel setting and a cooperative environment while being presented with unique problem solving situations. These situations may lead to feelings of accomplishment which are augmented by processing the experience which promotes generalization and transfer for future life endeavors. (p. 9)

A form created by the Dubuque schools for developing a unit of study was a second piece that was useful in our planning in language familiar to the teachers.

It was a challenge for us to make our work transparent. We wanted the teachers to have an Outward Bound course that would enable them to gain personally from the experience, and also understand an expedition. The teachers needed to understand the reasons for our actions, in order to transfer the relevant pieces to their own future classroom expeditions. These two desires, meeting teachers' personal needs and helping them understand the professional process, pushed us to go beyond our usual practice. We had to help the teachers understand the essence of what was happening while they were immersed in the process. We anticipated that they would be watching to see how and why we worked the way we did. We hoped the teachers would analyze whether we were doing what we said we were doing, and sort through the experience for points of transference. It became apparent immediately that, for us as instructors, it meant being open to questions at all times. We needed to be aware of and understand our own process in order to clarify it, and we had to be willing to join the teachers in mutual exploration. It meant that the teachers had to wear two hats: be an Outward Bound student and be an analytic teacher in training. We did not want them to go away being Outward Bound converts, but having a much broader vision and passion for their own work.

Besides transparency, new language also included "discovery learning" and "the having of wonderful ideas" (Duckworth, 1987). Learning how to structure sessions based on student discovery rather than instructor explanation was exciting and renewing. It became apparent that discovery was best done within structure rather than with no apparent boundaries. Determining what we needed as bottom-line adherence and articulating expected outcomes was an exercise that required us to creatively design learning opportunities based on knowledge and experience, tempered with new information and needs. Celebrating ideas was a wonderful way to validate ourselves and our potential.

Similar feelings of accomplishment were evident for our students as together we created the learning environment and fully immersed ourselves in the possibilities of each day. When we all came off course and spent time together reflecting on what had happened, it became evident that the instructors felt renewed, challenged, and successful in their own growth. One key to those feelings was realizing that we had shared power and were free of the usual feelings of responsibility for our students' learning. We were responsible for safety, created opportunities for learning, provided time and direction for reflection, and developed vehicles for transference while meeting VOBS's expectations for these courses. The freedom which was generated for both the participating teachers and the instructors gave space for everyone to be resource persons, seekers of involvement, and creators of options.

ECOEE Adds a New Dimension

My experience leading Expeditionary Learning training courses at VOBS led me to incorporate Expeditionary Learning Design Principles into the Environmental Conservation Outdoor Education Expedition (ECOEE). ECOEE, a Western Illinois University's field studies and travel program in the Department of Recreation, Parks, and Tourism Administration, aims to support professional preparation in recreation leadership through practical applications and scholarship. The program consists of a planning semester and a semester in the field. Eighteen students study theory and practice in the areas of leadership development, wilderness travel and ethics, adventure, interpretation, outdoor education, and camping.

ECOEE students desire to try their own ideas, apply what they have learned over their educational career, and become competent in areas of deep interest to them. They are developmentally ready to accept responsibility for their actions, although sometimes reluctant to do so. The instructors anticipated that, when the desire to learn and the ability to act responsibly were both present, students would take on a high level of involvement in designing their own content, determining how to learn the desired material, and assessing their progress.

In the sections which follow, the introduction of Expeditionary Learning into ECOEE is described. The first trial brought both satisfying results and difficulties. The second trial included important adjustments. Portions of a major student report are included to demonstrate the engagement of the students in their learning.

Promise and Problems
in the First Generation of Expeditionary Learning

Expeditionary Learning was first introduced during the field semester, after two weeks of classwork and one month of wilderness travel. The expedition phase put the students in a situation where their environment provided them with immediate consequences for their actions; even small details became important in light of their consequences. To function in this situation, students had little choice but learn the things they needed to know about themselves and the wilderness. As a result, learning styles and behavior patterns changed dramatically, shifting from other-directed to more self-directed. Students learned to oversee their own activities, care for each other, accept responsibility for the results of their actions with the group, and apply their skills to stay safe and travel comfortably with minimal impact on the environment.

Expeditionary Learning was received with enthusiasm, skepticism, reluctance, and relief. Students were given the option to redesign classes to better fit their career or interest needs. They were encouraged to tap into the resources within the group, work together on projects, modify the schedule for the following six weeks without compromising the integrity of the field studies program, and ask for help whenever needed. Once the students clearly understood the intent of each class, their responsibility for their own learning, and the requirements set by the university, they began to explore options and develop wonderful ideas. Using successful knowledge and procedures from the first six weeks of the program, the students began to create their own curricula. The proposals they presented to instructors included revised goals, breakdown of outcomes into feasible pieces, evidence of learning, due dates for work, and relative grade weights of their work.

The resulting curricula fit into four general modes. Some students set up a convergent process to compile information they already had into usable, accessible, and expandable form. The second group chose to take what they knew, identify what they wanted to know, and set about building knowledge bridges to connect the two in a career development context. For these students, the outcomes for the semester focused on gaining knowledge needed to realize their career goals. Accepting that the project would extend well beyond the semester, they became aware of continued learning possibilities. A third group wanted to explore areas of interest relative to individual classes, a very divergent process. Finally, a few minimized their options by choosing work of great comfort that would take little effort to complete.

Adjustments to the itinerary, generated by students, showed immediate effects. The original itinerary included wilderness trips, visits to agencies, and meetings with administrators in the recreation field. The students desired additional stops to access other resources. Positive results of the changes became evident during agency visits when some students demonstrated an enhanced interest and participated fully because of their personal focus. A less common, negative effect was lack of participation and professionalism when an agency was not perceived to be important to a student. Difficulties arose when such students were asked to be professional and support their commitment to the group itinerary. Many times the agencies were asked to flex to meet ECOEE needs rather than ECOEE adjusting to the agency's work. The group seemed to develop a general, self-centered mentality that was magnified by the student-centered Expeditionary Learning process

Another case of individualism in conflict with community appeared as students began to establish their own ways for meeting their needs by competing for agencies and resources. Some students were committed to accommodating others and meeting the needs of all, while others were more inclined to place themselves above the group, indicating that they did not accept the Design Principle of collaboration and competition. A common vision of commitment became difficult to sustain. The cooperative environment was compromised by competition for resources. Students were more individualistic than cooperative as learners. Johnson and Johnson (1990) indicate that individualistic learning is the less effective, and cooperative learning is more effective. This means that Expeditionary Learning requires that functional procedures for cooperative learning be implemented and upheld. The assumption that the students would transfer cooperative skills, developed while working together on a wilderness expedition, to a different setting without specific guidance and training to do so was faulty. The difference between those who were willing to work cooperatively and those who preferred individual pursuits raised issues which spilled over into the entire program.

The role of the instructors shifted from being primary information sources to being facilitators who, in helping the students connect to resources, clarified procedures and outcomes, validated ideas, and shared experiences as lifelong learners. Before the shift occurred, respect was associated with an instructor's position; afterwards, it was based on personal contribution to the process. In the former role, the instructors were responsible for evaluation of performance and outcomes. In the latter role, they were not primary evaluators but conferred with students on the learning that took place and the results of their efforts, jointly determining grades to be turned in to the University.

The process of evaluation and grading, even though framed early, was difficult because standards were not consistent among students. This caused instructors and students to ponder the complexity of evaluating the process and outcomes of experiential learning in standardized terms based upon institutional structures. The central dilemma was, how can we grade process and outcomes, which are mutually dependent factors, within a system that is concerned only with outcomes?

As students struggled to find ways to express what they were learning, they turned to familiar patterns that included papers, journals, notebooks, tests, adventure site management, storytelling, and skill development. Although these were not unusual, the students found more significant meaning in their work than they had in the past. The results of the students' efforts came to represent more than just a grade; the evaluation process became a way to verify that they were, in fact, learning and attaining their goals. This was evidenced by the students' enthusiasm and sincerity during the evaluation process. According to criteria developed by Gibbons and Hopkins (1985), the students were functioning in the psychosocial mode on the scale of experientiality. This schema indicates that this psychosocial mode, the highest level of experientiality, occurs when the "students gain understanding of themselves as unique individuals, and learn to direct their own activities effectively and responsibly" (p. 137). This understanding is the base upon which self-directed learning can take place. The ECOEE students had reached the highest level of experientiality but lacked ways to express and evaluate their learning in forms other than those which they had previously known.

Expeditionary Learning is a natural companion to academic field studies programs. It incorporates a high level of student responsibility and initiative, whether or not there is a wilderness expedition component. It requires the students to be involved in the planning of class work, invested in the process and evaluation of their efforts. The students are primary in all stages of curriculum development and implementation, and must be willing to accept consequences. The instructors are highly involved, but not the primary sources for the information or the dominant determiners of the value of outcomes or the direction of inquiry. These transitions from more conventional university relationships are not easy for students or instructors to achieve.

The Second Generation of Expeditionary Learning

Based on the evaluations and reflections of the experience of the first generation, instructors decided that Expeditionary Learning needed to be introduced during the planning semester prior to the field studies program. The students have always planned aspects of the field semester except the course content and structure, so this was a logical next step. A weekend retreat was organized to introduce Expeditionary Learning and to explore what students wanted out of ECOEE. They defined common interest in each of the content areas and established emphasis areas within each course that would satisfy student needs and university standards. A curriculum committee was established to continue the work for the rest of the semester with the goal of writing the syllabi based on desired student outcomes. Projects and concentrated learning experiences were planned into the itinerary, with the curriculum and itinerary committees collaborating on how to meet student goals within the constraints and opportunities of the field studies program.

Incorporating Expeditionary Learning in the planning semester caused the radical shift in the instructor's role to happen while still on campus amid a conventional academic climate. Instructors had to let go of their comfortable roles in planning a course without direct student input. This required learning how to share decision-making power. The process demanded continual adjustment as the instructors needed to retain responsibility for some tasks to prevent students being overwhelmed. For example, after struggling alongside the students for almost two months, the student curriculum committee and the instructors decided that six courses was too big a project for the students to take on. The students chose to take responsibility for three and asked the instructors to format the other three. Trying to give the information needed to build a foundation for the next semester while not fully determining the completed structure of that semester demanded mutual trust. Instructors did not have all the answers and found it stimulating to share in the discovery process along with the students. This style of instruction pushed them to grow both as people and as instructors. Their efforts brought them face to face with biases and procedures picked up from their own educations in more traditional settings. The experience was both freeing and puzzling. Their desire to provide a more positive learning environment, and the belief that Expeditionary Learning would work, prompted the instructors to take the necessary risks.

There was no time in the ECOEE preparation sequence for detailed instruction about educational design. As a result, the students had to struggle to understand Expeditionary Learning while they planned the coming semester. They were trying to use a model for which there was no precedent in their backgrounds. In many ways, the students and instructors experienced similar struggles. At times, all of us felt as though we were traveling in circles as we attempted to break free from old habits. Frequent meetings among students and instructors were essential to ensure that the whole group moved together into less familiar territory. In a sense, we were on a metaphoric expedition long before our real expedition began.

University Students
Reflect on Expeditionary Learning

This section is a compiled version of reports written by ECOEE students during their planning semester. It is a collective reflection on the process and outcomes of the students' experiences, the frustrations and triumphs of self-directed learning, and suggestions for others who may become involved in Expeditionary Learning. In keeping with the spirit of transferring responsibility to students, I have retained the students' voices in this section.

We students often have the smallest, yet most important, voice in determining the direction of our education and the processes through which we learn. This is our attempt to exert influence by evaluating Expeditionary Learning at the university level as a viable educational design which harnesses the student as a resource.

Imagine enrolling in a course about which you were already tremendously excited and then having your instructors ask, "What do you want to learn?" They were serious; it was not a rhetorical question. Although we were presented with what seemed to be a fairly simple task, we struggled to identify concepts and how we might make a bridge from concept to practice. We didn't know what to do; the experience was a mix of excitement and fear all at once. We wanted to know how this could be? What were our limits? How were we to be assessed? Perhaps most importantly, we wanted to know how would the instructors support us? If we could turn to them as a resource and for reassurance then, yes, we were interested, but we wanted a promise that they would be there and that they would not answer all our questions with questions. After most of these questions were answered, the class grew quiet; we began to let the concept sink in, to realize the endless opportunities while at the same time the tremendous responsibility we were taking on by becoming crew members, not just passengers!

We set aside time during a weekend retreat to begin to develop curriculum for six courses. The instructors asked us to group our interests into tracks and then identify the relationship of those tracks to our courses. The format suggested by our instructors was not successful. We began to succeed only after we had developed our own procedures for identifying interest areas, and had learned to understand our goals and the typical content of the various courses. We needed both to take responsibility for the process and to have some information in order to conceptualize what we were trying to achieve. It was through this process that we began to make use of our instructors as a resource. They contributed their expertise to help us create learning opportunities and clarify and focus our efforts. But instructors did not serve as our primary sources of information.

We were given the accreditation determinants of our Department, and those became the basis for the core components, usually accounting for 30%-40% of the course weight. We found we could legitimately pursue a tremendous range of ideas and areas of interest. At first, the number of suggestions was staggering. Feedback from the year before warned us against having too many directions of study, as this would become more than we could manage in one semester. As we discussed what we wanted to study, we began to see that it would make sense to work with others having the same interests to form more intimate groups for support, clarification of goals and ideas, balance, and evaluation.

Some of us were interested in therapeutic recreation, and that became a basic area of study with avenues of exploration reaching into other courses like camping, management of adventure recreation, and outdoor education. Others were interested in sharpening their Wilderness First Responder skills and chose that as one of their major foci for the management of adventure and wilderness leadership courses. A few students wanted to participate in multiple areas for each course. The weekend work resulted in common areas of study consolidated into tracks for each subject. Goals and objectives were written for each course, which resulted in the beginning forms of syllabi. A student's syllabus for management of adventure recreation, emphasizing a track in therapeutic recreation, might look like this:

Core Requirements 35%   Basic Rescue in Adventure 5%

Top Rope Climbing 15%   High Ropes/Teams Courses 15%

Therapeutic Recreation 30%   Resource Management 0%

Commercial Trekking and Trips 0%   Wilderness First Responder
skills 0%

Each student developed a unique mix of his or her interests, to be pursued in cooperation with other students sharing similar interests. We recognized that our interests were very complex and that our directions in life were not well defined. Many of us chose to include other areas of interest in order to broaden our awareness and opportunities.

It became evident that the formation of a student curriculum committee would be necessary to facilitate the development of our interests and goals. It would require too much energy and time for us to be continually involved in curriculum development while fulfilling the tasks required for each of the other committees. Being immersed in a conventional university setting made it difficult to function freely in planning to participate in an alternative education model. To be highly self-directed required time and energy beyond what many of us reasonably had to give. We often struggled to balance the demands of the present against the demands of our future. The feeling was expressed aptly by one of the curriculum committee members, Dawn Nivinski. She wrote:

> At times I find myself feeling like an old German shepherd, set in her ways, that just doesn't want to learn a new way, give me my money's worth and teach me. At other times it's like seeing a doorway opening with all sorts of possibilities. What may be even more difficult, it's accepting the fact that we are all vulnerable and highly dependent on each other.

To manage this struggle, we asked the curriculum committee to take the ideas and guidelines from the weekend retreat and work with the student itinerary committee and instructors to make sure that our educational goals could be met during the travel semester. We also decided to take on responsibility for designing only three courses. The committee accepted the challenge to prioritize our goals, find a balance between all our needs, and develop curricula, with our input and consensus. Although we were all aware that we were truly responsible for our own learning, something about the amount of time pressure and our constant contact with more customary academic situations prevented many of us from taking full advantage of this opportunity. Even so, the freedom to pursue our interests was exciting, and we looked forward to a semester of Expeditionary Learning.

It was clear that several Expeditionary Learning principles had been incorporated into our planning experience. "The primacy of self-discovery" was reflected in our attempt to set goals. The "having of wonderful ideas" was celebrated as we found we could legitimately pursue a tremendous range of ideas and areas of interest. "The responsibility for learning" during our planning semester varied. Some of us had adopted it more than others, depending upon our level of understanding, time, and energy. "Diversity and inclusion," "collaboration and competition," and "intimacy and caring" were all issues that we had to incorporate in order to develop the curriculum and plan for living together. We expected these principles to remain an integral part of our communal experience.

We found that we had accepted the Expeditionary Learning assumptions that "all students can learn" and that "success breeds success" (VOBS, 1993). For us, this meant that we needed to communicate how we best learn, and to create time in our schedule to build for success. This was not an easy task because there were so many things we wanted to do in our three months. We had to constantly refer back to our priorities in order to keep things in balance and provide for different learning styles and quality assessment. Another assumption of Expeditionary Learning is that "parents and communities play a role that enhances student learning." Community began to have an impact early in the planning semester. As we moved through the planning process, we found our group to be a source of both support and conflict; because of both, we began to feel connected. We knew from the accounts of past ECOEE programs that the twenty of us could develop into a community that would be very supportive and confrontive, enjoyable and frustrating, as well as all-consuming and temporary. We anticipated that, as with the past groups, the formation of our primary community would have a strong impact upon our courses of study. A secondary aspect of community involved our expectations for meeting professionals in the field, people with whom we hoped to work, in the very near future. We expected to extend community and enhance our learning through the agencies and the people we would meet along the way.

Conclusion

The principles of Expeditionary Learning, closely related to the philosophy of Outward Bound, form a process that is transferable to other educational settings. As implied by its name, Expeditionary Learning succeeds in creating a learning environment which closely resembles a wilderness expedition. The feeling of taking a journey into an area with many unknowns, teachers and students together, is duplicated. In pursuit of their goals, all are learners, all depend upon each other, and each must accept responsibility for their own direction. A sense of commitment is developed by the students who become actively involved in their own educations.

In the past, Outward Bound enthusiasts have searched for ways to transfer what they experienced to other educational systems. In this case, it was the Outward Bound instructors, dedicated to helping school teachers understand expeditions, who became learners themselves. In the process, they become committed to Expeditionary Learning. They also caught the excitement of the Dubuque teachers and realized the possibilities Expeditionary Learning presents for other settings.

Expeditionary Learning was intended for elementary and secondary students, but we have found that it excites students beyond that age group. A field-studies program in a university provided a dynamic environment well suited for Expeditionary Learning. Students and instructors recognized opportunities they had been unaware of and had the freedom to choose whether or not to investigate them. However, this flexible structure was difficult for some students to manage, especially those who were dependent upon clearly defined, authoritative assignments. Being a self-contained unit allowed ECOEE to pursue Expeditionary Learning undiluted by other institutional demands. The professional community in the field was valuable in helping to define and meet educational goals. It would have been a benefit to make better use of this resource by consulting outside practitioners during the planning semester. In the future, as a network supporting Expeditionary Learning at the university level develops, we anticipate that students will become much better equipped to be lifelong learners.

Acknowledgements

I would like to give special acknowledgement to Dan Perunko, Dan Caston, Richard Flor, Sharon Bassett, Martha McPheeters, and all the members of the VOBS Expeditionary Learning team for sharing their ideas and reviewing the early versions of this chapter.

References

Duckworth, E. (1987). *The having of wonderful ideas & other essays on teaching and learning*. New York: Teachers College Press.

Gibbons, M., & Hopkins, D. (1985). How experiential is your experience-based program? In R. Kraft & M. Sakofs (Eds.), *Theory of experiential education*. Boulder, CO: Association for Experiential Education.

Johnson & Johnson. (1990). Cooperative learning and achievement. In S. Sharan (Ed.), *Cooperative learning: Research and theory*. Westport, CT: Praeger Publications, Greenwood Publishing Group.

Nadler, R. S., & Luckner, J. L. (1992). *Processing the adventure experience: Theory and practice*. Dubuque, IA: Kendall/Hunt.

New designs for old schools. (1992, July). *Washington Post*, p. A12.

Voyageur Outward Bound School. (1993). *Manual for expeditionary learning*. Minneapolis MN: VOBS.

Chapter 11

CAN PROGRAM EVALUATION RESCUE SERVICE LEARNING?

Lyn M. Shulha and Jeffry Piker

Lyn M. Shulha, a former high school teacher and youth camp programmer, is an assistant professor of Evaluation and Planning at Queen's University, Kingston, Canada. She received an MEd in Curriculum and Instruction from Queen's University and a PhD in Educational Evaluation from the University of Virginia. Lyn is currently investigating, through site-based studies, the potential of program evaluation in facilitating program implementation and organizational learning.

Jeffry Piker is an educational consultant living in Kingston, Ontario, specializing in program evaluation, anti-racist education, transition to work, and labour education. Jeff completed an MA in Sociology at the University of Michigan and later, through his blend of academic and practical work, turned to high school teaching with a BEd from Queen's University at Kingston. His most recent work includes studies in cooperative learning and adult education.

Lyn and Jeff were closely connected with the service learning program, the success and failure of which they document. This chapter is an important contribution because, for all the lip service given to service as a learning opportunity in experiential education, it is relatively rare as an integral part of the curriculum. Here, two instructors in such a program tell its story and relate the part played by their evaluative efforts to demonstrate the program's worth. The fact that the program failed to survive is taken as a basis for learning lessons about the role and nature of program evaluation in any situation where unconventional program elements must reside within a more conventional institutional framework.

Introduction

This is the story of the rise and fall of service learning—one component of a teacher-education degree program in a university. This story will describe service learning's status within both teacher education and the community beyond the university walls. The history and evolution of our service-learning program contain the seeds of both its success and its eventual failure to survive. We think this story is worth telling because it reveals a pattern which may well apply to nontraditional experiential programs in other places.

In brief, service learning was a largely self-directed, community-based element within the student-teaching practicum. Students were responsible for matching their learning needs with placement opportunities within the community and then providing at least 30 hours of service. An evaluation of the program showed that it was meeting its mandate and confirmed that students valued self-directed, experiential opportunities as part of their professional preparation. Service learning was, nevertheless, deleted as a program component after 24 years of operation. The evaluation, an investigation of students' learning and the program's effectiveness, proved unable to help service-learning advocates contest the organizational agenda that ultimately shaped program policy.

What is the nature of community-based experiential learning? How can those responsible for the delivery of experiential programs avoid the dilemma and frustration of reporting that "the evaluation demonstrated program success, but the program died"? Our story is intended to guide those with the responsibility for both establishing and evaluating community-based experiential education programs such as service learning. The lessons we have learned, while hard won, may help to shed light on the complexity of grounding nontraditional learning in traditional educational settings.

Program Structure and Evolution

In 1968, Queen's University opened a new Faculty of Education, the primary function of which was to prepare post-baccalaureate students for teacher licensing and the BEd degree. (*Note*: The term "Faculty" refers to a major unit within a university, equivalent to the terms "School" or "College" in other jurisdictions.) Plans for the new Faculty reflected a progressive orientation toward teacher training. A community-based advisory board was established to support the planning process. Nontraditional thinking and innovation were encouraged. It was hardly surprising, then, that Faculty policy emphasized the professional commitment of educators to the broader social context, or that a service-learning project, called "Community Service," would be made part of the student-teaching practicum.

During the entire time that service learning was a compulsory part of teacher education, its basic format remained essentially the same. Within the general framework, however, some key changes did occur: in the educational philosophy that explained and justified the program to students, faculty members, and the wider community; in particular ingredients of the model's implementation; and in the general administrative and operational context of the Faculty itself. In any educational setting, the interaction between philosophy, delivery, and administrative context is important for analyzing the program's evolution within the broader context of experiential education and for analyzing the potential of evaluation to become a regular and desirable program activity.

Program Structure

Students were expected to select sites where they could assist in the delivery of educationally or socially valuable services. There was always a broad array of opportunities, within our city community and beyond: social and cultural agencies, healthcare institutions, correctional centres, religious organizations, and recreational programs. Students could also select schools, as long as the service-learning work did not duplicate their practice-teaching roles. A project undertaken by a student could be part of a site's normal routine, or it could represent a special initiative established just for this purpose. Each student's own project was expected to involve a minimum of 30-40 hours of service delivery. It could be scheduled over longer or more concentrated periods of time. Most students chose settings nearby, but to serve agencies in their home communities during weekends was also appropriate.

"Host professional" was the term eventually adopted to identify the individual at the project site who was responsible for directing and supporting the student's work. Host professionals interviewed student applicants and selected the successful candidate(s). Host professionals were expected to have sufficient training and expertise to supervise students in the tasks central to the service project. Ongoing feedback and support were key expectations of the host professional's role. As well, these individuals provided formal confirmation that the terms established in the initial learning agreement had been fulfilled.

The primary function of the University academic and secretarial staff allocated to the service-learning program was coordination of the process. This involved introducing students to the program's rationale and goals, clarifying its formal and informal expectations, facilitating initial contacts with potential placement sites, maintaining detailed records, reading and approving student journals and reports, and certifying successful completion. At times, project-related problems engaged staff in additional counselling and support both with students and with host professionals. Most placements, however, did not require any direct communication or intervention. Contact with the ever-changing group of active and potential host professionals was a central focus of staff work, primarily to encourage continued enthusiasm for the program, to facilitate understanding of its purposes, and to enhance the quality of its delivery.

Students had major responsibility for implementing the specific details of the program. They needed to assess their own professional development requirements, select the kinds of experience they wanted their service project to provide, locate sites that could be expected to provide such experience, schedule interviews, negotiate learning agreements, and perform the work they had agreed to do. They also managed the paper flow that was required to coordinate the program. In addition, students interpreted, through assigned reports and journals, the experience they had received, reflecting on its implications for their personal and professional development. Because it was actually a required part of their professional BEd program, students did not view their work as "voluntary."

Three general stages of the service-learning program's development can be identified: an early period, from 1968 to the late 1970s; a middle period, through the mid-1980s; and a late period, lasting until 1992. Although the reality of its evolution was far more incremental, some basic patterns emerged, making it possible—and analytically useful—to address each stage separately and to compare their characteristics.

The Early Period—Establishing the Program

During this time, the program staff established the role of service learning within the Faculty's teacher-training program, clarified the underlying educational principles, and focused the operations.

The dominant philosophy of learning that guided the early operation of Community Service was the view that schools and, therefore, teachers, were organically related to the people, groups, and social forces of their surrounding communities. It was essential, therefore, for beginning teachers to learn about the complexity and potential of these connections. Included in the program's own formal descriptions were comments about teachers "helping the community" to function and "giving back to the community" the kinds of service that would reflect and respect the resources and support it gave to them. Related to this was the explicit notion that teacher education needed to transmit understanding and respect for the "diversity" that existed in the wider society.

The field of experiential education, new and rapidly growing at the time, provided key input into the program's rationale. Crucial in this was the idea of locating training within concrete learning projects, in which comprehensive, task-focused activities would generate knowledge, skills, and attitudes in an integrated way. It was important that the contexts for such projects be applied and interpersonal, rather than abstract and purely academic, and that they generate a sense of genuine social importance and personal responsibility.

Although early documents described Community Service as a separate and distinct training requirement, its actual operation—functionally and physically—was allocated to the staff and facilities of the special program in Outdoor and Experiential Education (OEE). In reference to their Community Service activities, the staff described and viewed themselves as a "team"—a term, as well as a view, which continued to be used throughout the life of the program. The team members considered their primary role to be background support, distant from the learning that occurred at placement sites and focused on providing to students a balanced blend of planning and counselling. Although such input was fairly well distributed over the length of the service placements, its strongest impact on learning came when written reports and journals that students were required to submit were reviewed and commented on.

The pressure to change was consistent throughout the life of the service-learning program. In the early '70s, a large number of new teaching positions opened up within the Faculty. Not having participated in the development and expression of the Faculty's original ideals about community involvement and social responsibility, and often recruited from closer to the traditional centre than to the progressive edges of academic education, many of these new professors were not immediately convinced of the validity and relevance of any service-learning practicum component. In practical terms, it was a component that appeared to extract a sizable chunk of students' time—in addition to practice teaching—and crowded an already limited academic year.

The Middle Period—Institutionalizing the Program

Over a relatively short period during the early to mid-1980s, program personnel revised the general purpose and orientation. Renamed "Service Learning," the program delivery began to integrate more extensively with other specialized programs offered within the Faculty.

Although its total staff-time allocation remained essentially the same, the program was moved from its original home within OEE to a new location, much closer (in both physical and functional terms) to the Practice Teaching office. Responsibility for program coordination was also transferred from OEE instructors to other teaching and secretarial staff. This transition occurred at a point when the Faculty, itself, was undergoing substantial restructuring —a combined reaction to pressures from the university to cut costs, eagerness by some faculty leaders to orient teacher preparation in a more professionally orthodox direction, and the initiation of several, specially focused programs. The name change to Service Learning also reflected the alignment of the program within the general field of experiential education.

Influenced by the ideas and experiences of its new staff, and also in response to changes in the broader educational and administrative context, the program rationale was revised in several ways. Experiential education remained a key source of both general philosophy and specific terminology. Emphasis on the social responsibility of the teaching profession was maintained. Increased stress was placed on principles and practices from the field of adult education. Although self-directed learning had always been a major program theme, the steps and processes required to accomplish it had never been articulated clearly or emphasized strongly in earlier Community Service documents. The relationship between experience, reflection, self-insight, and personal growth was highlighted in greater detail—especially in information about the program that was provided to students, faculty members, and host professionals.

Staff began to suggest the potential of the program for career exploration beyond the teaching field, although care was also taken to reassure other faculty members about the continuing relevance of Service Learning for teacher preparation. Indeed, staff made several attempts to lobby their colleagues on behalf of the merit and worth of Service Learning. In response to doubts and questions concerning this kind of training experience, data were collected about the total hours of "free" professional experience and instruction that students were given by the community, and of "free" service that students gave to the community in return. Mention was made of the educational benefit that was accomplished on one side of this exchange, and the good will that was created on the other.

Although the job market for teachers remained tight during this period, the number of applications to the Faculty grew substantially. The response was a new admissions policy that weighted equally grade point average and applicants' experience in teaching-related activities. Administrative rationalization of the entire teacher education program began to favour a more orthodox view of professional preparation. As well, five specialized programs within the Faculty began to find new ways to use Service Learning for their own instructional purposes. While it was by no means inconsistent with experiential and adult education principles to integrate Service Learning with programs such as these, their own uses of Service Learning made it more difficult to generate a clear and coherent image of the program's unique purpose in the Faculty at large, and to sustain widespread agreement about its special value among students and faculty. The combined effect of all these substantial changes and pressures was to dilute institutional consensus about the purpose of Service Learning and to weaken commitment to its ongoing operation.

The Late Period—
Refining and Defending Service Learning

During a time when the program personnel were refining their analysis of Service Learning and identifying potential innovations in program delivery that could deepen and extend its role in professional development, they were continuing to struggle—unsuccessfully, as it turned out—to sustain broad support for the legitimacy and relevance of the program.

By far the most important contextual factor during this period was pressure on the Faculty to quickly and substantially reduce its total budget, based on severe cutbacks in funding to universities. This led to a comprehensive Faculty-wide review of its entire structure, content, and schedule of pre-service teacher preparation. Although Service Learning was by no means the only program to face serious questions of value, effectiveness, and relevance, its compulsory status, complex rationale, and nontraditional format made its situation more precarious than most of the others. It was during this period that we (the authors), as adjunct instructors, along with a new secretary, formed the Service Learning team.

This period also saw the rationale of Service Learning evolve in some important directions. The implications of self-directed learning for teacher training were clarified—as an appropriate and powerful model of professional development, and also as a necessary instructional tool for teachers interested in helping students become independent learners. Both the process of choosing the placement site and the dynamics of negotiating the learning agreement were given increased recognition and more detailed attention. The value of integrating service experiences with other aspects of the professional degree program was also emphasized.

Most importantly, Service Learning became definable in curricular terms. A program description, with clearly articulated goals, a rationale, objectives (experience, skill, attitude), and criteria for successful performance, was introduced as part of the orientation to the program. Service Learning was thus explicitly presented to students, faculty members, and the community as a formalized program component. In part this was due to our belief that the program's teaching and learning processes could benefit from a set of clearly stated and explicit intentions. In part it was our attempt to make the program a more integral part of the pre-service teacher education curriculum—that is, to answer in familiar and professional language the underlying question, "Why are we running a compulsory Service Learning program?"

During the late period, the structure and the substance—if not the solidarity—of the Service Learning team began to fade. Year by year, although the demands of the program remained the same, instructor time was depleted; the secretary's responsibilities increased accordingly. A decision was made to invest much of the available staff time into the preparation of students for the practicum. New student orientation sessions were instituted: a) to anchor the program within the overall BEd program; b) to emphasize the significance of self-direction in professional preparation as well as in teaching and learning in general; c) to introduce students to the conceptual and practical world of learning agreements; and d) to orient students to the procedural tasks necessary to complete the course.

Journals were by now assigned but not collected, and the "Progress" and "Final Report" forms were streamlined and shortened. Within the framework of self-directed professional development, the onus was placed on the students to identify to their host professionals or to program staff any placement problems that might require remedial counselling or personal support.

Because feedback, reflection, and mentoring were now centred almost entirely within each project setting, increased attention was given to collective communication with host professionals, clarifying with them the details of what was expected and acknowledging their important contributions to the teacher education process. Attempts were made—without much success—to include other members of the faculty in this process.

As the program closed the books on its 20th year of operation, it found itself in an eminently weakened and certainly defensive position. Forecasts of even more severe cutbacks had administrators and faculty members glancing more frequently toward Service Learning. Clearly, those who had been members of the program's instructional team understood the details and potential of the Service Learning model far better than did most of their colleagues, many of whom continued to refer to the program by its pre-1981 title, Community Service. Interestingly, most students—their extensive volunteer backgrounds notwithstanding—were still reporting informally and through program Final Report forms that they valued the contributions made by this program to their preparation as teachers.

The Evolutionary Process

Students enrolled in Service Learning in 1992 would probably have found the program to be very similar to that of their predecessors who had completed Community Service in 1968. The orientation they were given would have been better organized, located within a more systematically professional analytic framework, and focused on somewhat different objectives for learning. The number and format of the reports they were required to submit would have changed. They would have less ongoing contact with the faculty team and would play a more direct and active role in the negotiation of their own learning agreements. The instructors of their other courses would comment less often—and express less enthusiasm —about the importance of their nontraditional practicum experiences. More students would find the program directly tied to special programs, and fewer would establish their projects through independent contacts with agencies and institutions.

However, the firsthand experience of service and learning in community settings, and the professional development it thereby generated, retained its essential shape and form over the entire life of the program. While the distribution of placement sites evolved, increasing in number and variety, the general nature of students' tasks and responsibilities remained fairly constant. In their final reports, the great majority of students still commented, in concrete and detailed ways, about the learning they had accomplished, the personal growth they had noticed, and the professional development they had gained.

Thus, aspects of the program's rationale, structure, and context apparently changed more than its experiential content. In particular, the analysis by program staff of the role of experiential education in teacher development and their understanding of what was involved in such learning and how it occurred, acquired greater depth and clarity. The same insights, however, were not widely distributed among other faculty members.

After an early honeymoon period for Community Service, program personnel began what would continue to be a constant, if informally articulated, aspect of their role: the ongoing search for a rationale that would legitimate the existence of the program within a teacher education Faculty, and a manageable structure that would fully express that rationale. Over a succession of staff and instructor changes, there was a never-ending process of program development, usually informed by attention—sometimes anecdotal, other times more systematic—to program evaluation data.

Establishing Program Merit and Worth

Responding to Perceived Threats

As predictions of severe fiscal constraint and down-sizing continued, there was increasing informal talk that Service Learning had outlived its time. The first question the program team faced was whether we should, or could, be advocates for our own program. It was clear that testimonies from us about the value of the program would not be sufficient to sustain it. Because only one tenured faculty member was still connected to Service Learning, we understood that removing the program from teacher education would be a simple and relatively painless way to save money without causing trauma to the working life of the full-time community. It appeared to us that if the program was to stake a claim in the Faculty's future, it would have to demonstrate its value within teacher education and to our education students. This assumption—one that would be revisited—led us to our first investigation, the perceived worth of Service Learning as a component of progressive teacher education.

During the academic year 1988-89, we undertook two external tests of the program. In the first, the Service Learning as part of a teacher's training practicum was described by our university's representative to a Province-wide committee on teacher education with a request for comment and reaction. There was a very favourable response to the inclusion of this alternative type of community-based experiential learning. Our second step was to present the program for review and critique at the annual meeting of Canada's premier scholarly society for studies in education. There, we described both the program and some of the student-reported outcomes. The supportive comments and lively discussion from graduate students in education and practising teachers and academics were both encouraging and motivating.

The endorsements of these key stakeholders in teacher education gave us confidence that Service Learning could claim a legitimate place, at least philosophically, within teacher education. The remaining question was whether the program was achieving its potential. This question called out for a more formal program evaluation. We believed, at the time, that in the presence of accurate information about student and community experiences, faculty members and decision makers would be more likely to extend to Service Learning a fair hearing regarding its future. This belief was supported by administrative approval for a formal evaluation.

Getting Evaluation Started

A review of the literature revealed that almost all experience-based programs leave participants with personal satisfaction, enhanced social conscience, and increased measures of self-confidence (Warner, 1984). While we considered these to be significant outcomes, we realized that confirmation of these would do little to alter our colleagues' judgments of the program's value. We concluded that Service Learning would need to demonstrate outcomes specific to teacher education if it was to argue for a legitimate place within the Faculty of Education.

The literature also informed us that experiential learning for pre-service teachers was most effective when it a) did not replicate well-entrenched models of conventional teaching and learning (Law, 1982), and b) was accompanied by a framework of systematic reflection (Feiman-Nemser & Buchmann, 1983). We felt confident that Service Learning did have a strong history, at least in its intentions, of attending to these criteria. This could be traced through course descriptions, brochures, and student materials. What the evaluation needed to test was how fully students actually experienced the intent of the program. It would also be important to generate specific detail about how to strengthen these program features.

The question of how to actually carry out the evaluation proved to be complex. Warner (1984) had warned that those intent on discounting experiential education outcomes usually begin by targeting weaknesses, or at least controversy, in the research methodology. Since the fate of the program would ultimately be determined by a faculty vote, it was very important that faculty members perceive the information generated by the evaluation as creditable. We each came from different research backgrounds. By pooling our experiences, we were confident that we could design a thorough and reputable investigation. While we had only introductory experiences in evaluation, we speculated that information gathered from multiple methods would be the most convincing. This would mean including both outcome data (primarily quantitative) and rich descriptions of the experiences of students and hosts (qualitative).

Our first question was how to gain a better understanding of Service Learning as a learning process. Using the literature in experiential education as a guide (Warner, 1984), we determined that our methods would need to access the motivations, activities, decisions, and reflections of both our students and their hosts in the community. Observations and interviews grounded in the program settings would inform us about individual experiences. Collectively, these experiences could provide a description of the program, reveal patterns of meaningful participation, contribute to judgments about program utility, and, finally, guide decisions about program improvement.

Reminded by Dewey (1938) that not all experiences are equally educative, our second question was how students varied in their learnings and outcomes. Surveying the entire population of students following the completion of the program would, given a good response rate, allow us to talk about the experiences of students in general and to make some meaningful statements about the worth of the program.

Throughout this early thinking, we were sensitive to the possibility that an evaluation could be seen as an attempt on our part to produce "good news" propaganda. The Faculty's administration had already reported in general documents and in meetings that students from the previous year had complained about the relevance and necessity of Service Learning. We suspected that these complaints could be attributed, at least partially, to the forum in which the information was collected (an open meeting for feedback about the entire BEd program, attended by less than 20% of the students and held at a time when students were under great pressure to complete assignments).

While negative perceptions at this point in the students' year were not necessarily accurate indications of the program's overall efficacy, they did signal that some students found working through the program problematic in context with other course demands. An accurate and useful evaluation must, therefore, be able to account for the student dissatisfaction that had been publicized to faculty members as well as recommend changes that would improve the experience.

Designing an Evaluation

At first, we were perplexed by the seemingly impossible task of being both program implementors and program evaluators. If the evaluation confirmed our beliefs about the program's value, no matter how rigorous the methodology, results would likely be dismissed by many as self-serving. We decided that one way to bring credibility to the evaluation process and its findings was to form an evaluation team. Since students were the group that was supposedly most critical of the program, students appeared to be the ideal choice as colleagues for the project. From the 1989-1990 student body, eleven students expressed an interest in becoming members of an evaluation team. The six chosen had a sincere interest in trying to improve teacher education and in developing their own research skills.

Four of these students would work with one of us (JP) to map out a series of visits and interviews with both students and their host professionals. A total of 8 case studies were to provide an in-depth investigation of program processes, from students' introduction to Service Learning to their final evaluation report. As a set, these stories would reveal the extent to which activities and decision-making processes central to Service Learning prepared students for teaching.

The task for the other of us (LS) and two students was to generate information through a survey that would provide an accurate description of the characteristics and experiences of the affected student population in general. It would be important to determine not only the significance students attributed to Service Learning but the extent to which the intended outcomes of the program were being achieved.

The two research groups worked both independently and collectively. In October, we began by clarifying, through the literature and program documents, our understanding of experiential learning as it related to teacher preparation. This was followed by an investigation of the strengths and limitations of research methods, a sharpening of the evaluation questions, and a refining of the design. Even as the tasks of the two groups began to differ, we continued to meet collectively to review and critique each other's work.

By January 1990, instrument development and data collection had begun. Qualitative data were collected until early spring. The student population was surveyed following the completion of their entire BEd program. Data analysis was to be a joint responsibility, as time allowed, with both of us taking responsibility for submitting the final report.

Constraints and Compromises

One month later, by February 1990, the integrity of both the program and the evaluation was at risk. First, it was confirmed that one of us (LS) would be granted a one-year study leave starting in the summer of 1990. This was not problematic for the evaluation since the quantitative data analysis could be continued in this context. More significant for the program was the decision that her vacancy on the Service Learning team would not be filled. These events, however, were not nearly as perplexing as the loss of the remaining team member (JP) from the program because of the need to seek out a more secure professional future.

By April 1990, the staffing decisions for the next academic year were finalized. The Service Learning team would be reduced to one part-time faculty member and a senior secretary. These staffing decisions weighed heavily not only on the program's future but on the evaluation as well. Even if an evaluation could report significant findings in favour of Service Learning as a unique and valuable component of teacher education, it would be praise for a program that in practice no longer existed.

It is likely that experienced evaluators, under these circumstances, would have reassessed the feasibility and utility of continuing their work. With only a commitment to the idea of Service Learning guiding our decisions, the evaluation team continued working until the last day of the school year.

We eventually abandoned our hopes for a qualitative component to the evaluation report. Student members of the evaluation team had learned a great deal about selected placements and student experiences, but this task had absorbed all of their allotted time. With the students gone and their team partner no longer contracted by the Faculty, there was no one left to take on the responsibility of coding, analyzing, and interpreting the data. This, in turn, left the evaluation vulnerable to those who preferred to judge value using evidence grounded in context and the participants' own voices. Earlier plans to have some of the students and host professionals who had contributed to the evaluation also participate in reporting the results dissolved along with the entire qualitative segment.

Still, with a survey, developed by students, pilot-tested, and validated in hand, we decided to salvage the outcomes aspect of the evaluation. Throughout the spring and early summer, survey forms were sent out. We had never accepted the popular claims of colleagues that students were, at best, indifferent to Service Learning. For this reason, we felt somewhat vindicated when slightly over 73% of the 464 students surveyed responded. While we yet had no idea what students had said about Service Learning, they obviously felt strongly enough about their experiences and the program's future role in teacher education to register their opinions.

Reporting the Evaluation Findings

The first part of the evaluation report (Shulha, 1990) described the student body. The class of 1990 did report an average of four, volunteer, community-based experiences during the five years previous to their admission to the Faculty. This confirmed speculation that the new admissions policy was ensuring a student population with a rich background in community service. What needed to be determined was whether the accompanying argument, that students therefore viewed their Service Learning component as simply more of the same, was also true. On this question, most students (86%) reported that the Service Learning experience within their teacher education context had lived up to its name by providing them with unique service and learning opportunities.

Another rumour among faculty members was that most students found ways to get credit for Service Learning without putting in the required minimum 30 hours. We did find that about 16% of students got credit for Service Learning without completing the 30-hour requirement. We also discovered that most students (70%) met or exceeded the expectation for contact hours and 20% of students reported serving over 40 hours in their host setting. Some of the most encouraging findings had to do with students' perceptions of the program. One unique feature of Service Learning was the responsibility it gave students to determine how, when, and where preparation for teaching and learning might best occur. When the evaluation asked about the value of this approach to teacher education, almost all students (97%) said that pre-service teachers should be provided with opportunities to make these kinds of decisions about their professional development.

But, was this particular Service Learning practicum a useful addition to students' education? Half of the students confirmed that the program in its current form had been a significant element of their educational experience; three quarters felt that Service Learning had provided them with new insights into teaching and learning; and an even greater number (81%) felt that this form of experiential learning should be maintained as a credited part of pre-service preparation.

It is ironic that while we believed that the needs and experiences of students would guide us in making useful recommendations about Service Learning, students were telling us it was the needs and dispositions of faculty members that had the greatest influence on the program credibility. Students reported that few faculty members acknowledged Service Learning as a legitimate part of teacher education. Students talked about receiving little encouragement to link theoretical or practical issues discussed in classes to their alternative service setting. In the absence of institutional reinforcement, students tended to look to their peers for feedback and confirmation of their experiences. The students who declared they had completed the program without any formal or informal opportunities for reflection or integration tended to be the same 20% who recommended that Service Learning be deleted as a program component. The remainder (80%) encouraged the Faculty to maintain Service Learning as a part of pre-service teacher education.

Despite these findings, and students' claims that community-based experience within a context of professional preparation was different from traditional volunteer service, the argument that students were entering their teacher-training year with adequate related experience continued. In a vote of faculty members, the program was terminated.

Lessons Learned

On one hand, it seems unjust that a program with demonstrated value could be systematically reduced in the way that this one was. On the other hand, it is amazing that given the philosophical, political, economic, and personnel changes over 24 years, the program not only survived but continually found ways to be responsive to students and the community. What was it about this community-based practicum that made it viable for so long in the face of organizational inclinations to abandon it?

The success of this program was its ability to be responsive to changing times without losing sight of its primary purpose: to be educative. Learning, not service, was the one uncompromising cornerstone of the program. Even under the original name, Community Service, the seriousness with which program coordinators treated the importance of planning, reflection, and assessment demonstrated to students the connections between the program and their professional education.

Successive program personnel brought to bear their understandings of experiential education, adult learning, mentoring, cooperative education, curriculum design, and information management. The program's rationale and delivery structures benefited from all of these ingredients. As staffing resources, institutional interest, and connections with other faculty members diminished, it became essential to find structural ways to augment the essential activities of goal setting, reflection, and mentoring. Program guidelines became more explicit, providing students and host professionals with guidance in negotiating and decision making. These adjustments in program organization and delivery made it possible to sustain significant levels of student and community learning and satisfaction.

The reality remains that, in this example, the program was discontinued. Was there anything that we, as program personnel, could have done differently in those final years to preserve a niche for this nontraditional approach to teacher preparation? It is a question we have often asked.

We still feel strongly that a systematic program evaluation was an appropriate course of action, given the uncertainty we had about the effects on the program of diminishing resources and growing criticism from within the Faculty. What is much clearer with the benefit of time and distance is that our evaluation, in general, likely asked the wrong question. So intent were we in generating concrete evidence of the learning processes and outcomes of Service Learning that we neglected to fully appreciate the struggles of an organization under pressure to down-size and conserve.

In almost any program, but especially in nontraditional ones, an important analytic distinction can be made between insiders and outsiders. Several groups had a stake in the operation and continuation of Service Learning: the program team and students, certainly. But the presence of the program also had an impact on the community at large, host professionals (and indirectly, the clients of their organizations), and the Faculty's administration, as well as other faculty members and support staff. Although it is tempting to locate program personnel on the inside and everyone else on the outside, actually students and host professionals were insiders, too—at least part of the time. Even though students and hosts might not have developed as intricate and substantial an analysis (or theory) of experiential education as the program staff, still they had an experience-based understanding of the process. Not so for the bulk of faculty members.

Seduced by the unique features and outcomes of our program, we assumed that accurate information about the internal dynamics and consequences of Service Learning would be enough to influence the dispositions of teaching and administrative colleagues toward the program. Our belief was always, "Once you really understand the program, you will endorse it." The flaw in this approach was that it excluded the interaction of the program with the needs and values of those who would shape institutional policy. While educationally sound processes and outcomes were necessary for program viability, they were not sufficient.

The evaluation we conducted failed to examine the actual and perceived benefits and losses to the Faculty should the Service Learning program be terminated. Had we pursued this line of inquiry, program outsiders as well as students and host professionals would have become major stakeholders in the data-gathering and analysis activities. Instead, we produced a report of very little interest to anyone other than ourselves and other insiders. No evaluation can afford to focus on one group to the exclusion of others, especially if the power in decision making rests outside the program.

It is likely that in professional preparation where nontraditional programs and more conventional courses co-exist, tensions also exist. The extent of such tensions will be at least partially dependent on the degree to which the programs must compete for resources. In times of prosperity (such as the late 1960s and early 1970s), institutions can easily support both conventional and alternative practices. In times of diminishing resources (like the late 1980s and the 1990s) institutions begin to face difficult choices. At times like these, especially without influential program champions, programs such as Service Learning will benefit from evaluation, especially if it allows program personnel to participate in visioning the organization's future. Evaluation data could encourage discussion about the program's ability to contribute to overall organizational well-being. When an organization must reduce expenditures, evaluation results that suggest maintenance of the status quo may be self-defeating.

Given the Faculty's need to economize, more useful evaluation questions would likely have been: What contributions to organizational restructuring could be made by Service Learning? What would be the consequences to the Faculty of changing the existing program? These questions would have allowed an investigation of the role of Service Learning in teacher education and in the organization of a shrinking Faculty.

It is notable that since leaving Service Learning, we have both pursued, in quite different ways, career paths in evaluation. In coming together to tell this story, we have used more recent experiences to reflect on the complexity of having the responsibility both to operate a program and to periodically assess its worth. Conducting an evaluation to monitor and improve program effectiveness certainly attends to the needs of the program's staff and primary users. Conducting an evaluation to facilitate organizational learning and policy making requires that the context that surrounds the program also be addressed. As we have reported here, methods used in the first type of evaluation do not necessarily provide useful information for the second.

Can program evaluation rescue alternative experiential programs like Service Learning? Newer developments in evaluation practice encourage careful consideration of a) the structural, cultural, and political elements of organizations, b) the context these elements provide for programs, and c) the experiences and information that may be necessary if organizations are to learn from evaluation data (Cousins & Earl, in press; Stevens & Dial, 1994; Madison, 1992; Cousins & Earl, 1992; Larson & Preskill, 1991). Evaluations performed without this grounding run the risk of either being misused or not being used at all. By taking care "up front" to investigate the purposes that can best be served by evaluation, and by identifying the methods of inquiry that would adequately serve those purposes, we might have avoided the disappointment of learning that the program had worth but no context within which to operate.

References

Cousins, J. B., & Earls, L. M. (Eds.). (in press). *Participatory evaluation in education: Studies in evaluation use and organizational learning.* London: Falmer Press.

Cousins, J. B., & Earls, L. M. (1992). The case for participatory evaluation. *Educational Evaluation and Policy Analysis, 14*(4), 397-418.

Dewey, J. (1938). *Experience and education.* New York: Macmillan.

Feiman-Nemser, S., & Buchmann, M. (1983). Pitfalls of experience in teacher education (Report No. SP 023 408). East Lansing, MI: Institute for Research on Teaching. (ERIC Document Reproductive Service NO. ED 237 504)

Law, B. (1982). *Beyond schooling. A British analysis of integrated programs of preparation for adult working life in the United States* (Report No. NE-C-00-4-0010). Portland, OR: Northwest Regional Laboratory. (ERIC Document Reproductive Service No. ED 221 668)

Larson, C. L., & Preskill, H. (Eds.). (1991). *Organizations in transition: Opportunities and challenges for evaluation: New directions for program evaluation, 49.* San Francisco: Jossey-Bass.

Madison, A. M. (Ed.). (1992). *Minority issues in program evaluation: New directions for program evaluation, 53.* San Francisco: Jossey-Bass.

Shulha, L. M. (1990). *An investigation of students' attitudes and experiences in service learning: A required component of the pre-service education practicum.* Unpublished report, available from Office of the Dean of Education, Queen's University, Kingston, Ontario, K7L 4N6.

Stevens, C. J., & Dial, M. (Eds.). (1994). *Preventing the misuse of evaluation: New directions for program evaluation, 64.* San Francisco: Jossey-Bass.

Warner, A. (1984). How to creatively evaluate programs. *Journal of Experiential Education, 7*(2), 38-43.

Chapter 12

SCIENCE AND MAGIC:
A LESSON IN PHOTOSYNTHESIS

gary william rasberry

Gary william rasberry is a doctoral student at the Centre for the Study of Curriculum and Instruction, University of British of Columbia. As a poet and pedagogue, he is particularly interested in the ways that we use words to write our Selves into being. In a past life, he worked as an earth educator helping people to live more lightly on the earth. (Gary can still describe and define stomata and guard cells if someone points to them on a Giant Leaf.)

In this chapter, gary gives a beautiful example of narrative enquiry at work. He draws on a fictional account of Merlyn the Magician acting as tutor to the young King Arthur to illuminate his own experiences as a student and teacher. Those experiences are starkly contrasted in method and intent, yet in the end, even as gary reconstructs the educational values in two dramatically different modes of instruction, he finds that many unanswered questions persist and only the magic of imagination prevails.

To learn. That is the only thing that never fails.

Merlyn the Magician

From Grad School to Grade School:
Falling (Backwards) into Adventure

Lately, my life has been reduced to the blue phosphor glow of the word processor on the final drive to finishing a graduate degree. Complete with mountains of citations, an endless series of revisions, too much coffee, and not enough sleep, the academic life has begun to weigh heavily. I'm in need of a good distraction, a reasonable reason for further procrastination. My sock drawers are already organized, my books and records are arranged in alphabetical order, and the cat's nails are clipped. It's pouring rain, so any kind of outdoor exercise is out of the question. With no particular place to go, I unplug myself from the mainframe and wander down to the basement.

Before long, I'm opening old boxes filled with *Hot Wheels* and hockey sweaters, along with other long forgotten parts of my past. I fall into a box of school memorabilia and find Mr. Thompson buried in a pile of report cards and red ribbons, photographs, boy scout badges, and abandoned art projects. Mr. Thompson's name is printed clearly on the front page of a well-worn document. The lab report is organized and tidy, the handwriting foreign and familiar; I open the assignment to a complex and amateurish drawing of a leaf, carefully coloured and labelled (I must have used every pencil crayon I owned that year in Grade Seven). As if by magic, I find myself drifting back to another, almost forgotten part of my young academic life. (Cleaning the basement is fun.)

A Lesson in Photosynthesis:
The Mr. Thompson Story

Is it my imagination or is Mr. Thompson staring straight at me? He doesn't say anything so I guess it was just a false alarm. Still, I feel my face flush, and the lab stool I'm sitting on suddenly feels hard and uncomfortable. This room feels different from all the others. From where I'm sitting—in the back row closest to the door —I can see rows of smooth, black counter tops that run in sharp lines across the classroom. Most of us have our own sinks, complete with hot and cold running water. Strange valves and nozzles stick out at odd angles. Chromed and shiny, they remind me of science fiction stories I've read. (We've been warned not to touch the orange valves.)

The room is very wide from side to side, which somehow makes our teacher seem larger than life. The class goes silent and all eyes are on Mr. Thompson. Grade Seven science is serious business and Mr. Thompson, with his trademark crew cut and white lab coat, believes in a no-nonsense approach to revealing the systematic truths of science.

"All right, class, open your notebooks and copy this note on photosynthesis from the board. Make sure you leave room on the opposite page for a schematic diagram of the leaf which you will be responsible for drawing and fully labelling."

The chalkboard swims with terms, some of them underlined in red squiggly lines to emphasize their importance. I feel over-whelmed and thrilled at the same time. Everything seems so impor-tant and scientific. Mr. Thompson is bent on making sure we will remember mitochondria, guard cells, stomata, and chlorophyll for the rest of our lives. The note on the board we are all busy copying down disappears momentarily as Mr. Thompson, using his wooden pointer with the hook on the end, pulls down a large, colourful dia-gram of the leaf; it's on one of those strange roll-ups that hang on metal clips above the chalkboard. I've seen maps before, but seeing this huge leaf with billions of colourful parts really catches me off guard. I wonder if anyone else is as surprised as me? Mr. Thomp-son has a look of victory on his face; it's not a smile really, more like a twisted grin.

"I expect each and every one of you to know the names of all the working parts of the leaf as they relate to the process of photosyn-thesis. As I mentioned, you will be completing your own schematic of the leaf and it should appear exactly as it does here, accurately labelled and coloured."

A slight ripple breaks out and turns into a wave as it moves across the sea of heads in front of me. The "map of the leaf" fills me with an uneasy pleasure; the detail is so complex. Countless arrows lead to the many parts of the leaf. Almost every available space is taken up with long, mysterious-sounding terms. I'm drawn to the mystery but afraid I'll never be able to make my leaf look like something Mr. Thompson would approve of.

"You will need to know this information in order to perform the class experiment next week. If you have read ahead, you will already know that we will be covering leaves with foil, to see what occurs in the absence of sunlight."

The snapping sound of the amazing leaf being rolled back up into its resting place signals the end of science class. There is a sudden frenzy of activity as thirty Grade Seven students scramble for the door. Phys. Ed. is Period Six and photosynthesis is quickly left behind.

The steady rain outside remains the only constant as I continue to rifle through the rest of the contents of the box. Everything else is up for grabs. My life is a swirl of memories, facts and fictions. Forgotten and invented. There's no turning back. Pandora's box has already been opened and I'm in no position to close the lid and slip back upstairs to the safety of grad school. Grade School is only a skip away and I'm left to wander the halls waiting for the recess bell to ring.

As it turns out, the particular memories uncovered on this most recent basement excavation are stubborn and not entirely user-friendly. The neatly labelled leaf draws me into a remembered world, parts of which I am quite happy to have forgotten. Sure, I made it through Grade Seven science. I'm holding concrete proof: Mr. Thompson approved of my lab report (and my leaf). But there's something more to my dis-ease than Mr. Thompson's obsession with leaf terminology. (Cleaning the basement is tricky.)

In the Name of Science: Learning to be Objective

In my basement explorations, I've stumbled on to something, tripped over a big word. Objectivity. Yes, I think I learned how to be objective in Mr. Thompson's science class. Mr. Thompson was a strict and serious man—the first teacher I ever had who insisted on wearing a white lab coat to class. He believed in discipline and hard work. I'm thankful for the many work habits Mr. Thompson helped me establish. The lessons learned in his class still serve me well.

Now, however, I reflect back on some of those schooling experiences with a certain amount of resentment as I recall being told that any use of personal pronouns was unacceptable. It seemed an innocent game back then: I was trained to write in a style that avoided the use of "I" or "me" or "my" as I prepared reports and observations for science class. I can't recall how strange this procedure must have felt initially—trying to make my reports appear as though I weren't there. I have clearer memories of high school, from science as well as from many other subjects, where the challenge was to make my work appear more official, more academic, more acceptable by my teachers. I suppose somewhere along the line I stopped thinking about "The case of the Missing I's." In fact, I learned how to surgically remove any and all first-person pronouns with clinical efficiency.

For me, the more serious repercussion of losing my "I's" was a gradual loss of identity. I came to believe there was a mysterious and powerful force that possessed the right answers, a force that declared itself in the name of objectivity. As long as I aligned myself with The Force, I was safe. I hid behind the "Royal We" and stayed there for almost two decades.

I suppose I can't hold Mr. Thompson entirely responsible for my apprenticeship in objectivity; he just happened to represent the first exposure to the Pronoun Police I can remember. The process likely started much earlier and then became formalized and ritualized as I progressed through high school, and eventually completed an undergraduate degree in science. (Cleaning the basement is hard work.)

I came down here for a break from school and now I feel like I'm serving a detention. Enough. I should have gone for a run in the rain. But, if Mr. Thompson can be uncovered, I'm sure he can just as easily be buried again. I shove the report (I got a B+) back in the box. I'm just about to close the lid when I find something else that looks promising (and a lot safer than photosynthesis). It's an old copy of *The Sword and the Stone*. (Forget cleaning the basement.)

The Wart's Lessons: Magical Learning Adventures

Like Alice in Wonderland on an extracurricular field trip, I wander down the hall from Mr. Thompson's science class and into the castle where the Wart is soon to become King Arthur. The Wart is a likable boy who moves through childhood under the tutelage of Merlyn the Magician. Like many boys his age, the Wart has a spirited zest for life, and for learning. He is playful and adventurous, two admirable traits that help him on his journey seeking knowledge and truth. At the same time, the Wart possesses a healthy skepticism when it comes to classrooms and formal lessons and lectures.

> "Shall we go out?" asked Merlyn. "I think it is about time we began our lessons."

> The Wart's heart sank at this . . . "If only," thought the Wart, "I did not have to go into a stuffy classroom, but could take off my clothes and swim in the moat . . . I wish I was a fish," said the Wart . . . The Wart found he had no clothes on. He found that he had tumbled off the draw-bridge, landing with a smack on his side in the water. He found that the moat and the bridge had grown hundreds of times bigger. He knew that he was turning into a fish. "Oh, Merlyn," cried the Wart. "Please come too."

> "Just this once," said a large and solemn tench beside his ear, "I will come. But in the future you will have to go by yourself. Education is experience, and the essence of experience is self-reliance." (White, 1938, p. 52)

It becomes clear in the story that the Wart is well aware of the importance of getting himself a proper "eddication" (to use the word of his foster father). It is also evident that he has quickly learned to distinguish his own natural desire to learn and grow from his reluctant acceptance of being schooled. It isn't that the Wart is a difficult student; on the contrary, he is a good kid. (Just like I was in school.) He is motivated and eager to learn new things. It seems, however, that the lessons the Wart wants most to learn occur in life, not in the classroom.

The Wart's education is entrusted to Merlyn, a wise old wizard, who has most likely won numerous Teacher-of-the-Year Awards throughout his illustrious career. Despite his noted ability, however, the familiar situation still occurs in which Merlyn's credentials as an educator are inspected and questioned by a concerned parent. In the scene that follows, the Wart excitedly introduces his foster father to the man he hopes will become his new teacher.

> "Oh sir," said the Wart. "I have been on that Quest you said for a tutor, and I have found him. Please, he is this gentleman here, and he is called Merlyn."

> [The Wart's guardian, wanting him to have only the best of "eddication," then responds] "Ought to have some testimonials you know," said Sir Ector doubtfully. "It's usual."

> "Testimonials," said Merlyn, holding out his hand. Instantly there were some heavy tablets in it, signed by Aristotle, a parchment signed by Hecate, and some typewritten duplicates signed by the Master of Trinity. (White, 1938, p. 45)

To witness the questioning of Merlyn's reputation, despite his impressive list of credentials, brings humour to my often insecure musings over whether or not I will ever be well enough qualified to teach. (Despite the fact that I have been teaching now for over ten years.) I also see it as quite a wonderful feat for a student to be able to choose his or her own teacher. As luck would have it, the Wart and Merlyn are united and set out on a journey of magical learning adventures. Together, they are able to forge their own brand of education and transcend the limiting and narrow view that often separates life and learning. As well as becoming a fish to explore the mysteries of the underwater world, the Wart also turns into an owl to discover the beauty of flight, and a snake to learn the ancient stories and legends. He sets out on adventures that lead to a meeting with Robin Hood to learn of bravery, humility, and courage. He also visits a goddess and is presented with "The Dream of the Trees" and "The Dream of the Stones" in order to experience the wonder and awe of Creation.

These powerful field trips the Wart experiences as part of his schooling could hardly be considered extracurricular. Of course, the Wart also reads and writes and learns his Latin, along with all of his other lessons. The love and respect for learning that he and Merlyn share is indeed powerful.

> "The best thing for disturbances of the spirit," replied Merlyn, beginning to puff and blow, "is to learn. That is the only thing that never fails. You may grow old and trembling in your anatomies, you may lie awake at night listening to the disorder of your veins, you may miss your only love and lose your moneys to a monster, you may see the world about you devastated by evil lunatics, or know your honour trampled in the sewers of baser minds. There is the only thing for it then—to learn. Learn why the world wags and what wags it. That is the only thing which the poor mind can never exhaust, never alienate, never be tortured by, never fear or distrust, and never dream of regretting. Learning is the thing for you." (White, 1938, p. 254)

The story (the Wart's as well as my own) gets more complicated as it progresses. The plots thicken, yet already I seem to have strayed too far from chlorophyll and the production of carbohydrates by green plants. I bade farewell to Mr. Thompson at the end of Grade Seven (I moved to a new school). Life (and learning) continued and I succeeded through a series of parent-pleasing graduation ceremonies. Eventually, I found my way back to the world of white lab coats as an undergraduate science student in university.

The time came for the Wart to move on as well. He grew up and matured, and his lessons with Merlyn came to a close. Eventually, he "graduated" and moved on to the next phase of his life. Unlike my uneventful parting with Mr. Thompson, the Wart is deeply saddened by the knowledge that Merlyn will no longer be his teacher and companion in learning. He turns to other realities which he must now face and laments the fact that the adventures and joys he experienced as Merlyn's student were almost too good to be true. He feels that somehow he must now accept whatever new fate befalls him as a result of his privileged past.

> "Well, I am a Cinderella now," he said to himself. "Even if I had the best of it for some mysterious reason up to the present time in our education, now I must pay for all my past pleasures and for seeing all those delightful dragons, witches, unicorns, cameleopards and

such like . . . Never mind, I have had a good time while it lasted, and it is not such bad fun being a Cinderella, when you can do it in a kitchen which has a fire-place big enough to roast an ox." (White, 1938, p. 249)

The Wart experiences his convocation as though it were a trial. He awaits the next phase of his education as one awaits a verdict to be handed down. He appears quite willing to give up his innocence, as though there are no other possibilities.

Education, at least for the Wart and me, seemed to be a process that became progressively more serious and more difficult; the sooner we accepted this notion, the better. Maybe that's why I found Mr. Thompson's class so threatening. Science became something that took place only in a science room—and in my Grade Seven experience—by someone who wore a lab coat, by someone who was stern and serious. Gone were the days when we went out to the field beyond the schoolyard for science class. In Grade Seven, I learned to perform a series of scientific manoeuvres according to a newer and stricter set of rules.

How is it we learn to be like the Wart? What causes us to assume that our education must be painful in order to be satisfactory? When do we begin to dismiss the fun things as distractions to real education, taking part in them only with a certain amount of guilt, as well as an unspoken understanding that we will pay for our pleasure later? Where do we get the notion that it is important to grow up and out of our past experiences, instead of learning to use them as springboards to new experiences or as safety nets to fall back on when needed?

All these questions from just one box. I'm beginning to understand why the Wart's story has surfaced. There are many more questions to be asked, and many more lessons to be learned. It's likely not a coincidence that the Wart and Merlyn and Mr. Thompson share the same box. Discipline and seriousness are the backdrop to the Mr. Thompson story; adventure and magic are the elements in the Wart's story. The fact that the two stories seem so different from one another is also what draws them together as I begin to story and re-story my educational experiences. I can't imagine Mr. Thompson as the Wart's tutor, just as I find it difficult to imagine Merlyn as my Grade Seven science teacher. There is, however, much to be gained from imagining some of the possibilities that might stem from a marriage of plot and character in both of these two stories. How would Merlyn have taught photosynthesis? With some pomp and ceremony, Merlyn decreed, "The best thing for disturbances of the spirit is to learn—to learn why the world wags and what wags it." What would Mr. Thompson's famous speech on learning have been? How would the Wart have handled sitting on one of those hard and uncomfortable stools in Mr. Thompson's science room? How would I have reacted to becoming an owl to learn about flight? I carry these questions with me as I continue to reflect on experiences that have influenced my learning and, in turn, my teaching.

The Adventures of Teaching: Life at the Outdoor School

My first teaching job was far from the classroom. I became an environmental resource teacher, and, eventually, the program director of a large, outdoor education centre. We offered week-long residential programs to school groups that ranged in size from sixty to one hundred and thirty students per week. We worked closely with a group called the Institute for Earth Education (Van Matre, 1990). They were a nonprofit organization which designed and disseminated specialized, ecologically based programs structured on a holistic, deep connection with the earth and its life. Our centre, in conjunction with our affiliated school board, became heavily involved in piloting Earth Education programs designed to help people of all ages live more harmoniously and joyously with the natural world. A decision was made to implement *Sunship Earth*, an intensive residential program designed for twelve- and thirteen-year-olds (Van Matre, 1979).

The name *Sunship Earth* came from Buckminster Fuller's notion of the earth as a self-contained vessel travelling through space, a spaceship powered by the energy of the sun. The goals of the program included providing an understanding of how the planet functions in an ecological sense, nurturing deep feelings for the natural world and all its life, and crafting a lifestyle more harmonious with the earth and all its passengers (Van Matre, 1990). All of this took place against a wild and wonderful backdrop of creativity. The kids literally lived the program as they became passengers aboard our Sunship Earth in order to better understand its delicate operating principles. It was a carefully crafted program: every activity— every detail—focused on our roles as passengers and crew aboard the Sunship. Every facet of the program supported the original goals of providing better understandings, nurturing feelings and developing a lifestyle more in tune with the earth and its life. Our invitation to the students was, "Hey, we're on a sunship! How does it work and feel? We're both its passengers and its crew. What does this mean for you?" (Van Matre, 1979, p. 36). Much attention was given to even the most minute detail in order to capture the fancy and the imagination of the kids and teachers, and to make the learning of abstract ecological concepts more concrete for the learners.

All of the program's objectives translated to a wonderful and unusual learning environment. Visitors walking around the centre, unfamiliar with the Sunship Earth program, might feel as though they had stumbled upon another planet. The woods were filled with many strange sights: costumed teachers and students role-played in order to learn of the story of life on the planet. They were busy exploring "The Seven Secrets of Life," according to the formula "EC-DC-IC-A." These are the seven key operating principles—the key ecological concepts—that govern life on our Sunship: energy flow (E), the cycling of materials (C), diversity (D), community (C), the interrelationships of living things (I), change (C), and adaptation (A). The kids learned about EC-DC-IC-A on "Concept Paths" by weaving their way through the woods. There were three different concept paths, each one housing five concept stations. Kids became animals in a food chain as they visited "Mr. Sun's Restaurant" to learn about energy flow, or clouds in "The Sun's Bucket Brigade" to take part in the earth's great water cycle. They were birds in "Tools and Tasks" to experience how a beak is a tool that is specially adapted for performing certain tasks, or molecule messengers visiting the "Food Factory" to learn how sunlight is captured by green plants and turned into food. It was an impressive program to see in action.

Another Lesson in Photosynthesis: The Giant Leaf

[Somewhere in a sunlit forest . . .]

"Yeah, I think it's over this way. Who has the map anyway?"

The sun filters through the trees and splashes on to the trail in front of us as we wind our way along the forest path. A shout, "Kevin knows where we're going!" breaks through the collage of voices, all laughter and complaints and questions and commotion.

Our little group makes its way up a short, steep hill with a surprising amount of enthusiasm. I'm realizing that it's been an intense morning when my thoughts are interrupted by an imposing set of signs. **"Keep Out! Authorized Personnel Only. Top Secret."** By now, the kids know something is up and they look to me for some kind of hint of what's to come. The students and I exchange glances —looks that say that I know that they know that I know that all of this is part truth, part fiction, part fantasy. I believe it is an unspoken bit of madness that brings us here and propels us on this magical learning adventure together.

I scan the horizon with a worried look and then begin nervously glancing to my left and to my right. The kids pick up on this action and whether they are interested in humouring me or not, respond to my unspoken urgency by gathering around in a tight little circle. I motion with my eyes to a sign that says "Food Factory" (Van Matre, 1979) and begin to move cautiously down a narrow path that curves slowly and disappears up ahead. They don't need to be told to follow. Within thirty seconds we round a bend that takes us in between a set of imposing pines, and Chris spots a large cave-like structure with a low, rounded profile. It is covered in green canvas and camouflage and has a tube-like tunnel for an entrance.

"What the heck is it?"

"Only the most important thing on our planet," I say in a lowered voice. "It's a giant leaf. A food factory."

What do my eyes tell them? Still using my top-secret voice, I let them know that we're going to get the inside story on how we get our energy from the sun.

"You are all going to get a chance to go inside the food factory to find out how sunlight energy is turned into sugars, or carbohydrates, the food that we need to stay alive; the problem is that no one really knows exactly how it's done. This is a very important mission and you must all swear to secrecy."

"It's not really a leaf, I can see the canvas."

Ah yes, it's James again, stating the obvious. He's been making sure the group doesn't get fooled by any of this becoming-a-cloud or going-into-a-giant-leaf stuff. After we finish our secret oath, I explain that only half the group can go inside the leaf at one time, and that possibly James could lead the first mission.

"While the first group is inside the leaf, the rest of you have an important job. You are going to be 'Molecule Messengers.' You'll deliver the ingredients that the leaf needs to work its magic."

We walk over to an area looking like a bus stop with a sign that reads Molecule Messenger Waiting Area. I pull out three pouches labelled "AIR," "WATER," and "SUNLIGHT."

"The group inside the leaf will be communicating with the 'Chlorophyll Control Centre' and will be asking for these ingredients. When you messengers hear someone call for an ingredient, run over to the leaf with the correct pouch and hand in one of the envelopes from inside the pouch. Then return immediately to the Messenger Waiting Area."

"So what are we supposed to do in the leaf anyhow?"

That's Ian. His self-proclaimed title is junior executive in charge of role clarification and job descriptions. He wants to make sure everyone in the group knows exactly what is expected of them at all times. I give him the over-the-shoulder glance along with an accompanying shifty-eyed stare. He drifts a little closer, understanding that this is privileged information. The rest of the group eavesdrops.

"Listen," I explain, "I haven't actually been inside the leaf myself. What I've told you so far is what everyone knows about the food factory. Scientists know what goes into the leaf and they know what comes out of the leaf, but nobody actually knows exactly what goes on inside the leaf itself. Carbon dioxide and water go in and sunlight is around, too; then, after a while, sugars are produced and, eventually, we eat them in some form or other. But what happens inside the leaf is the real mystery—that's why you're being sent in there: to find out how the mysterious process of photosynthesis works."

In a slightly quieter voice, I tell them that they are going to be "chlorospies." "You'll need these green helmets to help camouflage you so that you are better able to spy on the chlorophyll."

A barrage of comments breaks the silence of the forest.

"I'm not wearing this stupid helmet, it'll wreck my hair."

"Cool; it looks dark in there."

"I'm going first!"

"When's lunch?"

"Like I said, I won't be going inside the leaf myself since I don't have the proper clearance, so you're on your own. The messengers will be passing the carbon dioxide molecules and the sunlight in the envelopes through the walls of the leaf. Water will also enter in the same way it does in a real food factory—up through the stem. Remember, only the chlorospies have security clearance so the messengers will have to wait outside. You'll receive further instructions once you are inside the factory. Good luck, everybody."

The first group of chlorospies disappear into the leaf. Things seem to be running smoothly. I wasn't being quite truthful about not having been inside the leaf myself. I have security clearance in the off-hours and, in fact, I know exactly what they'll find in there. I can picture it now as I stand quietly with the molecule messengers at the waiting area. Julia was right, it is dark in there, and as their eyes adjust, they will be greeted by a number of signs. One sign reminds them of their pledge to secrecy while another identifies a large green box with a slot in the top as the "Super Secret Chlorophyll Box." Another sign simply says, "Await Further Instructions." The three of them will have just about checked the whole place out, when a voice will speak to them from a tube lying on the floor.

"Attention. Attention. Can you hear me? This is Chlorophyll Control."

I always take pleasure imagining the look on their faces when this voice comes resonating through the leaf. The speaking tube leads out of the back of the leaf and runs unobtrusively into the woods where a volunteer parent is hiding behind some bushes a short distance away. The voice begins.

"Thanks for coming to work on the production line at the food factory. You will have to follow my instructions carefully, OK?

Now, here in the food factory we need some important ingredients in order to make food-energy, or carbohydrates. Together, call to the molecule messengers for the first important ingredient, AIR. Ready? One, two, three: AIR!!!"

I'm snapped out of my little daydream by a sudden scrambling of molecule messengers. The AIR messenger sprints off to the leaf, delivers his package, an envelope containing two ping-pong balls —one marked carbon and one marked oxygen—attached together by velcro. Things should begin to "cook" in the leaf right about now.

"Tell me when you've got it," the Control Centre voice drones. "What do you find in the envelope? [pause for the kids' response] That's carbon dioxide—C for carbon, O_2 for oxygen. At the food factory we get our carbon dioxide directly from the air."

"OK, call for the second important ingredient, WATER. . . . Got it? Great. What's in the envelope? [pause] That's hydrogen, H_2, and oxygen, O, the parts that make up water. Now listen very carefully. Pull off the carbon, C, from the carbon dioxide and pull off the hydrogen, H_2, from the water. Try to stick the carbon, the hydrogen, and the single oxygen ball together to make a carbohydrate, the food energy for all life. The three balls should all stick together like links in a chain. How are you doing?"

By now the water and the air messengers have done their job and we're all standing around chatting.

"When do I get to go?" Gail is the SUNLIGHT messenger and she is not too happy about not being called.

"I'm not sure," I reply calmly. "Let's just wait a bit longer, something definitely seems to be going on in there."

"What's wrong?" Chlorophyll Control asks, sounding somewhat alarmed. "You have the hydrogen and oxygen stuck together, but the carbon won't stick to the hydrogen?"

I can't really tell Gail that I do know exactly what's going on inside the leaf. They are trying to fit a round peg into a square hole right about now. That is, the placement of the velcro strips on the ping-pong balls (I mean molecules) is such that it is impossible to attach the carbon molecule to the hydrogen molecule no matter what mark you got on your last science test. (I'm not worried though; nature will provide the solution.)

"This is impossible!"

"How do they expect us to do this?" Julia and Nicole cry foul.

"Something must be missing." The Chlorophyll Control speaks with the voice of reason. "OK then, call for SUNLIGHT. Now, using the sunlight, try to stick the carbon and hydrogen together. Got it? Congratulations! You've just completed the process known as photosynthesis. That's the process that takes water, air, and sunlight and makes energy-rich food for all life. Just put your completed carbohydrate into the box and your work shift is over. Oops—there's one last thing you need to do. Push your leftover oxygen (O_2) out the 'Oxygen Exit Tube.' Well, thanks for helping out on the production line here at the Food Factory. You can go out now. This is Chlorophyll Control Centre signing off."

Julia, Nicole, and Brian emerge with shielded eyes from the giant leaf; they look like celebrities who have just finished a press conference. I recognize my own voice asking the first question.

"Well, what happened—did you find out the secret?" I'm drowned out by other urgent queries.

"How hot is it in there?"

"Where's the sugar?"

"What took you so long?"

"We couldn't bring the sugar out because we had to leave it in this special top-secret box, and yeah, it was boiling in there," says Brian.

A little disappointed at not getting the information I was hoping for, I suggest the Molecule Messengers switch roles with the Chlorospies and we try the whole thing again.

The students add their newly acquired information about the concept of energy flow to their passports. They also draw and describe other examples that exist around us here in the forest.

At the end of it all, the elusive inner workings of photosynthesis still remain a secret. It seems that photosynthesis really is part mystery and may remain so for quite some time, despite determined efforts on our part. "I guess we shouldn't feel badly," I tell them. "Even the most brilliant women and men in science don't know exactly how the process works." (Not even Mr. Thompson, I'm thinking to myself.)

Nothing Up My Sleeve: A Closer Look at Magic

It's difficult, though not entirely impossible, to envision Mr. Thompson as a molecule messenger. Some of the Sunship Earth activities might have ruffled his white lab coat, but I don't think he would have disagreed with the educational objectives of this particular Earth Education program.

> What sort of frame or goals did we have in mind? First, like a surveyor, we wanted to cast a point of reference for each of our learners—to convey something about their place in the universe. We hoped to establish this sense of place forever in their understandings, or perhaps more accurately in their feelings, for we wanted it to become embedded inside them, where it would be a continued source of awareness about who and what they were. Second, like a friendly wizard, we wanted to convey to them a feeling for life's wondrous mysteries—the awesome, yet joyous, systems in which they are bound up with every other living thing on earth. And we hoped that this recognition of miraculous interrelationship would become a mental touchstone against which they could forever check their actions. (Van Matre, 1979, p. xvi)

I have been quick to point to Mr. Thompson's (lack of) magic in conveying the wondrous mysteries of life on our planet. I have been just as quick to align myself pedagogically with Merlyn: a "friendly wizard [conveying to his students] a feeling for life's wondrous mysteries—the awesome, yet joyous, systems in which they are bound up with every other living thing on earth" (Van Matre, 1979, p. xvi). Like the Wart, I would have preferred to become a fish rather than to dissect one. But magic, as it turns out, is not all that it's cracked up to be. As an educator, committed to connecting understandings with feelings, I stumbled and (eventually) tripped over magic on more than one occasion. I now wonder whether my pursuit of magic wasn't also a kind of reactionary running-away from Mr. Thompson.

After enjoying much success with programs like Sunship Earth and discovering the delights of teaching and learning as though they were part of an adventure, like Wart, I wondered, "Must I now pay for all my past pleasures?" For teaching all those weird and wonderful activities. For becoming a squirrel to find out how animals must solve problems and adapt to find food. For becoming a cloud in order to take part in the earth's great water cycle. For going inside a giant leaf to discover the mystery of photosynthesis. For roaming through the dangerous forests of King Snoyd's kingdom to find out about the interrelationships of living things. For shrinking down to the size of a bug to explore the world from a new perspective.

Surely these activities were kid's stuff, right? It was a lot of fun doing all those crazy things, but that's not how real learning takes place. Is it? The Sunship Earth program was just a diversion from regular school. Wasn't it? I got to be outside—to explore and adventure with kids. Together we learned the story of how life works on our planet. So why did I feel like the Wart at the end of it all—waiting to "graduate" to more serious learning? What went wrong?

Was I trying too hard to wear Merlyn's cloak? I wanted the kids to have experiences like those of the Wart's, but in fact I am not a magician. Creating magical learning adventures is hard work. It involves paying close attention to every detail. Perhaps part of the illusory quality of magic is that things appear—as if by magic—with the wave of a wand. Closer scrutiny, however, usually reveals the detail, the precision—careful and calculated—required to make the magic. (In the end, Dorothy meets the man behind the curtain who doesn't seem like much of a wizard at all.)

I don't mean to strip away the magic by looking at it too closely. I am simply aware that creating a giant leaf for a group of kids to stumble upon, as if by accident—as if by magic—out there in the forest in order to learn the intricacies of photosynthesis requires a great deal of work. So do Mr. Thompson's carefully crafted lesson plans. The giant leaf, it seems, requires a cautionary note similar to the one given Mr. Thompson's science lab: "Don't touch the orange valves and don't forget to close the door to the leaf on your way out."

Is the magic of the Food Factory misleading? Does the translation from molecules to velcroed ping-pong balls clarify or confuse conceptual understanding? Is the trip inside the leaf an invitation to, or a distortion of, further learning? Is learning lost in the excitement of the molecule messenger-to-chlorospy exchange? Can a process as complex as photosynthesis be simplified to a disembodied voice (Chlorophyll Control Centre) providing a set of instructions to a handful of kids huddled in the dark? Yes? No? Maybe? Sort of? It depends? Why? Why not?

Surely Mr. Thompson's plasticized map of the leaf is also a distortion—torn·from a tree and left to flap above the chalkboard in a series of unnatural colours. My capacity to memorize the various parts of the leaf and the countless terms involved in photosynthesis did little to convey the wonder of such a process. Isn't Mr. Thompson simply another (disembodied) voice providing a set of instructions to a handful of kids huddled (in the dark) behind desks?

The answers will not be pinned down like parts of a frog in this particular reflection. I feel like Calvin (of Calvin and Hobbes fame), who, in one particular episode, begins to experience life from a "neo-cubist perspective." Sparked by a debate with his father, Calvin begins to see both sides of everything; multiple views provide too much information; chaos rules as his world fractures into unrecognizable fragments. Calvin resolves the problem quickly, as only Calvin can, then turns to his father and says, "You're still wrong, Dad."

Mr. Thompson Meets the Giant Leaf: The Many Faces of Photosynthesis

Although I admire Calvin's style, my task does not seem quite as simple. At the same time, I am not necessarily attempting to resolve anything, or prove anyone wrong. Multiple views are part of my (chaotic) world; I try to accept them, even embrace them.

There are a lot of ways to learn about photosynthesis. My experiences with the process, as a student and eventually as a teacher, certainly represent two very different possibilities; in hindsight, these differences don't seem at all bad. In fact, it's a luxury to be able to reflect on the unique and contrasting approaches to the teaching and learning of such a magical process.

In my schooling, I happened to first learn about photosynthesis from the confines of Mr. Thompson's classroom, where sunlight was conspicuously absent from the whole process. I learned partly out of fear, partly out of fascination. I was intimidated by

Mr. Thompson's apparently cold exterior; I felt compelled to learn and memorize the multitude of facts that he presented in strict fashion. I was a good kid in school, impelled to please parents, teachers, and peers. If the assignment was to draw and memorize every part of the leaf, then I would do exactly that. Yet, I was also intrigued by the large and mysterious schematic diagram of the leaf with its complex circuitry. Maybe the plastic roll-down chart was simply another kind of magical giant leaf.

I must also admit that there was something compelling about Mr. Thompson's style. Perhaps it was his white lab coat and his pointer. Or maybe it was how serious and scientific he made everything seem. He was the living image of the scientific method—an impressive and striking model for a kid just out of elementary school. Our class was held in a real science room—a special place designated for experiments of all kinds; it was filled with glass display cases that contained beakers and test tubes and all manner of laboratory supplies.

With Mr. Thompson, science (and photosynthesis) seemed impressive and official; he brought the scientific method to life. Mr. Thompson helped to lay the foundation upon which the rest of my scientific inquiry in schools would be constructed. At the end of Grade Seven, I couldn't imagine photosynthesis spelled any other way.

But what would have happened if the process had been the other way around? What if I had crawled inside the giant leaf—as the Wart might have—as a chlorospy in Grade Five before arriving in Mr. Thompson's Grade Seven science class? What if I had learned about photosynthesis—the capturing of sunlight energy by green plants—by wandering and exploring in a rich, green forest where the process was taking place all around me? What if I had been introduced to photosynthesis by a person in shorts and a T-shirt instead of a white lab coat? (By someone I thought was cool, not scientific.) What if I had been able to handle the "molecules" and then push an extra oxygen molecule out of the leaf, giving me a concrete memory of green plants releasing oxygen? What would it have felt like to have been a twelve-year-old messing around inside a dark, cave-like structure, and suddenly have a voice speak to me from out of nowhere? What if?

And how would Mr. Thompson have reacted to the Giant Leaf? Would he have eagerly crawled inside? What would the map of the leaf he unveiled so impressively in the classroom have looked like to me and my classmates after having been chlorospies? Would I have been intimidated or bored? Would I have been completely turned off by the map of the leaf after having been inside one, or would I have been more curious to explore the complex parts of the leaf because of that fact? How would I have felt about Mr. Thompson's photosynthesis experiment, performed in his windowless room—in which we attempted to discover what happens to a leaf when it is covered in foil—having already walked through a sun-splashed forest to the giant leaf in Grade Five.

I'm not sure what part of my Grade Seven experience led me to want to teach photosynthesis in the way that I did. Mr. Thompson provided the pieces to the process of capturing sunlight energy without regard for the bigger picture of how life on the planet works. Maybe that came in a later unit that we never got to. I don't think so. My memories of those pieces taught to us by Mr. Thompson are sharp, like those parts of the leaf that stood out in "living" colour at the front of the room. I can incorporate the pieces into the broader picture of life I now possess, thanks to the giant leaf and the Sunship Earth program.

Of course, I'm no longer a student of Mr. Thompson. I'm a teacher—a colleague of his in a sense. We both put our efforts toward helping kids learn about science in the ways we saw fit at the time. We share much in common as a result. It would be interesting to talk shop with Mr. Thompson today—to discuss our practices, our beliefs, our thoughts on why we do what we do.

Experience into Story:
Lives Remembered and (Re)invented

The narratives I have told up to this point must be taken for what they are: stories. From the dampness of my basement, I have attempted to write myself out of the box, on to the page, into existence. The word processor seems not only an appropriate tool, but also an excellent metaphor with which to help me sort out the thoughts that tumble forth looking for places to land.

Words. The signs and symbols, the codes I use to invent and reinvent myself. Words. Processed. Words. Sorted, scrubbed, sanitized, subjected to filters, both kind and harsh. Words. Remembered, forgotten, made up, manufactured, managed, make-believe. My words fall on to the page and build stories from sentences that conflict and contradict one another. Didn't I say that Mr. Thompson's white lab coat and specialized science room might have been problematic in alienating me from my own learning? (Only to wonder if they didn't also appeal to my newly forming scientific sensibility.) In writing and remembering, I am engaged in a process that is as much about self-construction as self-discovery.

I seem to have come full circle from my Grade Seven lab report. (Or have I?) Mr. Thompson wanted structure, order. Science was spelled using upper-case. I was discouraged from clouding the results with my own "I." Today, I resist the pull of order in my writing, yet my stories remain neat and tidy. If things get too messy, I can always put them back in the box, close the lid. I push against convention, interrogate Mr. Thompson's attempts to toilet-train me into objectivity. Yet, I now question my own intentions as a story-maker. Am I being too subjective? I build my life with, in, and through words. I paint stories using colours of my own choosing. My intentions are good; I strive to find sense, to make meaning of my life experiences, but the search for Truth, the life as it was really lived, is a misleading one. The life I (have) live(d) is the one I make up. I am caught up in language, in word-making, constantly striving to create the world.

I once worried about losing my identity under Mr. Thompson's resolve to remove all personal pronouns; now, I struggle over which "I" is me. Merlyn said, "To learn. That is the only thing that never fails." Currently in Grade Twenty-four, I continue to celebrate my own ways of learning and knowing. And through it all, I continue to word my world—as if by magic. Merlyn would be impressed.

This is Chlorophyll Control Signing Off: A Final Reflection

All of this reflecting has helped me to make explicit what was once buried and tacit (like the box in the basement). I discovered parts of me that emerged through my practice, of which I am both proud and embarrassed. I still wonder about Mr. Thompson. I wonder what stories he might tell about the classes he once taught. I wonder what stories my former classmates might tell. Do they even remember Mr. Thompson? Perhaps they have forgotten about the map of the leaf. Maybe photosynthesis only rings a faint bell when it appears on Jeopardy: "All right, contestants, this one for $10,000.00 . . . Answer: The production of complex organic materials from carbon dioxide, water, and inorganic salts, using sunlight as the source of energy and with the aid of chlorophyll and associated pigments. Question: What is photosynthesis?"

Personally, I don't feel cheated for not having had the opportunity to be a molecule messenger as a twelve-year-old. Like the Wart, I seem to have "had the best of it for some mysterious reason." Just over a decade after leaving Mr. Thompson's classroom, I was crawling around inside the giant leaf. I was busy making sure the molecules were in order, the instructional signs in place, and that the voice for Chlorophyll Control was out of sight and ready to go. I was out in the natural world, surrounded by living things, and by kids, and we were learning together. I'm not sure it would have fit Mr. Thompson's vision of the scientific method but it certainly was an experiment.

Perhaps in some strange way I was doing it for Mr. Thompson. Not in spite of him, but because of him. I am a product of all of my combined experiences. Whether it was Mr. Thompson's white lab coat, his pointer, his map of the leaf, his adherence to scientific principles, or whether it was crawling around inside of the giant leaf as a chlorospy, I will always think of photosynthesis as a magical process.

References

Van Matre, S. (1979). *Sunship earth: An acclimatization program for outdoor learning.* Martinsville, IN: American Camping Association.

Van Matre, S. (1990). *Earth education: A new beginning.* Warrenville, IL: The Institute for Earth Education.

White, T. H. (1938). *The sword in the stone.* London and Glasgow: Collins Clear-Type Press.

Chapter 13

AN EXPERIENTIAL ADVENTURE SCHOOL FOR SEXUALLY ABUSED ADOLESCENTS

Thomas E. Smith

Dr. Tom Smith, founder of the Raccoon Institute, is a retired psychologist and wilderness guide. He was formally educated at the University of Wisconsin, but he also studied for many years in what John Muir called "the University of the Wilderness." He has written four books *(Wilderness Beyond . . . Wilderness Within*; *The Theory and Practice of Challenge Education*; *Incidents of Challenge Education*; *The Challenge of Native American Traditions*).

In this chapter, Tom draws on his experiences as the Psychologist and Director of The Fresh Start School for sexually abused and exploited adolescents. The chapter is important because it describes a deliberate attempt to integrate home life, schooling, and psychotherapy for wounded young men and women who are not well served by piecemeal help. Tom gives considerable detail about the nature of the curriculum and therapeutic content. Out-of-school experiences and adventures lie at the heart of the joint educational and therapeutic work.

Throughout the 1980s, the challenge adventure methodology was the fastest growing variant of the experiential education movement. The roots of that methodology are complex, as it has drawn from a variety of professional orientations (Smith et al., 1992). Challenge adventure sequences have been offered for many different client populations, usually as part of a broader educational, therapeutic, rehabilitation, or training program. This paper summarizes a comprehensive education and therapy program for sexually abused and exploited adolescents which was designed with experiential challenge and adventure methodology as its core.

The Problem

The efforts of police and family service workers to crack down on perpetrators of sexual abuse and sexual exploitation of children have resulted in identification of numerous youths with special needs. For example, whenever police move in on a child prostitution ring or a child pornography movie producer, there are a number of young victims identified. By the mid-1980s, the state of Illinois had identified many adolescent boys and girls who had been victims of sexual abuse and/or exploitation. These youth had been "recovered" from the streets, or had been identified by criminal justice and family service investigations. They were victims of sexual abuse and had been sexually exploited by adults. They had emotional and behavioral problems, and a history of poor social adjustment. Most of them also had significant learning problems, and many had not been in school for 2–3 years. Few of them had any interaction with their biological family, and there was very limited possibility for any rehabilitation of family constellations. They needed to be placed in foster homes or supportive group homes as they grew toward adulthood. Most of the youth had also been involved with drugs and street crimes, and were "street smart" survivors in the urban environment.

Previous efforts to provide psychotherapeutic treatment and educational remediation had failed. Many of the youth had strong anti-school attitudes, and their trust in adults was extremely low. Some had a history of running away from foster homes, group homes, and residential treatment centers. Most tended to be manipulative in interpersonal relationships. Some were depressed, and all had been diagnosed as having very low self-esteem. Most of the case workers, therapists, teachers, and previous caregivers who had been involved with these youth suggested that they do have potential for rehabilitation. They noted that the youth were of average or above intelligence, in good physical health, and capable of demonstrating pleasant personality and positive adjustment at times. While most workers agreed that the prognosis for readjustment was guarded, they still felt that these youth could be helped—**if they were given a fresh start in the right program.**

The problem, then, was to find some way to turn the page for these young people, to create a program which would provide such a fresh start.

Early Planning

An informal planning committee with representatives from the State Departments of Family Services, Mental Health, Criminal Justice, and Education set out to develop an experimental program for these youth. After soliciting the input of a number of field professionals, a plan, which was to become The Fresh Start Program, began to unfold. An early decision was for the youth to be placed in foster homes which were patterned after the "Teaching–Family Model" for improving family living and social adjustment skills. The original development of this behavioristic model was the work of Ellery and Elaine Phillips at the Achievement Place in Lawrence, Kansas (Levitt, 1981). Essentially, it involves training couples to be "teaching parents" for foster homes, learning to use an intensive, structured program of behavior modification to eliminate negative behaviors, followed by procedures to teach appropriate family interaction and social adjustment patterns.

It was also decided that the most appropriate location of these foster homes would be at some distance from the city, in hopes of reducing temptations to run away. Since the child service agency that could train and supervise the foster parents owned a camp in the northwoods of Wisconsin, two residential units would be constructed there. Each of these homes was to be staffed by a married couple trained as the family teachers, and one additional adult to help with their program. One home would house a maximum of 8 boys, and the other, a maximum of 8 girls. This experimental population would range in age from 14-18, and would be multicultural. Placement in the program was to be of a full year's duration.

Two possibilities existed for providing the youth with an appropriate educational and therapeutic program. First, they could be sent to the local schools, working with available special education services to develop a remedial educational program, and counseling services could be contracted through the County Mental Health Center. Second, a comprehensive therapeutic school could be operated at the camp, providing a tailor-made program for the youth in residence. The planning committee decided that since the local school district and area mental health center, which would have the responsibility for serving the youth, had very limited resources, the more feasible option would be to develop a special school for both educational and therapeutic intervention at the camp setting.

Since previous programs, based on traditional patterns of educational and therapeutic intervention, had had very limited success with these youth, the planning committee suggested that alternative models be explored. As all of the youth to be assigned to the program would be considered eligible for special education placement, there was opportunity to plan for reduced class size and increased staffing. The school was therefore designed to have two certified special education teachers, two teacher aides, a full-time psychologist, and a part-time administrator. This would provide for a staff-student ratio of 2:5.

After considering a number of possible program designs, it was decided that the appropriate model would be the experiential, outdoor adventure alternative. With this choice in mind, the planning group contracted a clinical psychologist who was an advocate of the therapeutic potential of experiential methodology and who had an extensive practice in outdoor therapy. (*Author's note*: I was on my way to a new adventure. My role would be that of the psychologist for the school and psychotherapist for the youth, but I would

The Program Design

From the outset, there were two separate but related components to the total program. There were the family living homes staffed by the teaching parents and adjunctive staff, and there was The Fresh Start School which was responsible for providing education and therapy. An early description of the program noted these two components by describing the experimental project as a "living and learning therapeutic milieu."

The school program was developed with the outdoor adventure component as the core of the whole psychoeducational intervention. That program was designed to offer special off-campus adventure trips of 4–5 days' duration each month, and much of the school-based curriculum would be related to those trips. It was also expected that all of the school staff would accompany the group on all adventure trips. Still, it was obvious that a comprehensive school program would have to involve much more than the outdoor adventure trips. Specifically, there would have to be attention to three components of intervention: behavior management, academic curriculum, and therapeutic intervention, with experiential outdoor adventure as the core of the overall program.

The Behavior Management Program

An effective behavior management system is the priority starting point for any psychoeducational program dealing with youth who have behavior disorders and parallel learning problems. Only after symptoms are contained can meaningful academic instruction and therapeutic intervention unfold. The priority of starting with a meaningful behavior management program in an integrated program can be shown as in Figure 1.

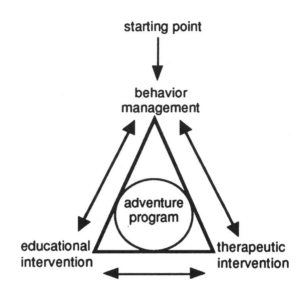

Figure 1. The three components of the program with adventure challenges at the core.

Recognizing the value of having *consistent behavior expectancies at both home and school,* The Fresh Start School developed a modification of the points-and-privileges system used by the family education home. That system also contributed to another desirable goal, that of *frequent communication between home and school.* The school management system provided for a "school note" which gave the teaching family a daily report on the student's behavior. In addition, there were periodic meetings between the teaching parents, the school staff, and the students themselves, focusing on the setting of individual behavior goals.

The Academic Program

The age and grade achievement range of the youth in the school was extreme, so instruction had to be highly individualized. As there were two teachers and two teacher-aides, individual and small-group instruction was provided as needed. Still, all the students were of high school age, so it was deemed important to have them all earning regular high school credits which could transfer at a later date. The school staff therefore organized meetings with representatives from each student's home high school district to develop the Individualized Educational Program so that their course work would keep them on track toward graduation from high school. Course work was designed to satisfy the requirements of high school courses in mathematics, English, social studies, science, health, and physical education.

The curriculum units were developed with emphasis on the experiential learning model. There was to be a considerable variety of curriculum units of study that would make up the various courses offered, and examples are listed below:

- A curriculum unit on the geology of the state of Wisconsin, focusing on the period of glacial flow, was taught prior to an adventure trip that involved exploring caves in southwestern Wisconsin.

- The physical education curriculum included instruction in basic relaxation and breathing exercises, which were later facilitated by challenge education sequences and as part of group processing time.

- A basic mathematics curriculum was often presented by price shopping for food to take on the outdoor trips, and in the measurements required for baking and preparation of meals.

- A social studies unit focused on various patterns of physical, mental, and emotional disability, offered prior to a winter camping trip with a group that included people with disabilities.

- The English curriculum included vocabulary-building classes that emphasized "affect words" which could help the students better understand, reflect on, and express their inner feelings, confusions, and conflicts in group processing and group counseling sessions.

- The health program included experiential teaching of First Aid and C.P.R., and covered topics of preventive and interventive attention to problems of frostbite and hypothermia.

- Creative writing was taught by having the students keep journals when on adventure trips and field experiences, and then write stories when they were back at the school.

- A history unit on the logging industry included visiting a paper mill and a logging museum, and backpacking on trails in both virgin and new growth forest.

- A social studies unit on the Native American Indians involved a visit to a reservation, opportunity for sharing both interactional activities and discussion with Indian youth, and participating in a powwow where students learned drumming and dancing.

Some of the instruction at the camp-based school was more conventional, in that students used ability-appropriate workbooks in mathematics and English. There was also a program of 1:1 tutorial and remedial teaching for those students with academic deficiencies in math or reading. In addition, the staff developed a program of peer tutoring, which involved higher achievement students pairing with lower achievement students on partnership projects. This required that the higher achievers coach and assist the lower achievers. As often as possible, the teachers would offer instruction to the total group, and this was usually the case when there were hands-on learning experiences.

The Therapy Program

Like the academic program, the therapy program was designed to be related to the total living, learning, and adventuring environment of the youth. It was recognized that each student should have opportunity to resolve psychological conflicts through an intensive individual psychotherapy sequence, but it was also recognized that such an approach is not always productive for every person. The program for therapeutic intervention rested on the assumption that there is no single therapeutic method that is appropriate for all. Some adolescents will grow psychologically and socially with only a behavior management approach; others will not. Some youth will respond meaningfully to group processes or peer culture systems; others won't. Some youth, especially when basic trust in adults has been shattered, will not respond well to the individual therapy sessions. From the beginning, the design of the program called for a multidimensional program of therapeutic intervention which paralleled the multidimensional educational program.

Eight different methodologies for therapeutic intervention were included in the total program. Each has a unique theoretical foundation. The eight avenues for therapeutic intervention have been described in a previous paper (Smith, 1987), and are shown as a multidimensional model in Figure 2.

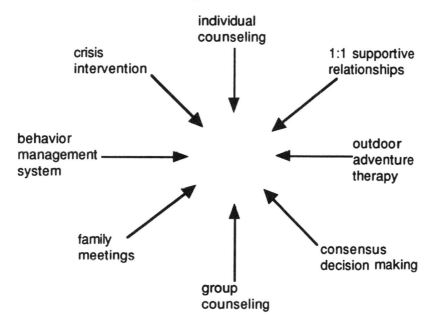

Figure 2. A multidimensional model for therapeutic intervention.

Individual Counseling. Many professionals have become aware of the limitations of the individual counseling model, especially with young persons who have cause to fear and distrust adults. Such counseling is often offered on a voluntary basis. At Fresh Start, individual time was set aside for each youth every week, hoping that he or she would use the developing trust with the therapist to really work through his or her problems.

Group Counseling. This is the second, most standard offering of therapeutic intervention. Over the past few years, counselors have found the group methods to be most effective for some clients. At The Fresh Start School, there was a regular, weekly, counseling group session for the boys and another for the girls. Each of the classroom teachers served as co-therapist for one of the groups.

1:1 Supportive Relationships. The program recognized that a very special relationship could develop between any member of the school staff and a student. Historically, such a situation might be considered as "lay therapy" (counseling provided by an adult with less than complete professional training as a therapist). In order to maximize the therapeutic impact of such relationships, the program identified and encouraged them, even setting aside special time for the two people to interact. In addition, the psychologist met regularly with staff members who were doing this to provide consultation and support.

Daily Family Education Meetings. In the Family Education model for foster homes, there are daily family meetings facilitated by the teaching parents. While these meetings are basically designed to review the youth's progress toward family living and social adjustment goals, they often lead to clinically therapeutic interactions. As trust between the young person in placement and the family teacher builds, the family meetings become a place where members can discuss personal issues. In order to coordinate the therapeutic aspects of the family meetings with the total multi-dimensional therapy program, the Fresh Start psychologist met periodically with the teaching family parents.

Crisis Intervention Therapy. When the psychologist is available to assist other staff at times of a student's emotional or behavioral outburst, the whole situation can be turned to meaningful therapeutic growth. At Fresh Start, the psychologist would usually be on hand to help with any crisis situation and would always be available for a follow-up, 1:1 session with the youth to explore emotional learning.

Behavior Management as Therapy. Behavior modification enables the student to get continuing feedback on appropriate and inappropriate behaviors, and can lead to many personal growth gains. In addition, a good behavior management system enables the students to set individualized goals, allowing them to work out problems and patterns from their previous adjustment. At Fresh

Start, there was keen appreciation for the importance of the behavior management system as part of the total therapy program.

Consensus Decision-Making Groups. The program offered a special weekend privilege for all students who achieved their personal goals under the behavior management system. However, there was the additional requirement that the students would agree to, and organize, that special reward session. Using consensus decision-making, the youth had to talk over possible activities and deal with all the details, including timetable, need for special equipment or funds, transportation, and the appropriate behavior rules and consequences. The method requires that the appointed youth leader recognize all voices and guide the group to decision. Consensus cannot be bought or attained by threat, but must be arrived at by negotiation and appropriate attention to the wishes of others. Many peer conflicts develop and require the attention of the group in order to reach consensus. Any one person can block the planning of the others, and the group must then deal with that person's issues in order to move ahead.

Outdoor Adventure Therapy. The concept of outdoor therapy is perhaps the most unique aspect of The Fresh Start School's multidimensional, therapeutic intervention. Basically, the theoretical basis of outdoor therapy is that sequences of outdoor adventure, such as exploring the darkness of caves, climbing and rappelling on rock bluffs, cold weather camping, group initiative problems, and teams course activities can enhance awareness of self, others, and the self/other interdependency. The theory and practice of adventure therapy has become a recognized tool for work with troubled youth (Gass, 1992). For adolescents who have become detached from close interpersonal relationships, the outdoor-adventure group sequence tends to re-establish connections with others. When the staff responsible for the other dimensions of therapeutic intervention are also involved in the outdoor adventure program, trust relationships build so that the other components of the total therapy program can be more effective. Many barriers between psychologist and client are quickly reduced when that therapist holds the belay line for a youth scaling the walls of an 80-ft. cliff, or when they sleep next to each other on a tarp under the stars.

The Adventure Core

The challenge education model and the monthly adventure trips provided the core for the total educational and therapeutic program to unfold upon. An early differentiation among different domains of adventure supported the program's comprehensive approach. Four different types of adventure were distinguished: adventures outdoors, in the community, in the school, and in the psychological arena.

A distinction was made between outdoor adventure (hiking, camping, caving, and canoeing) and community adventure (service projects, visits to museums and historical sites, vocational education visits, for example). The adventure trips typically involved both the outdoor and community aspects. Adventure activities were not confined to trips; when the group was at home base, there was still school adventure (teams course, climbing on the water tower, and cross-country skiing, for example). Finally, the whole concept of adventure was used as a metaphor for the important introspective and therapeutic journey of each student—the psychological adventure.

The monthly 4- or 5-day trips away from the school provided a focal point for much of the rest of the program. Each trip followed the same pattern. Skills were progressively taught and practised. There was challenging travel in new terrain. Students met local people along the way and performed various acts of community service. Teachers gave daily lessons, relating academic content to the region being visited, and the psychologist maintained the therapeutic interventions with daily group sessions, crisis management, and debriefings after challenging events. Trips included both physical and social challenges. A brief outline of the content of each trip is given below.

September. A basic camping trip, teaching camping skills. There were hikes, tree climbs, environmental awareness sessions, and classes about wilderness survival.

October. A canoe trip, traveling wilderness waterways, and hiking into virgin timber forests. Along the way, the students met with loggers and forest rangers. The community service project was cleaning campsites at a state forest campground.

November. A backpacking trek along Ice Age trails, camping in handmade trailside shelters. Visits included a college geology museum and a reconstructed historical village; in parallel to the latter, the students interviewed elderly local residents.

December. A caving trip which involved sleeping in one cave and exploring two others. At the live-in cave, the group did a thorough clean-up. In the remote depths of one of the wild caves, there was a special psychological, introspective exercise.

January. A cross-country skiing, backpack trip traveling to the icy shores of Lake Superior. The group trekked to an abandoned iron ore mine, fished through the ice, tracked wildlife, and made large snow sculptures on the lakeshore. A highlight of the return trip was instruction at a pizza parlor, where the students baked their own pizzas.

February. A winter camping expedition to the Canadian border, with travel by dogsled, cross-country skis, and snowshoes. This trip paired the group with physically disabled campers. Students interviewed their traveling companions on the subject of their abilities, compensations, and attitudes. Sharing a special activity session with a group of foreign exchange students at Minnesota's Audubon Camp was a highlight.

March. A rock-climbing and rappelling trip. Through the school year, the group had experiences on the ropes course, the climbing tower, and various tree climbs. They were ready to move to actual rock bluffs. Along the way there were experiential visits to a taxidermist, a wilderness art studio, the emergency room of a hospital, a radio station, and a State ranger's fire tower.

April. A horsepacking trip through a National Forest. There had been pre-trip classes on horses, riding, and horsepacking. This trip also involved a very extensive service project of clearing unused riding trails in the forest. By the end of the trip, the students had cleared deadfalls and cut back brush along a 7-mile riding trail.

May. A wilderness waterway canoe trip, and whitewater rafting experience. This adventure provided opportunity for the group (by that time, quite experienced outdoor travelers) to share the excitement of the wilderness beyond and to maximize their own journeys to the wilderness within. A highlight of the journey was to camp near an Indian reservation, and to be guests at a special ceremony with Native American young people. An early morning sequence of sun exercises beside a northwoods lake provided a fitting climax to the trip.

June. The final trip of the school year was a backpacking hike to a remote lakeside campsite. Students occupied solo campsites to spend time in reflection on the whole year and to record thoughts about the whole adventure. On the third night, the whole group gathered to share feelings, learnings, and therapeutic insights from the year's adventure—especially the psychological adventure.

In these sorts of ways, adventure programming provided a connecting thread and central core for the academic curriculum, the therapeutic interventions, and the behavioral management aspects of the program. The overall effect of these constituted the "fresh start."

Evaluation of the Program

The progress of the youth in placement at The Fresh Start School was assessed by a number of evaluation tools, with results as follows.

Academic Achievement

Two different academic achievement tests were administered to the students before they started the program and again at the end of the school year. Both the Wide Range Achievement Test and the Peabody Individual Achievement Test were individually administered. The entry data suggested that, while the average age and grade of the students was of 14.5-year-old high school freshmen, their academic achievement was only at the 4th- or 5th-grade level. Attitudes toward school and learning were quite negative, and the students were reluctant to risk academic output for fear of failure. In the early months of the program, the goals of the behavior management system were often in terms of basic behaviors necessary for learning in the classroom (e.g., listening, following instructions, staying on task, completing assignments).

As attitudes and behaviors which interfered with learning were modified, academic instruction could have more impact. Comparison of pre-program and post-program test results (Smith, 1992) showed that the students had made worthwhile academic gains in all areas of evaluation. The average of grade-level gain was 1.5, although some of the individual students had demonstrated almost three years of achievement performance. The data suggested that the academic program at Fresh Start School had been successful.

Behavioral Change

During the first few weeks that the youths were in placement, four different adults who had interaction with them filled out the Jesness Behavior Checklist (JBC). Usually the JBC was completed by two adults from the home placement (teaching parents or adjunctive staff) and two adults from the school program (teachers or teaching assistants). These four evaluations were averaged to provide a base-line behavioral profile for each student. During the last weeks of the school year, four adults again rated each youth.

The vectors of the JBC are scored from items that ask about observable behaviors, such as the tendency to interrupt, complain, or clown around, or tendencies to be angry, nervous/anxious, or withdrawn. A composite student profile was obtained by averaging the evaluations. The pre-post JBC profile of the average student at The Fresh Start School showed that, at the end of the school year, the students were more responsible, more considerate and trusting of others, more independent, better able to establish rapport with adults, better able to control anger, more enthusiastic about life, more relaxed and calm, and capable of some insight into their problems (Smith, 1992).

Self-Concept

There was also pre-post evaluation using the Tennessee Self-Concept Inventory. Again, the pre-post comparison of an average student profile showed that there were self-concept gains in three different areas. First, the students seemed to make gains in the area of identity awareness. This implies more knowledge and awareness of themselves, their feelings, their conflicts, and their potentials. The counseling activities, both individual and group, as well as the sequences of challenging adventures, would be expected to contribute to this gain. Second, the data suggested that students made gains in their concept of themselves as physical beings. This makes sense, given the large amount of demanding physical activity in the program. Other things were also involved. All of the young people in the program had been victims of sexual abuse and exploitation, and tended to view their bodies negatively. As they learned to use their bodies in more productive ways, and even to share hugs with others, one would expect them to feel better about their physical beings. Third, there were changes in the student's social self-concept, which reflects feelings about one's perceived value to, and connectedness with, others. This finding matches the program's emphasis on interdependency, interactional trust, and positive social exchange. One student summarized this aspect of self-concept in her journal: "I feel so close to everybody here. This is my family—all of you are like brothers and sisters. I love you all, and I know that I am loved by you in return."

Conclusion

The Fresh Start Program was an experiment in providing a comprehensive educational and therapeutic program for sexually abused and exploited adolescents. The program was based on the theory and practice of experiential, outdoor-challenge adventure education. The experiment involved 16 youth in a living and learning environment in the northwoods of Wisconsin. The youth lived for a year in foster homes staffed by trained "teaching parents," and attended school staffed by special education teachers, teacher aides, and a clinical psychologist who also coordinated the adventure program.

During a 180-day school year, the students and staff spent 45 days in adventurous trips that involved backpacking, canoeing, rock climbing, cave exploration, horsepacking, and dog sledding. These experiential trips to the wilderness were all less than 200 miles from the home-base school. The whole school staff accompanied the group on the adventure trips, so educational curriculum and therapy were designed into the whole sequence.

How does one summarize and evaluate a program of such complexity and intensity? Evaluation of the youth showed valuable gains in academic achievement, and improvements in both behavior and self-concept. Still, no amount of quantitative data could really summarize the impact of the program. Perhaps the whole experience is best evoked in the words of two of the people involved.

At year's end, one of the teachers noted:

I always loved the outdoors, and I have come to love being a teacher. Before I started at Fresh Start, I knew very little about experiential education. Now I have come to realize that it is the most powerful methodology available. I always thought I was quite involved with my students, but I have learned new depths of caring and sharing. There is no doubt in my mind that from now on I am going to be an outdoor experiential education advocate.

One of the students wrote in her journal:

I'm worth something. I know that now. I used to think my life had been a waste, and that was what my future would be. I don't know where I'm going from here, but I know I'm on the road to making something good out of myself. Maybe that's how I would summarize what I've learned—I was nothing, and now I am something. I wonder if it is too much to say I know that I'm something special?

Fresh Start, despite apparent success and cost efficiency, was closed down after five years of operation. There were two major reasons for the closure, bearing in mind that the program was essentially a curricular and therapeutic experiment. First, Fresh Start was very demanding on staff members. In the fourth and fifth years, the strain began to take its toll and staff changes became necessary. It was hard to find certified, special education teachers willing to spend 5-6 days in every month in 24-hour-a-day program involvement on a sustained basis. At the same time, it proved very difficult to adequately replace the one person who served both functions of staff psychologist and coordinator of the adventure program.

Second, funding sources in Illinois began to question the need to move children to the northwoods of Wisconsin for placement and treatment. Could not a similar program be offered closer to home? The answer was "Yes, of course." A comparable integrated program emphasizing agricultural and vocational themes was subsequently opened in western Illinois.

References

Gass, M. L. (1993). *Adventure therapy: Therapeutic applications of adventure programming*. Dubuque, IA: Kendall/Hunt.

Levitt, J. L. (1981). Achievement place—the teaching family model in a group home setting. Washington DC: U.S Department of Justice, Juvenile Justice and Delinquency Prevention Institute.

Smith, T. E. (1987). Multi-dimensional therapeutic intervention for problem youth. (ERIC Document Reproduction Service No. ED 268 443)

Smith T. E. (1992, January). *Evaluation of a comprehensive challenge/ adventure program for sexually abused/exploited youth*. Paper presented at the First Outdoor Education Research Symposium of the Coalition for Education in the Outdoors, Bradford Woods, IN.

Smith, T. E., Roland, C., Havens, M., & Hoyt, J. (1992). *The theory and practice of challenge education*. Dubuque, IA: Kendall/Hunt.

Chapter 14

NO STRINGS ATTACHED: PERSONALIZING MATHEMATICS

Rena Upitis

Rena Upitis holds degrees in psychology, law, and education from Queen's University and an EdD from Harvard. She is a practising musician and has taught music in inner-city schools in the U.S. and Canada. Her wide interests lead her to seek connections among the worlds of nature, the arts, computing, and teaching. She is a prolific writer, performer, and workshop leader whose publication credits include four books: *This Too is Music*; *Can I Play You My Song?*; *Cold Feet and Chicken Curry: Reflections on Teaching*; and *I Made it in Math: Moving Beyond the Use of Manipulative Materials in the Mathematics Classroom.* Rena is Dean of Education at Queen's University in Kingston, Ontario.

Rena's chapter is important because it comes to grips with the two serious dilemmas in experiential education. One dilemma is to truly make students responsible for their learning, yet develop knowledge and insights within a particular discipline. The other is to evaluate learning, having regard for its deeply personal locus, especially when the learning is derived from individual pursuits. Rena uses a narrative account of her own teaching to highlight the joys, troubles, and adventure of personal projects with would-be teachers of elementary mathematics.

It's midwinter, but the sun shines boldly as if it were early spring. The window frames a cerulean blue sky, and it hurts my eyes to look at the melting snow. Icicles cascade over the eaves' troughs and shatter as they hit the ground. Smoke curls from my neighbour's chimney, and I remember I must go downstairs and add another log to the woodstove. But not just yet. I am painting the shadows of a glass jar and a red wooden horse, and I must work quickly or I'll lose the moment. Watercolour painting is tricky. A few seconds too soon or too late and the magic is gone. But no matter. Even if these shadows lose their translucence, I have more paper and more time. The afternoon is mine for painting—time I have set aside to play with this passion.

I began watercolour painting just over a year ago. It was something I always wanted to learn. I started with paper, paint, and a book for beginners. After a few months of joy and frustration, I found a teacher. I've been taking lessons—and painting—ever since.

I teach at the Faculty of Education at Queen's University. The courses I teach are varied—including elementary mathematics, music, arts-based education, and computers in education. Despite the diversity of these offerings, I have one assignment common to all the courses I teach: the personal project. Recently, I chose watercolours for my personal project for a math course I was teaching. Watercolour painting has been one of my most successful personal projects to date, for not only was I able to come to understand mathematics in new ways, but I loved what I produced—and I still paint.

The personal project, simply put, requires students to learn something they have never tried before and to document their progress in whatever manner best suits their needs. I also take part by completing this assignment, believing, as Herndon (1971) so aptly pointed out, that I should only ask of my students what I would willingly do myself. Herndon was a writer and educator who provided rich and powerful stories of teaching in the tradition of Kozol (1975) and Dennison (1969). He claimed many school structures stand in the way of learning, one of which is the presence of grading—another issue I deal with in the context of the personal project.

While the experience of the personal project has similar outcomes regardless of the course for which it is assigned, the discussion in this chapter focuses on how the personal project works in the area of mathematics teaching. My reason for picking this area over the others is that mathematics, at first blush, is perhaps one of the least likely candidates for experiential learning—at least in terms of the traditional ways that mathematics (or arithmetic) has been taught (Papert, 1993). I will describe the features of the personal project and the kind of learning that takes place as a result of these undertakings. Implications for teaching and learning mathematics in light of school expectations and practices will also be discussed.

Features of the Personal Project

The most central aspect of the personal project is that students are asked to learn about something new or do something *they have never done before.* They are given the opportunity to become fully engaged in a pursuit of their *own* choice, with no strings attached. By giving students this opportunity, I am not asking for a list of curriculum topics that could be taught in the formal setting. I am simply asking them to learn about something new, on their own initiative, and by whatever means they see fit. Many lessons are learned outside of school, and by asking future teachers to concentrate some of their learning efforts outside the school setting, they are reminded that as classroom teachers they affect some, but by no means all, of their students' learning.

In giving students this opportunity, I must be prepared to support projects that I would not be interested in pursuing myself. For that matter, I may find myself supporting projects in which I think there is little room for significant learning. (In this latter case, I often find I am wrong—just because I can't imagine the learning that will take place, doesn't mean the project isn't worthwhile for the student.) I must also be prepared to give students time to choose their projects—sometimes it takes up to two months for students who make four or five false starts to settle on their final project. In fact, I often try one or two ideas myself before settling in—and I have been giving myself this assignment for some years.

The projects are personal in that the students make their own choices, but "personal" does not mean "alone." Sometimes students will work on personal projects together—when several people find they are all interested in knitting, for example, they may choose to work at the same time on their individual projects. Sometimes the actual product is a joint effort—for example, a group of students making a quilt. In any case, the personal projects almost always involve a larger learning community in that the students usually find they need the help of others to complete their projects. Even those students who prefer to work alone will want to share their work with peers at some point in the process.

Reflection on one's own learning is one of the expectations—students are asked to keep notes, a log, or a journal—some record of their work, the people they used as resources, the frustrations and joys they encountered (if students made false starts, a record of these trials is to be kept as part of the process of making a personal choice). This record is then used to write a summative reflective piece in the hope that students will be able to articulate something about their own learning. In the math course, I ask students to find the math in their personal projects (see excerpt below); this could be done with other disciplines as well.

The personal projects take several months to complete. At various times, I ask students to share their work, in groups of four or five, discussing the progress they are making on their respective projects. I also join one of the groups for this ongoing sharing.

I believe it is vital that I undertake a personal project along with the students, partly because I believe in the strength of modelling, but more so because it puts me in a better position to understand the nature of my students' undertakings. Besides, going back to Herndon's (1971) point—why should I ask of my students something that I won't do myself?

Finally, the personal project brings with it no threat of evaluation—there are no hidden hoops to jump through for the final grade (Falbel & Higginson, 1985). The personal projects do not get marked. Students are told at the outset that they will be expected to share their project, if possible, and to write journals and a reflective piece. They are also told they will get an "A" for their efforts (or whatever a high mark might be in the particular context; when I did something similar with high school students, I gave them all 96%). But giving a high mark at the outset does not mean that I don't ask for hard work or, indeed, that the students don't ask it of themselves. In fact, students often report that they've worked harder for the personal project than for other courses, despite the pre-assigned grade. I like to think of it in terms of a phrase coined by Papert, where a situation of "demanding permissiveness" is created. Students are expected to work hard on their personal projects once they settle on an idea, but they are given extremely wide latitude in choosing their projects (Papert, 1993, p. 124).

In every way possible, then, the personal project puts learning in the hands of the students—with no strings attached.

Description of the Personal Project Assignment

The following excerpt describing the personal project assignment is taken from my course outline for a primary-junior mathematics curriculum course for pre-service teachers.

Learn about something new or do something you have never done before. It should be something that matters to you, something that you think might be useful, something that you would enjoy (and not classify as one of life's "busywork" assignments). Oh yes—it would be nice if the "something" was related to mathematics. You could . . .

• make a quilt	• try watercolours
• make stained glass	• compose some music
• try Thai cooking	• learn Spanish
• take ballroom dancing	• build a robotics wonderland
• learn sign language	• take a life-drawing class

As you engage in your personal project, keep a log or a journal or set of notes, if only haphazardly. From these notes, generate a brief description of what you found—what the experience was like, what you observed, felt, wondered about, liked, disliked, marvelled at—and learned. I'd also like you to identify the mathematics involved. . . .

People choose a variety of personal projects—making a cribbage board, ballroom dancing, making stained glass, woodworking, making twig furniture, learning to bake bread, making wine, print making, photography development, and learning to fly an airplane (some personal projects gave "risk-taking in teaching and learning" a whole new meaning). I encourage students to choose a project for the love of it, rather than worrying about the mathematics involved. I assure them that we'll play "Where's the math?" (a distant cousin to "Where's Waldo?") as the term progresses, and not to worry if they are concerned that there will be little math in their projects. This is one of the functions of the small-group discussions; often one's peers can see some of the math more readily than the person directly involved with a project.

Initial Reactions

The feelings and learning we encounter through this experience are as varied as the projects themselves. Some students' initial responses to the personal project are nothing short of gleeful. They speak of how it is wonderful to be given this kind of chance, and list many ideas that leap to mind for possible projects. Later, many write about this initial response, reflecting that rarely have they been given an opportunity in school to truly pursue their own learn-ing. For example:

> When we were first asked to do a personal project as an assignment, I was absolutely elated! Finally, someone is interested in what we want to learn. I came up with all sorts of ideas. . . . (Roy Choudhury, 1993, p. 1)

> When I first realized this assignment would be something I actually enjoyed doing, I was surprised. In my nineteen years of schooling no one has ever given me complete freedom of choice. There were

many teachers who provided me with choice, but somewhere in the assignment there was always a catch. (Philpot, 1993, p. 1)

Students like these are enthusiastic about taking charge of their own learning. Perhaps they have already done this outside school, which leaves them poised to take advantage of the personal project assignment. Papert (1993) makes the convincing argument that if children practice taking charge of their own learning, then as adults they will have developed a sense of intellectual identity and will be able to "define and redefine their roles throughout a long lifetime" (p. 24). Papert describes how his own personal projects—starting a newspaper as a child, learning to juggle, learning to fly a plane— have affected him profoundly, and given him the opportunity to observe and theorize about his own learning. He further argues that school tends to inhibit the possibility of children taking charge of their learning, as they are more often than not in a "position of having to do as they are told, to occupy themselves with work dictated by someone else . . . [work] that has no intrinsic value" (p. 24).

One wonders if the school experience explains, in part, why other students respond to the personal project in less than enthusiastic ways. Some students are frightened by the open-ended nature of the assignment, and approach me in private after class saying, "Just tell me what to do." Others find the assignment interesting in principle but, because they fear mathematics, they cannot imagine how they could learn something new *and* deal with the mathematics involved. Usually about a third of the students are uncomfortable with the personal project, either because of the potential mathematics involved or because they have had few opportunities to make their own choices throughout their schooling, and are therefore unprepared to make a choice. As Illich (1983) so aptly argues, the pervasiveness of school as a public institution creates a dependence on school and its practices for learning; as Papert claims, a "superstitious belief in its methods" (p. 141).

Some students complicate the issue even further by wondering how they could apply their personal project to a classroom setting. To these students, I find myself frequently stressing the "personal" part of the "personal project," reiterating that the project is for them, not for their future students. This phenomenon of wanting to relate everything to a classroom situation is also described by

Papert (1993). In a workshop setting, he found himself frustrated with participants who thought of themselves as "teachers-in-training rather than as learners . . . [where] their awareness of being teachers was preventing them from giving themselves over fully to experiencing what they were doing as intellectually exciting . . . in its own right, for what it could bring them as private individuals" (p. 72).

In the last two math courses I have taught, from which the excerpts in this chapter are taken, the students uncomfortable with the assignment designated a spokesperson to talk to me about their discomfort and confusion. In both cases, the women speaking for the larger groups have themselves been delighted by the assignment, but have well understood the confusion on the part of their peers. I assured these students that there were truly "no strings attached," and with that assurance, they returned to the disgruntled group, explained the features of the assignment once again, and watched the confusion slowly turn to engagement and enjoyment. Some of the students who were initially uncomfortable with the personal project wrote:

> My first reaction to this project was utter panic. I felt somehow threatened by the open-endedness of the assignment, and could not decide what the project should be. This panic was fuelled by the conflict between my desire to fulfil the requirements of the course to the letter and my desire to find creative fulfilment in a tried-and-true, safe activity, like writing. . . . It would have been much, much easier for me if there had been guidelines other than "do something you have never done before." I needed to know what the teacher's objectives were before I could come to a final decision. (Burbidge, 1993, p. 1)

> When I first heard that we were to decide upon a personal project...I thought, "Oh no, how am I ever going to decide what to do?" I am a product of the school system where children are told everything that they are to do for every class, and when a decision like this is left up to me, my initial reaction is to panic. Fortunately, once I calmed down . . . I began to come up with a few ideas. (Bitterman, 1993, p. 1)

A third, very small group of students, aren't threatened by the prospect of making a choice, but feel that the assignment can't have any significant value for a course in mathematics. This tends to happen most often with students who have excelled at traditional mathematics curricula, often taking a number of math courses in high school and university. For these students, the personal project is not real math. A case in point appears below.

> I came into this course very excited. I have always liked math and couldn't wait to try teaching it myself. To me math was "textbook math." I have always liked math because there was a right or a wrong answer and not a "how much can I B.S. my way through this" answer. Math was something that always boosted up my self-esteem. I was always proud of my math abilities, especially since most of my friends practically broke out in tears anytime they saw a math book. . . . Then came the personal project. Being the math textbook person that I am, I thought, "What a dumb thing to have us do. How are you going to learn math by making something?" OK, so I put off the project as long as I could. First I was going to make a kite. . . . I decided on a gingerbread house . . . but I still thought, ". . . I can't believe I'm making a gingerbread house for a math project." My friends laughed at me and said, "So that's what you do in University nowadays." (Tomasevic, 1993, pp. 1-2)

I admit that as I was reading this piece, I was worried. I was unaware of the upheaval the personal project had caused this student. I was even more concerned about her choice of a personal project. As I stated earlier, sometimes "no strings attached" includes supporting projects that I think may not be the most enlightening in terms of mathematics. I felt that the gingerbread house would be that kind of project—that the student and her peers would build the house without difficulty, and they would all be left wondering why I had created such an assignment, convinced that "textbook math" was the only legitimate vehicle for teaching mathematics.

As it turns out, I needn't have worried. Even building a gingerbread house—which to me seemed a much simpler undertaking than, say, making a stained glass window, resulted in important learning for the student. Kathy continued:

That just goes to show you [my friends] were just as cheated as I was out of what could have been a wonderful math education. It is no wonder so many of them hate math. How could you not hate something that involved doing pages and pages of the same type of work day after day? Some of us only liked it because of the self-esteem thing. . . . Ask me to do something that involves math skills that are not so obvious; I am no longer good at math . . . [e]verything was moving along nicely until we had to assemble the parts of the house . . . and realized the roof [would not] cover the house. . . . I sat there in disbelief and began to wail. . . .

What I am trying to say is that my view of math and how it should be taught has completely changed. . . . I can't stop looking for math in everything I do. (Tomasevic, 1993, pp. 2-3)

A more detailed look at how students journey through the personal project follows.

Early Stages

One of the most common occurrences in the early stages of the personal project is that students (myself included) often change their minds about the projects they will undertake. Having decided to try something "simple," they often find that their simple ideas are not so simple and, for one reason or another, abandon them. Sometimes they abandon projects because they turn out to be too costly; sometimes they want to take a course—say in pottery—that is already full, and consequently need to choose something else. Sometimes students abandon projects out of frustration—and sometimes because they simply don't like what they're doing. Of all of these reasons, the last is perhaps the least acceptable in school terms. When I was visiting a tourist turn-of-the-century schoolhouse on Prince Edward Island, I read on the blackboard:

If a job is once begun, never leave it 'til it's done;
Be the labour great or small, do it well or not at all.

My sense is that this little ditty still reflects the sentiment of many teachers. While I believe it is often right to ask a student to persevere and complete a project he or she begins, I believe it is even better to help him or her recognize when the best decision is to abandon the project. Often the personal project causes students to reflect in a similar manner, and they relate how they will try to recognize when it makes sense for one of their students to stop or give up, even though a job isn't completed. One student wrote:

> At this stage, I clued in that if a reasonably normal adult can change her mind so frequently . . . then as a teacher I should remember this when [a student] decides to scrap a struggling plan for a new one. (Theilmann, 1993, p. 2)

One of the other aspects in the early phases of the personal project is the prospect of gathering the materials required to do the work. Some approach this phase with excitement; purchasing the materials gives them a positive feeling about the entire undertaking. I certainly fall into this category—I love the feeling of going on a shopping expedition for a new adventure. For others, however, there is real trepidation involved, as even buying materials can expose one as a learner. This makes some people feel uncomfortable and vulnerable. The same student quoted above wrote:

> Straight ignorance gave me the willies as I entered [the art supplies store for my materials]. . . . [Since I was] obviously looking lost, a very kind lady approached me to see if I needed assistance. . . . I told her my sister likes to make jewellery and I wanted to purchase supplies for her for a Christmas gift—an outright lie! (Theilmann, 1993, p. 1)

Mid-Phases

Once the project has been chosen, materials have been secured, and some initial attempt has been made on the personal project, difficulties and frustrations invariably set in—even when people choose what they deem simple projects. The following comment was made by a student who decided to make a cribbage board out of driftwood from a beach near the university:

The journey was much rougher than I expected. . . . [I] began with a simple idea . . . yeah, right. This idea soon became not so simple. . . . (Brown, 1993, p. 1)

Since adult students generally expect some difficulties to occur, they are surprised by the impatience they feel when their projects cause them anxiety. This leads some students to change their projects entircly, while others stick with their projects despite the difficulties encountered—"when one is deeply involved in something, 'easy' is not what one wants" (Papert, 1993, p. 48). The following journal excerpts, written by a woman learning to crochet an Afghan, illustrate well the cycle of enjoyment-frustration-enjoyment:

24/10/93

I am starting to get really excited about this. . . . I have beautiful blue wool. . . .

25/10/93

So far, so good; only worked for 2 hours.

6/11/93

I am very frustrated but I don't want to give up on this pattern. . . .

11/11/93

Looked at it again, pulled it out and started again. No luck. I am a glutton for punishment.

12/11/93

What a relief. Now I am getting somewhere. . . .

14/11/93

Piece of cake! I know how to crochet!

16/11/93

This is very relaxing. . . . (Rothmuller, 1993, pp. 1-4).

Yet another group of students experience anxiety when they begin to discover the kinds of tools they will need to produce their piece. One student wrote of his healthy respect for a router, having put a hole through a piece of pine he was sculpting. Another student, learning to upholster furniture, commented:

> My bubble burst abruptly when my husband informed me I would need to buy some upholstery tools. I wrote in my journal, "The idea that there might be tools involved means this is going to be technical. Technical scares me." (Burbidge, 1993, p. 1)

Personal projects invariably take many more hours than expected—even I am surprised by my inability to gauge the time I need for a new undertaking. In one of my papers, I wrote:

> I've done a fair number of personal projects over the years. So, by now, I should be getting good at them. . . . It still takes me a long time to do each project, always longer than I think. (Upitis, 1993, p. 1)

There is nothing wrong with taking a long time to learn something. In fact, taking the time to learn is something we rarely do, and school tends not to encourage this because its very structures cause the "chopping" of time (Papert, 1993, p. 89). By making the personal project the major assignment of the course, I can give students time they may not give themselves—the time they would normally take completing four or five other assignments for the math course can be spent for the personal project—it is time students have already budgeted for school work; the personal project changes the nature of that school work.

Learning Issues

One of the most important revelations students have as they engage in the personal project is that there is a great deal of mathematics involved in their pursuits. Students are always surprised by this and, further, many realize that it is important to articulate the mathematics involved. That is, just using the math to accomplish the project goals is not enough. After all, as several students have pointed out, many people use math successfully for years—especially women doing "women's work" like sewing and cooking—and yet see themselves as math illiterate or describe themselves as math-phobic. Part of the reason for this is that they have never thought of these pursuits in mathematical terms. Some related quotations follow:

> You can see all the math that was needed to design and make this. . . . I couldn't believe it until I started to write this. (Patrick, 1993, p. 2)

> I was also a little worried that I wouldn't be able to find a lot of math in crocheting—I was wrong. Right from the start, I jumped into math. (Hick, 1993, p. 1)

> I've thought of something else. At the most basic level, we are also dealing with left-right/up-down/and side-to-side concepts. These are so automatic we don't even think about them. But we would be continually thinking about these concepts if we had a learning disability and had to struggle with them. (Senra, 1993, p. 3)

Another equally important learning issue was the role of learning through social interaction. Some people found it preferable or even necessary to involve others in their learning. Many wrote about how they involved their fiancés, friends, and family members in their work, often noting that this was the only school assignment they found useful and helpful to share. One woman said that she had her 3-year-old daughter help her decorate the musical instruments she had constructed, and commented further that she would not have involved her had the personal project been like other assignments and faced the grading process upon completion. Interestingly, this student noted that her end product was more engaging and artistically successful with her daughter's input—even though she feared that her daughter might ruin the work, and wouldn't have risked having her help had the project been marked.

Some other comments regarding the importance of involving others appear below:

> I knew that the initial teaching [for knitting] had to be done by a very patient friend. (Duncan, 1993, p. 1)

The social aspect of the [watercolour] course was a significant element in my enjoyment of the course. The atmosphere was so casual
and friendly . . . not only did I discover a love of painting and of
drawing during the course, but I met some really neat people as
well. (Grant, 1993, p. 2)

While some students enjoyed and even depended on the involvement of peers and family, others took the opposite approach, either
because they feared exposing themselves as new learners, or
because they revelled in the time they could spend alone. One
woman falling into the latter category said she used her crocheting
time for personal thought, wandering from one topic to another in
her mind. Every Friday night she had a date with her Afghan and a
pot of chamomile tea. Someone falling into the former category,
that is, not wanting to show her vulnerability as a new learner,
wrote:

Considering my complete lack of experience with painting anything
other than the walls with a roller, learning from a book seemed the
best method for avoiding embarrassment. (Craig, 1993, p. 1)

Certainly the time spent on the personal projects became valued
time for most students. The comment below made me realize how
few assignments give students the opportunity to make something
with their hands; small wonder that so many personal projects
involve handwork of one form or another. This comment comes
from the student quoted earlier, who was frustrated with the tools
required to upholster furniture:

It was therapeutic to work with my hands after frustrating days of
discussing theories of education. . . . (Burbidge, 1993, p. 1)

I certainly concur with this observation. As I described at the outset, watercolour painting for me has become an outlet—a way of
balancing the teaching, marking, and yes, chapter writing, with
other ways of engaging my hands, heart, and mind.

Implications

In terms of general implications, perhaps the most important one dealing directly with mathematics is that almost all students report that, as a result of the personal project, they are now seeing math everywhere:

> Meanwhile, I learned about tessellations in math class. Tessellations are now taking over my life; I find them everywhere (I'm beginning to consider therapy). My project just had to tessellate! (McWhirter, 1993, p. 1)

> When we introduced ourselves on the first night of the course, we all announced why we were taking the [watercolour painting] course. I said that part of my reason was to fulfil a component of my math course, and that I was here to find the math in watercolours. Everyone, of course, looked at me as if I were crazy. I was a bit doubtful myself. However, one of the first exercises we did that night was to draw, conceptualizing everything as one of four three-dimensional shapes—a cube, cylinder, cone, or sphere. . . . I realized in doing this personal project that math lessons do not have to be ditto sheets, but that math really is all around us. (Grant, 1993, pp. 1-2)

Along with "seeing math everywhere" comes an increased level of confidence with one's own math abilities. This is crucial for future teachers of mathematics, many of whom come to the first math class with visible anxiety on their faces and in their body movements. I am convinced, as are the students who write below, that exploring one's math abilities in a real context does far more for elevating one's self-confidence than passing achievement tests.

> It was great to have the opportunity to use math in a real life context. By doing something I was interested in, I didn't mind doing the math. In fact, it was rather enjoyable searching for the math—like a game. . . . This personal project has definitely increased my confidence in my mathematical abilities. (Smith, 1993, p. 3)

> Strange—this personal project taught me to find the math in "normal" activities. . . . However, it is still difficult for me to "find the math" in an activity because, basically, doing so threatens my enjoyment of the activity. Now, I didn't say *ruins* my enjoyment, because

I am now comfortable enough with math to find it and use it . . . but my old (and still very present) fear of math makes me automatically shy away from it. Now that I know I can do it, I have to learn how to feel that I can do it. That will be my goal during my next personal project. (Duncan, 1993, pp. 1-2)

I'm sure you know these personal projects have not only affected our class, but everyone we come in contact with. In a building full of future teachers, many now understand that math can be found everywhere in everything we do. And even if there are some who didn't understand what we have told them about finding the math in our personal projects, they'll be perplexed now. They weren't perplexed before. (Assinck, 1993, p. 1)

As mentioned earlier, for some students, this notion of math ability or talent was closely tied to gender. Many of the women students noted that not only could they "see math everywhere," but felt more confident in their abilities because they realized they had been doing math all along in their daily lives. Two particularly strong excerpts in this regard appear below:

When I was thinking about what I would do for my personal project and [Rena] mentioned in class the option of knitting, I immediately thought "Where is the math in that?" As I started to crochet my baby's blanket I began to see what [Rena] [was] talking about...[this project] made me realize how much math we use in everyday life. It made me feel, and now here comes my quasi-feminist statement, how undervalued many things have been in the past. Sewing, crocheting, and knitting were traditionally thought of as "women's work." . . . [The personal project] showed me how many skills, especially mathematical ones, women possessed and were traditionally considered incapable of possessing. My maternal Grandmother taught me how to knit and sew when I was a small child. I do not think my Grandmother realized she possessed a number of math skills in order to make her crafts; I think these skills were viewed by her and most people as "real-world realities," as something you just knew. (Haines, 1993, pp. 1-2)

These observations are like those made by Lave (1988), a cognitive anthropologist who has demonstrated not only that women know and use mathematics in household tasks, but that the mathematics they use is often qualitatively different in form from "school math."

In a similar vein, another woman who learned to crochet wrote:

> I have always been fairly conscious of the lack of participation of women in math and science. I have researched the topic and seen many suggestions for dealing with this problem. However, I was never sure how to make the necessary changes in my own classroom. From this assignment I learned many things. I chose an activity which is considered "women's work" or a "women's pastime" . . . there was tons of math in this activity . . . therefore, even if women are only actively participating in things that are deemed "women's work," they are being exposed to math all the time. This suggests that the way we are teaching math—the examples and the tools—is gender exclusive. . . . I learned a lot about myself and a lot about the kind of teacher I want to be. (Philpot, 1993, pp. 3-4)

It is clear that the personal project has value for students beyond fulfilling the requirements of a university assignment or, for that matter, beyond being able to "see math everywhere" or be more confident in one's math abilities. The personal project has value because it has the potential to reach into other important parts of one's life—because it goes beyond the classroom walls and curriculum containers. A group of women made a math quilt—each square had significance for mathematics, ranging from simple manipulatives attached with velcro to the recognition of female mathematicians. When Terri, a six-year-old, was told that her family would be looking after the quilt for the summer, she exclaimed as she wrapped the quilt around herself, "I love the quilt. I'm going to set it down in the living room and play, play, play, play"—what a fine way for Terri to embrace and explore some math ideas. Another quilter found that her project was not only full of mathematics, but realized it would serve as a gift for her parents' fiftieth wedding anniversary. A student who wrote a book for her personal project describing a game called Cows! Cows! Cows!, related her plans of taking it to a publisher (Parent, 1993). Others who had made jewellery of various kinds commented that they had received commissions for jewellery, stating how this made them feel that their work must be good. Yet another student, who made a cross-stitched quilt for her unborn child, wrote:

> Well, I'm in the middle of doing letter "C" and my back hurts, my fingers ache, and I've lost sight in both eyes because the holes are so tiny, and oddly enough, I still love what I'm doing. . . . Aside from realizing that I will develop acute arthritis when I'm older, I will have something pretty spectacular to give my child when he or she is born. . . . Every stitch in that quilt and every letter represents a certain time in my life. It's like a diary . . . letter "E" was completed with my best friend at my side, "H" was done when I was teaching and learning to teach, and letter "I" was completed during a time of confusion about my teaching and the teaching I was seeing around me. This quilt is a story about me and I look forward to sharing myself with my child, and this is where I begin. (Senra, 1993, pp. 5-7)

This kind of undertaking invariably involves thinking about one's own learning. Many of us are able to comment on our learning, and the kinds of conditions and teaching methods that work best for us in a given circumstance. What is interesting is the diversity of teaching methods that people find appropriate. Some students, for example, state how they are unable to follow diagrams, as in the following account:

> There were three diagrams to complement these instructions. Immediately, I became tense. I hate trying to follow diagrams. This was the first self-realization with which I was faced regarding how I learn. (Wells, 1993, p. 4)

Others describe the opposite experience, stating that the diagrams were the most helpful part in a set of written instructions:

> I ignored the written instructions and followed the diagrams and models . . . let's try this and see if it works. I did not want to "waste" time reading about how to do it. (Burbidge, 1993, p. 2)

What is most important, of course, is not whether a given learner likes one method over another, but that he or she is able to find a way that works. As future teachers, this is particularly important, for a method that works well for the teacher, and indeed for some of the students, will not necessarily work for others. Many of the math students came to grips with this—and other learning issues—through the personal project, and by sharing their views in the small-group discussions.

Numerous other features of the learning environment were raised as well, including the role of structured expectations and directions, the need to feel the work had real educational value or practical purpose, the need for approval (even applause) from teacher and peers, and the importance of taking a hands-on approach to solving the practical problems of the personal project. One student also talked about how she was highly motivated by the end product, even though she realized the importance of process in this assignment. She talked of her fear of failure and preoccupation with the final product, stating:

I feel these views may have been influenced or even created by my socialization to the process and expectations of the educational system. Since I consider these negative points, I would hope, as a teacher, to influence my students in other directions. (Burbidge, 1993, p. 3)

Thinking about one's own learning invariably led to new ways of thinking about teaching. Pre-service teachers, along with their more experienced colleagues, are well aware that people learn in different ways and at different rates. But it is one thing to know about learning styles intellectually, and another thing altogether to *feel* what those differences mean. Since the personal project involves learning something new, many students find that they are given a context for experiencing what they know—in short, by putting themselves in the shoes of a learner, they better understand what it means to be taught. For example:

I felt like I had lost all control in my hands and fingers. At first, it was extremely awkward . . . and frustrating, because I couldn't remember what I was supposed to be doing. I also had to practically count out loud to keep track of what stitch I was on. (Kimmett, 1993, p. 1)

I always knew that people learned in different ways, but I never realized how subtle the differences could be. . . . An interesting lesson I learned was that everyone has bad days. Some days I would start crocheting and I just could not follow the pattern. It may have been that my mind was somewhere else . . . regardless, I couldn't complete a row. This . . . is something I will definitely need to take into consideration when I am teaching. . . . (Philpot, 1993, p. 3)

Many continued with specific plans for their own teaching—like providing a variety of ways of introducing new concepts and tasks—oral, written, diagrams, models—but not enforcing the use of one method over another. Others noted that they would try not to interfere with students' work unless they were asked for assistance. There is nothing earth-shattering or novel about these approaches. Many educators advocate the use of multiple representations for teaching, based in part on the work of psychologists like Gardner (1983) who have demonstrated different kinds of intelligences or strengths in making sense of the world. Likewise, educators have stressed the importance of offering help to students only when it is solicited, rather than providing unasked-for help at every turn (Falbel, 1989). What is significant here is that these pre-service teachers are making these same conclusions on their own, on the basis of an experience which is strong enough to shape their view of mathematics and teaching and learning.

The significance of the personal project to students is further demonstrated by the fact that many describe future personal projects they plan to undertake, realizing the importance of giving more than lip service to the notion of lifelong learning:

> [T]he most important thing I learned by doing this project was the fact that I need to *make* time for those important things that I want to learn. I have even started to decide what my project will be next term! (Wells, 1993, p. 2)

The personal projects are worth doing, in and of themselves. That there are learning outcomes related to mathematics—or any other number of disciplines, for that matter—is secondary. One does not engage in personal projects because there is mathematics to be learned through them. One engages in the projects because they are a worthwhile way to spend some time. Although I ask students to articulate the mathematics so that they become more aware of the math involved, I do not ask them to choose the project with math in mind—the math emerges. One student echoed this sentiment in terms of how she would pick an activity the next time for herself, and for her students:

> I think that is the trick: to find learning outcomes that relate to what I have done, rather than trying to find an activity that fits the outcomes. (Duncan, 1993, p. 2)

Too often our approach is the opposite—instead of beginning with a worthwhile idea, we begin with things we want to teach, and try (often in vain) to find activities to fit. Or as Papert (1993) writes, "Geometry is not there for being learned. It is there for being used" (p. 17). And geometry is there for being used in personal ways— just because a quilt turns out to be a good project for one person doesn't mean an entire class should now engage in the same activity. Again, quoting from Papert, "significant engagement [is] too personal to be expected to operate as a mass effect . . . reasons [for engagement] are as personal and in a sense as unreproducible as those that determine any kind of falling in love" (p. 27).

Finally, I would like to raise the issue of how many of these worthwhile activities, chosen out of personal interest rather than out of their potential mathematical riches, turned out to have something to do with visual art or music or, generally, had an important aesthetic component. When we are given the chance to learn something new, nearly everyone gravitates toward making something, and trying to make something beautiful. The beauty of mathematics and its strong relation to the arts is often underplayed in traditional curricula. Yet, this is perhaps the most convincing way to make mathematics real for our students. One teacher wrote:

> I see art and math together, and these are the two [subjects] that are the most often [at] opposite ends of the spectrum. In schools we [often] disengage these two subjects, when in reality, they complement and support each other at the most basic level . . . neither can escape the other . . . instead of spending all our time dividing and isolating things, a more sensible . . . [approach] would involve an integration of thoughts and processes. (Senra, 1993, p. 6)

Another student shared the following quotation by a mathematician named Morris Kline, found somewhere in a book of phrases about learning mathematics, the source of which, unfortunately, has been lost.

> A mathematician, like a painter or a poet, is a maker of patterns. The mathematician's patterns, like the painter's or the poet's, must be beautiful, the ideas, like the colours or the words, must fit together in a harmonious way. Beauty is the first test. There is no permanent place in the world for ugly mathematics.

The personal project provides a window for teachers to see the beauty of mathematics.

References

Assinck, B. (1993). *Drawing on the right side of the brain.* Unpublished manuscript, Faculty of Education, Queen's University.

Bitterman, M. (1993). *Personal project: Cross-stitch.* Unpublished manuscript, Faculty of Education, Queen's University.

Burbidge, M. (1993). *Furniture upholstery.* Unpublished manuscript, Faculty of Education, Queen's University.

Brown, C. (1993). *Making a cribbage board.* Unpublished manuscript, Department of Math and Science Education, University of British Columbia.

Craig, S. (1993). *Personal project: Watercolour.* Unpublished manuscript, Faculty of Education, Queen's University.

da Rosa, V. (1993). *The quilting club.* Unpublished manuscript, Department of Math and Science Education, University of British Columbia.

Dennison, G. (1969). *The lives of children.* New York: Vantage Press.

Duncan, A. (1993). *Knit one, purl two . . .* Unpublished manuscript, Faculty of Education, Queen's University.

Falbel, A. (1989). *Friskolen 70: An ethnographically informed inquiry into the social context of learning.* Unpublished doctoral thesis, Learning and Epistemology Group, Massachusetts Institute of Technology.

Falbel, A., & Higginson, W. (1985). *Hoopla about curriculum.* Unpublished manuscript, Learning and Epistemology, Media Lab, Massachusetts Institute of Technology.

Fodor, N. (1993). *Music composition.* Unpublished manuscript, Faculty of Education, Queen's University.

Gardner, H. (1983). *Frames of mind: The theory of multiple intelligences.* New York: Basic Books.

Grant, J. (1993). *Watercolours and math.* Unpublished manuscript, Faculty of Education, Queen's University.

Haines, T. (1993). *Crocheting a baby's blanket.* Unpublished manuscript, Department of Math and Science Education, University of British Columbia.

Herndon, J. (1971). *How to survive in your native land.* New York: Simon & Schuster.

Hick, L. (1993). *Crocheting.* Unpublished manuscript, Faculty of Education, Queen's University.

Illich, I. (1983). *Deschooling society.* New York: Harper & Row.

Johnston, K. (1993). *Personal project.* Unpublished manuscript, Department of Math and Science Education, University of British Columbia.

Kimmett, M. L. (1993). *Knitting.* Unpublished manuscript, Faculty of Education, Queen's University.

Kozol, J. (1975). *The night is dark and I am far from home.* New York: Bantam Books.

Lave, J. (1988). *Cognition in practice.* Cambridge: Cambridge University Press.

McClelland, C. (1993). *Quilting—A personal project.* Unpublished manuscript, Department of Math and Science Education, University of British Columbia.

McWhirter, S. (1993). *Stained tessellations.* Unpublished manuscript, Department of Math and Science Education, University of British Columbia.

Papert, S. (1993). *The children's machine: Rethinking school in the age of the computer.* NY: Basic Books.

Parent, L. (1993). *Cows! Cows! Cows!* Unpublished manuscript, Faculty of Education, Queen's University.

Patrick, H. (1993). *Rug hooking.* Unpublished manuscript, Department of Math and Science Education, University of British Columbia.

Philpot, M. (1993). *A baby blanket for my niece or nephew.* Unpublished manuscript, Faculty of Education, Queen's University.

Powers, S. (1993). *Learning to play chess.* Unpublished manuscript, Faculty of Education, Queen's University.

Rothmuller, C. (1993). *Crocheting an afghan.* Unpublished manuscript, Faculty of Education, Queen's University.

Roy Choudhury, I. (1993). *Adventures in cross-stitching: A personal project.* Unpublished manuscript, Faculty of Education, Queen's University.

Senra, H. (1993). *Cross-stitching.* Unpublished manuscript, Faculty of Education, Queen's University.

Smith, J. (1993). *Making wine.* Unpublished manuscript, Faculty of Education, Queen's University.

Theilmann, K. (1993). *Papier maché earrings.* Unpublished manuscript, Faculty of Education, Queen's University.

Tomasevic, K. (1993). *Gingerbread house math.* Unpublished manuscript, Department of Math and Science Education, University of British Columbia.

Upitis, R. (1993). *A watercolour aquarium.* Unpublished manuscript, Department of Math and Science Education, University of British Columbia.

Wells, J. (1993). *Crocheting.* Unpublished manuscript, Faculty of Education, Queen's University.

Chapter 15

"THE STUBBORN PARTICULARS OF GRACE"

David W. Jardine

David Jardine has a background in philosophy and religious studies and currently teaches Early Childhood Education at the University of Calgary, Alberta.

He brings this background and a fine poetic sensitivity to the experiences of children and teachers in trying to make sense of mathematics in the world. David takes us from the surfaces of things into the depths of reality and meaning. He invites us to attend to particulars of practice as persistent symbols of unity. He seeks to have us see the everyday business of teaching as a whole. In doing so, he holds up a mirror to practice which is lyrically beautiful, critical, and hopeful.

Prelude

Poet Bronwen Wallace entitled her third collection of poems *The Stubborn Particulars of Grace* (1987). Reference to this title comes up in a poem called "Particulars" which is full of the meticulous details of memory and reverie ("those Sundays at my grandmother's table") and which shows the way that our lives are always lived right here, in the face of these stubborn particulars. Wallace's work gains its deep resonances, its sense of wholeness, not through nebulous talk of grand things, but because it consistently "argue[s] the stubborn argument of the particular, right now, in the midst of things, *this* and *this*" (p. 111).

This stubborn argument of the particular is reminiscent of a fragment of William Carlos Williams's "Spring and All" (1991, p. 224):

> *So much depends*
> *upon*
>
> *the red wheel*
> *barrow*
>
> *glazed with rain*
> *water*
>
> *beside the white*
> *chickens.*

Here, an ordinarily insignificant object is portrayed with such spacious clarity that the insight becomes unavoidable: somehow, *everything* depends upon this red wheelbarrow. Somehow, from out of a mindfulness to *this* and *this*, the particular object, in its very particularity, becomes like a sacred place where the whole Earth comes to nestle in relations of deep interdependency.

This is one of the secrets of ecological mindfulness. To understand what is right in front of us in an ecologically sane, integrated way is to somehow see this particular thing in place, located in a patterned nest of interdependencies without which it would not be what it is. Differently put, understanding "the whole" involves paying attention to *this* in its wholeness. This rootedness in the particular is what helps prevent ecology from becoming woozy and amorphous—a disembodied idea that misses the particularities in the flit of *this* ruby-crowned kinglet pair in the lower pine branches and how their movement is so fitting here, in the coming arch of spring in the Rocky Mountain foothills.

Math Facts on a Teddy Bear's Tummy

During practicum supervision in a Grade 1 classroom over the past year, I witnessed again a common sight. The children are in the middle of a bear theme. In order to integrate with this theme and in order to make the work "more fun for the kids" (as one teacher put it), mathematics addition facts are printed on the stomach of a cut-out line drawing of a teddy bear.

Such activities—where the mathematics questions are answered and the bears are coloured in and posted on the wall of the class-room—are certainly carried out with the best of intentions. Blaming teachers for engaging their children in such trite activities in the name of curriculum integration belies the fact that we are all "witnessing the inevitable outcome of a logic [of fragmentation, severance and dis-integration] that is already centuries old and that is being played out in our own lifetime" (Berman, 1983, p. 23). More strongly put, we are all, however unwittingly, living out this logic. Teachers, children, administrators, University academics—we have all, in our own ways, been victimized by the uprootedness and "unsettling" (Berry, 1986) caused by this logic. Such classroom activities should, therefore, not be taken up as occasions for blame, but as interpretive opportunities that give us all ways to address how we might make our pedagogical conduct more integrated and whole.

What we see occurring with these math facts on a teddy bear's tummy is what could be called an "urban sprawl" version of inte-gration. To integrate one subject area with another, one begins with the clear, unambiguous, univocal, literal surface features of a par-ticular activity (for example, "5+3= __" as a so-called "math fact") and moves laterally, adding more and more (clear, unambiguous, univocal, literal surface feature) activities from different subject areas. We can hear in teacher's talk such as "I wanted to make the math stuff more fun for the children by linking it up to things they were already doing," the understandable desire to rescue 5+3= __ from its flatness and isolation. Understood and presented merely as a math fact, it is rather severe, so we find ways to remedy this malady by dressing it up through combining it with cut-out line drawings of teddy bears (which the children supposedly find cute and interesting).

The problem, however, is that such integration, if one could call it that, works precisely because it operates with the thinnest veneer of each area. Curricular integration becomes akin to formulations of post-modernism which well describe the mood of so many elementary schools: a hyperactive play of surfaces juxtaposed at the whim of the subject (whether teacher or child), juxtaposable with facile ease precisely because we are dealing with uprooted surfaces which offer no real resistance and demand no real work. Integration in such a post-modern milieu becomes formulated as little more than surface co-presence or co-occurrence, bereft of any fleshy, experiential immediacy.

If we begin with a surface understanding of 5+3= __ , our efforts at integration can easily fall prey to the bizarre cultural-capitalist equation of the achievement of wholeness with the consumptive accumulation of "more." One makes 5+3= __ (or any other curricular fragment) whole, not by sticking with it, deepening it, opening up its "necessities and mysteries" (Berry, 1983, p. vii) but by adding more and more activities to it—surrounding and crowding it with other equally isolated, unopened particulars but, we might say, never housing it. In this way, to re-formulate Wendell Berry's (1986) critique of the motto of the Sierra Club, our interest in math facts becomes *scenic*. Mathematics becomes akin to a tourist attraction, something to look at but never enter into, open up, and learn to live with well. And we, in turn, become akin to curricular tourists, ready to be momentarily entertained and amused. However, since we just see the thin, tarted-up, presentable surface of things, we, along with our children, become equally subject to boredom, frustration, and eventual violence. Given what is presented to us, it is little wonder that our attention is fleeting.

There is an odd logic at work here. Since, as a math fact, 5+3= __ affords only the briefest consideration, what we begin to witness is the attempt to attain integration, not simply through the *accumulation of co-present surfaces*, but through the *acceleration of such accumulation*. One need think only of the typical tempo of early-grade elementary school classrooms. What appears on the surface as vigour and enthusiasm is also readable as a type of hysteria and panic. Given that 5+3= __ is understood to be an isolated curricular fragment (i.e., it is "un-whole"), there is no time to deepen it and dwell on it, to slow it down and open it up, because there is simply so much else to get done and so little time. As Wendell Berry suggests, for this way of being in the world of the classroom, "time is always running out" (1983, p. 76). As such, we can witness in so many classrooms (and, in fact, in so much of contemporary life) an ever-accelerating "onslaught" (Arendt, 1969) of ever-new activities and the odd equation of some sort of fulfilment with becoming caught up in such frenetic consumption. Many teachers and children are thereby condemned to constantly strive to keep up, and to take on the failure to keep up as a personal, pathological problem involving lack of effort or lack of will. Talk of slowing things down, dwelling over something, and deepening our experience of it begins to sound vaguely quaint and antiquated.

An urban sprawl version of curriculum integration thus becomes convoluted with both a metaphysical and an eschatological belief. First, it is premised on the metaphysical belief that each curricular fragment (e.g., 5+3= __) is what it is independently of everything else, independently of any sustaining relations. In this view, wholeness cannot be a matter of meditating on how the whole of our course might be refracted through *this* fragment or *this*, since it is precisely such refraction that is denied by this metaphysical assumption of severance and fragmentation. Second, and following from this metaphysical assumption, an urban sprawl version of curriculum integration suggests that wholeness and integrity is always yet-to-arrive. Education thus gets caught up in a type of eschatological anticipation—"an occult yearning for the future" (Berry, 1986) when integrity and health and wholeness might finally be achieved through the final accumulation of all the pieces of the picture.

Placing "5+3=8" Back into all its Relations

In a recent Early Childhood Education methods course, we considered the following examples of Grade One children's math-facts work:

1) 5+3=8

2) 5+3=8

3) 5+3=8

It was proposed that we had found these three samples in the files of three different children who have just entered our classroom. The following questions were posed: What do we now know about these children, these samples? What do they mean? What do they show? As expected, the answer, for the most part, was "very little." One student ventured that "these children know how to add."

Through a combination of considerations of Jean Piaget's notion of operations (1952), working ourselves with manipulative materials, and, especially, frequent visits to a wonderful, Grades 1–4, multi-aged classroom, what slowly became visible underneath the surface-presentation of "these children know how to add" was a roiling nest of multiple operations, multiple voices: "threads interweaving and criss-crossing" (Wittgenstein, 1968, p. 32). Rather than reading each 5+3=8 pathologically, as an isolated *fact*, we slowly became able to read each as a *sign* pointing beyond its isolation to a whole world of implicate relations, a whole "chaos of possibilities" (Hillman, 1987).

One child holds five and counts on. A second counts them all out, showing us not only his own ways of working in mathematics, but showing us also that the child who can hold five is holding not just a math fact but a crystallized and stabilized nest of operations that this second child still needs to concretely re-embody and re-enact. Differently put, "5" is itself a doing full of underworlds of relations and connections and threads (for example, the accomplishment and stability of 1-to-1 correspondence and ordinal numerical sequences, the infinite iterations of relations of 4+1, 3+2, 12–7, the square root of 25, and so on), some of which this child who holds five understands, some not, but all of which surrounds and houses and makes understandable and locatable his work, his efforts, and his experiences. This child's work lives in these implicate relations and is deeply meaningful and sustainable only *within* them (and this in spite of the fact that some of these relations are, from the point of view of the child's own experiences, beyond him at this juncture: this is a profound and difficult ecological point— our lives and actions are sustained in part by what is beyond us, beyond what we know, experience, or construct). Another child "just knows" the answer but cannot articulate the operations she performs. Another gets caught up in such articulations and takes on the task of filling out all the permutations of operations embedded in the question at hand, verging, for a moment, near calculus and the formulation of functionally defined sets.

What occurred here was a wonderful but also rather disorienting phenomenon for many student-teachers in this class. They began to see that being stuck in the present tense with the three surface samples and then rushing to accumulate more and more in order to understand "the whole child" (or in order to "cover the whole curriculum"), was somehow potentially misguided and unhealthy, for it skitters over the deeply experiential ecology of *just this*. Underneath the surface of each stubborn particular was an almost overwhelming richness, diversity—hitherto unnoticed communities of relations. But more than this, once opened up, we could begin to see how each stubborn particular—*this* child's work and *this* child's work—becomes reflected and refracted through all the other stubborn particulars, giving all the others shape and place and sense. Differently put, once *this* 5+3= 8 becomes interpretable, it is no longer an isolated given which simply is what it is independently of everything else, like the unread work samples found in the children's files. It becomes readable as a multivocal sign which portends a whole nest of sustaining relations that are always already wholly at work and without which this stubborn particular would not be what it is. Each stubborn particular thus becomes placed within a nest of possibilities that house and sustain it. It becomes, in this deeply ecological sense, *whole*, through the slow, meticulous, disciplined working out of its relations.

Here we have a wonderful inversion of the metaphysical assumption of the urban sprawl version of curriculum integration. Each curricular fragment is what it is only in relation to the whole, a whole now readable in and through the stubborn particulars of our lives.

It is important to add that this does not mean that every child should be relentlessly inundated with relations, possibilities, and articulations at every turn. This would simply turn our interpretive efforts into another version of urban sprawl which acts irrespective of where we are and what particular relations are at work "*here* and *here*." This is the profound sense in which the particular is stubborn: there is no way that we can replace the exquisiteness of *this* particular (child's work, for example). *This* work—*this* 5+3= 8— occurs at an irreplaceable intersection between the world of mathematics, this child's life and breath and attention and experience, the life and relations of the classroom, the hopes and actions and experience of the teacher, the working out of our curriculum and our culture in and through the institutions of schooling, and so on.

Differently put, *this* work—the delicacies of this child's slow counting out of 5—is the centre of the whole of these relations. It is, in its own way, "a sacred place where the whole of the Earth comes to rest in relations of deep interdependency."

However (and this cannot be overemphasized, given our culture's tendency to inflate "child-centredness" to ecologically disastrous proportions), *this* work is, at the very same time, peripheral to (yet still housing of) the work of this next child and this. This stubborn paradox is at the core of curriculum integration. On the one hand, "the universe is a fabric of interdependent events in which *none* is the fundamental entity" (Nhat Hahn, 1986, p. 70): curriculum integration is not child-centred or teacher-centred or subject-matter-centred, but rather gives up the fundamentalism that underwrites such centration in favour of a world of relations. And yet, at the same time:

> *The centre is [also] everywhere.* Each and every thing becomes the centre of all things and, in that sense, becomes an absolute centre. This is the absolute uniqueness of things, their [stubborn] reality. (Nishitani, 1982, p. 146)

The arrival of each new child in one's class, the arrival of each new piece of work is thus potentially fecund. Each stubborn particular carries the potential of re-opening and thus revitalizing what I have heretofore understood the whole web of delicacies surrounding 5+3= __ to mean. This particular child always counts by twos and seems stuck there in a loop. She disassembles 5 and 3, re-sorts them, and adds them two by two by two by two by setting out pairs of small wooden blocks in rows in front of her. This child brings a uniqueness and individuality and irreplaceability to this activity. But her actions are not just that. Her work cannot simply be accumulatively added to the whole of what we have heretofore understood 5+3= 8 to mean. Rather, because of her work, that whole now "waver[s] and tremble[s]" (Caputo, 1987, p. 7). This fecund new case refracts and cascades through each particular relation that we took to be a given, giving each one a renewed and transformed sense of its relations and place in the whole. Without the arrival of such fecund new cases, and the portent of transformation and renewal that they bring, mathematics would become simply a given set of memorizable (but not especially memorable) facts and rules and would lose its sense of potency and possibility. It would thus lose its integrity as a living system.

What we have come upon here is a discipline of mathematics which is both open and closed, which has its own patterns and structures and operations, its own arrays of possibilities and potentialities, but which somehow is renewed and made whole by the arrival of the young. If we pay attention to the stubborn particularity of *this* 5+3= 8, this arrival need not be caught up in an onslaught of accumulation and acceleration. Our attention to *this* 5+3= 8 is slowed and held in place by the wisdoms and disciplines and sustaining relations of this place called mathematics. Conceived as a living system (one hopes that this is a warrantable image for our curriculum), mathematics is not a fixed state (whether already achieved or yet-to-arrive). It is, so to speak, a *way* which must be *taken up* to be a living whole. There is thus a way to mathematics. Learning its ways means entering into these ways, making these ways give up their secrets—making these ways telling again, making them more generous and open and connected to the lives we are living out. Understanding mathematics thus becomes a type of ecological intimacy which always already contains images of children and the passing on of the wisdoms of the world to the young. Consider this passage as describing the world of mathematics and all its sustaining interdependencies:

> Some people are beginning to try to understand where they are, and what it would mean to live carefully and wisely and delicately in a place, in such a way that you can live there adequately and comfortably. Also, your children and grandchildren and generations a thousand years in the future would still be able to live there. That's living in terms of the whole. (Snyder, 1980, p. 86)

Living in terms of the whole requires somehow making the world of mathematics livable. As such, it is not enough to simply delve into its indigenous operations and patterns; nor is it enough to simply abandon children to their own devices and, so to speak, let them have their way with mathematics and not teach the difficult lessons of how to pay attention to where they are and what mysteries this place offers.

It is here that we encounter a paradox: making the world of mathematics livable requires going beyond mathematics itself into the deep, patterned relations of the world which house and sustain the possibility of pursuing mathematics *at all*: patterns of experience and breath and bone and blood. It is in this deeper, fleshier discipline of repeated patterns of operations and structures and doings, that mathematics becomes integrated. It becomes whole.

Interpretive Descent and the Mathematicity of the World

The patterned doings of mathematics are themselves not simply isolated facts. Rather, we find in the patterns and structures of mathematics "an anciently perceived likeness between all creatures and the earth of which they are made" (Berry, 1983, p. 76). Consider how the following passages describe the patterned doings of the human body (pulse, breath), the patterns of our Earthly lives (daily and seasonal cycles and rhythms), and the structure of language itself. Consider how these passages show that each of these refracts through all the others:

> The rhythm of a song or a poem rises, no doubt, in reference to the pulse and breath of the poet. But that is too specialized an accounting; it rises also in reference to daily and seasonal—and surely even longer—rhythms in the life of the poet and in the life that surrounds him. The rhythm of a poem resonates with these larger rhythms that surround it; it fills its environment with sympathetic vibrations. Rhyme, which is a function of rhythm, may suggest this sort of resonance; it marks the coincidences of smaller structures with larger ones, as when the day, the month and the year all end at the same moment. Song, then, is a force opposed to speciality and isolation. It is the testimony of the singer's inescapable relation to the earth, to the human community, and also to tradition. (Berry, 1983, p. 93)

Or, even more mysterious:

> Rhyme leads one no doubt to hear in language a very ancient cosmology. Rhyme is not only an echo from word to word. Arrangement for arrangement, the order of language evokes and mimes a

cosmic order. In realizing itself, rhyme is tuned in to [this cosmology]. Rhyme and meter are praise. An indirect theology. (Meschonnic, 1988, p. 93)

Given this, we can see how curriculum integration cannot involve concertedly *adding on* language alongside mathematics or vice versa. Rather, it requires delving into the mathematicity of language itself—its patterns and structures and rhythms and tones and operations and grammars. And, once we crack the literalist surface of mathematics that might render it an isolated discipline, a cascade of implications ensues: the rhythm of mathematics, mathematicity of language, the language of music and rhythm, the interlocked music, patterns, and rhythms of the world, and, in the end, the profound mathematicity of the shifts and flutters in a bear's gait as it breaks from a walk into a run. Differently put, deep in the underworlds of $5+3=\_\_$, we find a strong and sustainable integration of mathematics into a bear theme. Or, better, we find the integration of bears *and* $5+3=\_\_$ into a whole which embraces them both, each in their own way and refracts each through the other—structure, pattern, rhythm, operation.

This is an exhilarating movement—a type of meditational and imaginal descent into the crawling underworld of the particularities of our lives. Every thing—even just this red wheelbarrow, or that child's holding five tight in her fist for fear of losing it—abounds with connections, dependencies, relations. Every thing, every word, every curricular fragment is a potential opening in to the whole—"*this* and *this*" (Wallace, 1987, p. 111). More strongly put, only through a deliberate and disciplined attention to the stubborn particulars is the whole anything more than simply a floating, and, in the end, unsustainable *idea*.

However, there is also a fearsomeness attached to the realization that the world is not a flat, clean, literal surface and that our sanity and healthy wholeness cannot be had by skittering across such surfaces, however safe and secure they might appear at first glance. There is a fearsomeness attached to the realizations that the world is *interpretable*, alive with implications and complicities that are always already at work in the intimacies of our everyday experiences, and that we cannot always control and predict what relations we might stumble on in the dark, no matter how well-laid our (lesson) plans might be.

But none of this goes quite far enough. The mathematicity in the gait of a bear as it breaks from a walk into a run is, in the end, a topic which still simply floats. We could just as easily have mapped out the parabolic curve of its shoulders or counted its toes or graphed its offspring or lifespan in relation to other animals. The sort of interpretive descent that curriculum integration requires of us is far more fearsome and more experientially immediate than this allows.

In dwelling upon the mathematical changes in the gait of a bear as it moves from a walk to a run, I cannot avoid coming to reflect on my own living involvement in such Earthly rhythms, an "anciently perceived likeness" (Berry, 1983, p. 76) that embraces us both and makes the life of each complicit in the other. In walking up this hill and feeling the fluttering mathematical patterns of breath and pulse and steps, I come to better understand this creature and its mathematical being in place, housed by flesh and humus, housed by a mysterious immediacy. And, in understanding this creature in this way, I come to understand myself and my own living involvement in the ecological conditions under which this creature lives and which I live with it, pulling hard at this same air as it curves up the steep valley sides. It is the fleshy mysteries of my own life and my own wholeness and integrity that this bear and its steps pace out. And, it is mathematics—the very mathematics which I now teach my child—which has underwritten technological images of severance, fragmentation, commodification, and mastery that have ravaged this place, this bear's life and, thereby, mine along with it. To teach mathematics in an integrated way, therefore, requires more than simply dwelling in its indigenous intricacies and patterns. I must help children (and myself) place mathematics back into the embrace of the Earth (into the embrace of its kin, like the symmetries of these pine branches). Such embrace will help make it more generous and forgiving and livable than it has become in the severities of our curriculum guides and the severities and violences of our unsustainable beliefs in its dominion as a "Father Tongue" (LeGuin, 1987) which silences all others.

It will help make it (and ourselves, and our children, and this bear, which paces out a life beyond our dominion) whole.

Concluding Remarks

It is impossible to divorce the question of what we do from the question of where we are—or, rather, where we think we are. That no sane creature befouls its own nest is accepted as generally true. What we conceive to be our nest, and where we think it is, are therefore questions of the greatest importance. (Berry, 1986, p. 51)

Just as it is my own wholeness and integrity that this bear and its steps pace out, so too it is my own wholeness and integrity that are foretold in whatever actions I do here, with these children in the classroom. In another Grade One classroom, children are completing subtraction equations on a white sheet of paper. When they are done, the rectangles, each with one equation, are cut out, curled up, pasted on Santa's beard, and posted for parents to see during the Christmas Concert and classroom visits that surround it.

If we meditate for a moment on this activity, there is a sense in which it is, frankly put, insane. This is not to say that some children might not enjoy it. It is it to say that fostering such enjoyment abandons children to a flickering, hallucinatory vision of the Earth, of mathematics, of the events surrounding Christmas that is, in the end, an ecological and spiritual disaster that no amount of acceleration and accumulation can outrun. Such activities suggest that we no longer know where we are. Such activities, too, are disturbingly suggestive of where we might think we are.

In this chapter, I have been suggesting that curriculum integration requires a concerted, thoughtful resistance to such skittering hallucinations. To prevent the woozy visions often associated with such matters, curriculum integration and the wholeness it portends must not sidestep a disciplined, mindful attention to the stubborn particulars of grace. But there is another suggestion here: these examples of math facts on a Teddy Bear's tummy and Christmas subtraction equations bear witness to a terrible logic that many teachers and children are suffering on our behalf. This is one of the agonies of ecological mindfulness: my own life is implicated in these very examples—*this* and *this*—as is my son's. This difficult knowledge, more than anything, is at the heart of curriculum integration and the ecologies of experiential education.

References

Arendt, H. (1969). *Between past and future.* London: Penguin.

Berman, M. (1983). *The reenchantment of the world.* New York: Bantam.

Berry, W. (1983). *Standing by words.* San Francisco: North Point Press.

Berry, W. (1986). *The unsettling of America.* San Francisco: Sierra Club.

Caputo, J. (1987). *Radical hermeneutics.* Bloomington: Indiana State University Press.

Hillman, J. (1987). Notes on opportunism. In J. Hillman (Ed.), *Puer papers.* Dallas: Spring Publications.

LeGuin, U. (1987). Introduction. In *Buffalo gals and other animal presences.* Santa Barbara: Capra Press.

Meschonnic, H. (1988). Rhyme and life. *Critical Inquiry, 15,* (Autumn 1988).

Nhat, H. (1986). *The miracle of mindfulness.* Berkeley: Parallax Press.

Nishitani, K. (1982). *Religion and nothingness.* Berkeley: University of California Press.

Piaget, J. (1952). *Origins of intelligence in children.* New York: International Universities Press.

Snyder, G. (1980). *The real work.* New York: New Directions.

Wallace, B. (1987). *The stubborn particulars of grace.* Toronto: McClelland and Stewart.

Williams, W. C. (1991). Spring and all (1923). In *The collected poems of William Carlos Williams* (Volume 1: 1909–1939). New York: New Directions.

Wittgenstein, L. (1968). *Philosophical investigations.* Cambridge: Blackwell's.

Chapter 16

EXPERIENCE
AND THE CURRICULUM

Bert Horwood

The purpose of this chapter is to comment on the preceding chapters and to pull them together by providing a broad curriculum context. To do this, Bert points to common patterns among the essays and to unresolved and emerging issues. His reflections are grounded in the conviction, coming from many sources, that the world at the opening of the 21st century, is a world in transition, and that education must play a leading part in helping people find the abilities to cope with a bewildering and possibly destructive future.

It was one of those stairwell conversations, casual at first, then turning serious. I was struggling to give a colleague a respectable explanation of what an experiential educator did. She retorted, rather acidly, that no one taught or learned anything except through experience, and what was all the fuss about? At the time, I did not have any answer. Now, years later, it is possible to be somewhat more articulate.

Dewey (1938) made a critical distinction between experiences which were educative and miseducative. He did not mean that one would not learn from the latter, only that the learning would fail to contribute to the person's education and possibly even inhibit it. My colleague's sharp comment echoed in my head when, as part of my work as a teacher trainer and educational researcher, I watched students and teachers at work in classrooms and in the outdoors. It became easier to see what the students were experiencing and to reckon what it might contribute to their educations.

Students, I noticed, spend most of their time doing and experiencing certain things. Students mostly watch, listen, and imitate. They are highly experienced watchers, listeners, and copiers. This is what the commonest styles of instruction teach. It doesn't matter much whether students watch canoe portaging or a mathematical proof. The experience is of watching someone else do something. Usually demonstration is accompanied by verbal description. Sometimes, there is verbal description alone. Again, the subject of the words is irrelevant, whether they tell how to arrange wood for a fire or relate the story of Magna Carta. The experience is of listening to someone else expressing ideas. Imitation works the same way, although here the student is closer to performing the central act — portaging the canoe, proving a geometrical proposition, writing an essay, and so on. But their action on the material before them is not their own; it is simple mimicry. And from those experiences, students learn to be good imitators. As Bill Patterson (1995) says, "School does a good job at preparing people for more schooling" (p. 27).

It would be a mistake to underestimate learning from watching and mimicry, for these are powerful, natural ways which can be easily observed in any schoolyard in the spring when skipping ropes appear. But it is a mistake to limit learning to this model and especially to restrict a person's tendency, having observed a desirable action, to try it for herself or himself. In the schoolyard, or on the street where most children learn to skip rope and shoot baskets, watching and listening are rapidly alternated with personal attempts at action. Furthermore, those attempts are chosen by the learner with respect to timing, intensity, and degree of difficulty. Schools do right to employ demonstration and mimicry, but there is much more to learning from experience.

My colleague was right. Students do learn what they experience, including processes and values which are of limited educational value. And I was right, too. There is a mode of teaching which puts the student in the thick of experiencing the subject matter with no, or absolutely minimal, intervention by an instructor. This mode of teaching, plus the learning that ensues, is what is meant by experiential education. It is particularly difficult and is relatively rare in publicly supported schools and colleges; it is sometimes rare even in schools which espouse the centrality of student experience in their programs.

In this essay, I will explore the possibilities and realities of an experiential curriculum as revealed by the preceding chapters. That exploration will summarize common elements and dilemmas of practice. Because this summary constitutes an account of the state of the art, there are implications for the future in teacher education and renewal, research in education, and the social changes in which we find ourselves. These implications will also be examined.

Common Practices

Models of Experiential Education

A much better answer for my colleague, though not at all suited to casual conversation, is the contents of this book. The nature of experiential education is not so much a matter of definition as a matter of seeing what teachers and students actually do. There are several, well-documented models of experiential education. These have in common a mechanistic or mechanical ideology, namely that a complex reality can best be expressed as a simplified mechanical model, usually as a flow chart. The chapters by Tom Herbert and Rogene McKiernan refer to these. Such mechanical models (mechanical, because they treat the teaching-learning axis as though it was a machine) are useful because they are simple, and they gain credence to the extent that they serve as maps which point to features visible in the descriptions of practice by other teachers.

Mechanical models are popular for a more important reason. They reflect the scientific world view which has driven thought in most of the West for the past three hundred years. Most of us are accustomed to this view of the world and have been trained to believe it. However, there are cracks appearing in the dominance of that world view. Alternative, and ancient, ways of knowing and understanding are being rediscovered and reclaimed. We are learning that there is a truth which lies between the facts (Perkins, 1983). Chapters like that of Rena Upitis and David Jardine illustrate this holistic, integrated view. The fact that Jiddu Krishnamurti could be held up as a hero in this field (Ed Raiola's chapter) is a sure sign that values are in transition.

This integrative tendency, the desire to be inclusive, the recognition that experience is more additive than analytic, or isolating, is a fact that rings throughout this entire collection. Gail Simmons demonstrates the creative and imaginative power available when students combine their reading of literature with related action in the world. Gary rasberry's chapter reveals the same unlocking of potent forces of imagination, only in a more directed context. Bill Patterson and Gary Shultz display the gains that come from increased exchange between schools and communities. Rick Gordon and Thomas Julius show that the creative power of experience is independent of grade level. Tom Smith's abused adolescents respond best to a multi-sided program in which teachers, foster parents, and therapists participate in each other's work.

The special ingredient here (I nearly wrote the "magic ingredient") is emotion. The emotional aspect of engagement is clear in the account of Karne Kozolanka, and reaches its fullest expression in David Jardine's chapter. Students are cited in some chapters (e.g., Shultz, Upitis, Kozolanka, and McKiernan) and there is always emotional content present. The lesson from all these accounts is that experiential education, at its best, engages the emotions, intellects, and bodies of both teachers and students. Here, the language is letting me down. The words "emotions," "minds," and "bodies" imply a kind of internal taxonomy that subdivides a human being into discrete entities. That's not what I deduce from reading these chapters together. What I'm trying to say is that the teachers and learners are engaged all over. The curriculum becomes lived experience, and lived experience is absorbed into the curriculum. Exactly as Whitehead (1929) would have it.

Students at the Centre

While the nature of educational engagement may be in transition, there is still the practical, everyday, down-to-earth business of going to work and spending time with one's students. Teachers find value in sharing highly specific procedures for accomplishing the ends of experiential education. They are acting like good cooks for whom, no matter what theories of nutrition and aesthetics they hold, specific recipes have a value which no amount of general principles can replace. In this respect, chapters like those by Deborah Millan and Tom Herbert provide examples.

One of the strongest lessons in these chapters is that students are at the centre in making decisions and living with the natural consequences. There is a hard, double-edge in this aspect: hard, because it is difficult for students to choose. It is especially difficult for students to choose if their previous experience in schooling has been to accept the choices of others. As evidence, note the difficulties described by Rena Upitis, Rick Gordon, and Rogene McKiernan when adult students are required to make independent decisions. Double-edged because, while one edge is challenging for the student, the other edge is troubling for the teacher. What if the students, as is highly likely, do not choose wisely? These writers reveal the great courage it takes for teachers to deliberately abandon their authoritative and controlling ways. Teachers, too, must live with the natural consequences of students' choices. In most cases, the results are wonderful. But there are nerve-wracking moments of tension and uncertainty. Uncertainty, diversity, irregularity, novelty, and other unpredictables are the most difficult consequences of this aspect of experiential education. Successful practitioners learn to live with ambiguity.

The centrality of students and learning from experience does not relieve teachers of the responsibilities that go with being adult professionals. Students must be kept emotionally and physically safe. Somehow, mandated curriculum content must be honoured in ways that will not cheat the students. Teachers have critical roles to set experiences within limits that make sense. In this respect, the sequence of instructional events is shown by these writers to be crucial to success. Rogene McKiernan gives the most vivid account of this in canoe instruction and Deborah Millan discusses the significance of the placement of field trips in the classroom instructional sequence. The lesson is that the earlier the experience, the more convincing is the message to students that they are to take responsibility for making sense out of it. If the sense has previously been delivered by vicarious experience (such as watching a paddling demonstration, or reading about the field trip site before visiting it), learning out of the experience has been more or less preempted.

It is no accident that the essays in this book say virtually nothing about the desirability of exhaustive sets of curriculum resource materials. These teacher voices are different from many in that they do not cry out for more packages of materials, media, or software. Similarly, the work described is remarkably free from the influence of commercial and corporate agendas which infiltrate the flood of resource material entering schools. The reason for this impressive freedom is closely related to putting students at the centre of the educational enterprise. Teachers who conduct their classes experientially do need libraries and community resources, but student decision making obviates the need for pre-digested and pre-planned materials. The concept of curriculum is broadened beyond subject-content details to include critical issues of being human, like that of gender identity as described by Karne Kozolanka.

Students in experientially oriented classes have placed on them a burden to make meaning out of their current (and past) experiences. James Raffan (1993) has described that kind of learning as making personal meaning. He claims it as a major consequence of out-of-school experience that is set in a deliberative curriculum context. My colleague, of the stairwell conversation, was quite right in her assertion that everyone learns something from experience. For some students, their experience of school is construed into a personal conviction that school is not a good place for them to be, that books and teachers and writing waste time. The chapters in this book all show the central characteristic of experiential education, namely, that participants, and instructors, too, are expected to make personal meaning. It is important to distinguish between personal meaning and private meaning because, in much of the practice described here, personal meaning is often expected to be made public, at least in part. Students in the highly individualized service-learning program described by Lyn Shulha and Jeff Piker, for example, are nevertheless expected to declare their learning. Thomas Julius's Grade Three students are expected to choose samples of their work to present to their families. There is a social context that cannot be ignored.

Rena Upitis made the observation that when students are required to choose an activity, even in a mathematics education class, there is a tendency to pick one which is an art or a craft, rather than, say, learning a new branch of mathematics. This observation is supported by the kinds of choices made by Gail Simmons's high school English students and the profound learning about gender, work, and job satisfaction described by Karne Kozolanka. In a similar way, it is no accident that David Jardine found the most potent expression of his ideas in the hard particulars of poetry. The arts and crafts are the converging roads which connect all learning. Thus, the integrative, whole-making tendency of experiential education is best expressed in the arts. The frequency with which students choose such modes of expression may also be related to the paucity of their opportunities to be expressive in conventional academic prose.

Evaluation

Individual student responsibility, artistic expression, making personal meaning within a community context, and divergence in activity and specifics of learning all contribute to make evaluation a major problem. The problem is even greater when one considers the unique treatment given to student failure found in experience-rich settings. Events that go wrong, which might be rated as failures in another school's context, are treated as valuable occasions for learning. In the stories from Expeditionary Learning, Tom Herbert's practice, portfolios, and projects, we see the constructive, creative, and educative treatment of error which in other settings might result in a student's being marked down. Reframing error from being something shameful and discreditable into a natural occasion for further exploration is a wonderful feature of those practices which we call "experiential."

By evaluation, I mean that peculiarly "schoolish" process of issuing a letter grade or number to assign value to a student's learning. Evaluating a school program is equally problematic, as Lyn Shulha and Jeff Piker show, but for clarity I'll treat it as a separate issue. There are four devices described by our authors. One of them is to use portfolios as a combined teaching and evaluation tool. Another is to dismiss grading as a discriminatory tool and, at the same time, express high confidence in the students by giving them, in advance of the course, a uniform and high grade. A third device has students select the weighting of grades among their various courses, which weighting will reflect the student's interest and commitment to parts of the program. Things like the public celebration after a *History Comes Alive* unit constitute informal valuing of learning which parallels the more formal school system grades. Despite these pragmatic, creative, and valuable methods, they are still essentially stunts being played on the pervasive and oppressive reliance on grades.

Experiential teachers have yet to come to grips with this central issue. Grades or marks determined by conventional testing and examination are inimical to experiential education. It is not possible, using these devices, to discover what each individual student has learned from their school experiences. Neither is it possible to discover what collective or communal learning there may have been. It follows that it is equally impossible to assign a numerical value, whether absolute or comparative, to learning that can never be discovered. This truth is very hard to deliver in a culture which grades eggs, wheat, and beef, and evaluates to the finest degree the performance of all new model cars. The delightful thing about the writers in this book is that they have found ways, in various degrees of subversion, to live with the problem.

It is instructive to examine a form of report developed by Kurt Hahn (Ewald, 1977, p. 31) for use in his schools. Hahn did not shy away from the evaluative process, but he did put it into the broad framework of human development which he wished his schools to promote. I do not urge that teachers use this form; rather, it is an example of putting the standards of achievement of school subjects into the context of the rest of a student's life. The particular items being assessed also reveal how much any evaluation system, when it is honest, reflects the value system of the evaluator.

Esprit de corps

Sense of justice

Ability to state facts precisely

Ability to follow what she(he) believes to be the right course in the face of:

> discomforts
>
> dangers
>
> hardships
>
> mockery
>
> skepticism
>
> impulses of the moment

Ability to plan

Imagination

Ability to organize her(his) own work and work with younger students.

Degree of concentration when the task interests her(him)

> And when it does not

Conscientiousness in everyday work and in special assignments

Manners

Manual dexterity

Standard reached in school subjects

Practical work, crafts, etc.

Arts (music, drawing, theatre)

Physical exercise, reaction time, endurance . . .

Implications for Teacher Education and Research

Given that there is an established body of practice, albeit divergent and only fuzzily defined, which can be termed "experiential education," what are the implications it has for professional training and for research in education? The following sections explore these questions.

Teacher Education

One of the most nagging questions arising from reading teachers' stories of their work is, "How did they learn to do that?" My own experience as a student teacher, and later as a teacher educator, convinced me that there was very little, if any, direct training, study, or practice of experiential methods in the education of most teachers. Some exceptional programs do exist, but they are small and happen not to be the programs in which most of the authors in this book were trained. The question persists: Where and how do we learn to teach in this way, a way which was once identified to me by a student as a "strange manner of teaching?"

One answer is that when a teacher is dissatisfied with her work, and determined to make changes, inventiveness and creativity drive the search for greater satisfaction. A classic account of this motive is found in Wigginton's (1986) story of the origins of the Foxfire program. Equally vivid is Gail Simmons's discovery of experiential teaching out of frustration with the lifelessness of her geography lessons, and Rogene McKiernan's stimulation from working with Expeditionary Learning. In Gail's case, it is especially significant that she made the discovery while teaching a subject in which she was not particularly expert. I interpret this as further evidence that expertise is overrated and may even inhibit the search for solutions. This pattern of thoughtful reflection and search stimulated by dissatisfaction is evidenced in several other chapters; examples are those by Tom Herbert, Ed Raiola, and Lyn Shulha and Jeff Piker. In short, by reflecting upon the experiences of practice, especially when there is attention to the dissatisfying aspects, teachers learn to practice experientially by themselves.

Another possible answer lies in experiential practice, often unsung and unlabelled as such, at any stage of a person's learning life. There are indications in the work of Rena Upitis, Rick Gordon, and David Jardine that their students may well teach in a different manner than they would have done if they had not encountered portfolios, projects, or math facts on a teddy bear's tummy. In the same way, I wonder what sort of teaching practice will be found among Thomas Julius's Grade Three students when they re-enter schools as teachers? Will the graduates of Expeditionary Learning programs incorporate the principles into their practice, should they become teachers? Schools of Education are not the only possible place for discovering the role of experience in teaching. The point is that teachers may well teach mostly in the ways in which they themselves were taught most effectively and pleasantly. Experiential teaching may be infectious: caught more easily than taught. And the place of infection need not be a school. As speculation, I offer the proposal that some of the best experiential teachers learned their craft as much on the family farm, at summer camp, or in the workplace, as in school.

This book is a strong case for the roles of reflection and narrative in bringing experiential methods into greater awareness. Confidence is also increased through professional internal and external dialogue. One is not alone in these "screwy things," as Keith King calls them. Teachers telling their stories to one another is an important part of their own learning from the lived experiences of teaching. It is a sort of meta-experiential education. It is quite right that the teachers writing in this book have not spared themselves from the demands for thoughtful reflection and meaning making which they placed on their students.

Research in Education

There is a gap between the academic and commercial research community and the community of teachers. Few teachers read research reports and fewer still use them to guide practice. There are several possible reasons. One is that the results of research are published in relatively inaccessible forms. Another is that the results are not seen to be relevant to the concerns of practice. A third is that research is regarded as "theoretical," which must somehow always be transferred into "practice." One of the things that emerges clearly in this book is that teachers do not first learn theory and then put it into practice. The reality here is that there is continual dialectic between practice and theory. The former, when considered reflectively, leads to the emergence of the latter, which, being relevant, informs changes in practice. And so on.

Fortunately, there are two trends apparent in this book that suggest the gap may be narrowing. One of those trends is to conceive of research more broadly than has been done in the past. Donald Schön (1983) provides a lovely example when he assigns status as a researcher to any professional who is struggling to redefine and reframe the dilemmas and puzzles of practice. The conversation of Rick Gordon and Thomas Julius, and Ed Raiola's search for models and guides, are examples. So is Bill Patterson's reframing of community members as partners of the school. The concept of research has also been broadened to include qualitative investigations alongside the previously dominant, quantitative experimental studies. Thus, Karne Kozolanka's description of gender as a factor in the education of students on a building site counts as a legitimate and useful way of learning new things about education. This is not to disparage quantitative research as a less legitimate way of discovery.

The second trend is the recognition that narrative constitutes a powerful research tool (Connelly & Clandinin, 1994). The stories of practice reconsidered, of success and failure, of hopes and fears, make practice malleable and transparent. Malleability is important because it attacks the notion that teachers boringly do the same thing over and over again, ad nauseam. Malleability shows that, while there is enough form and structure for consistency, there is also the ability to flow, to be plastic, to take another shape. Transparency is critical if the discovery made by one teacher about practice is to be learned by another teacher. Rogene McKiernan describes the struggles of one group of teachers (Outward Bound instructors) to make their work as expedition leaders transparent to the school teachers who were Outward Bound students. The heart of a teacher's work, like any artistry, is often concealed to observers. Narrative is a way to reveal that which has, up till now, been the hidden secrets of practice.

There are further questions which emerge from these narratives of practice. One is to better understand the process of reflection and invention which enables teachers to be innovators. Another is to learn more about the sources of teacher energy and satisfaction. A book like this one does not attract writing from teachers who are tired, disenchanted, frustrated, and isolated. The ways of teacher renewal and refreshment are poorly understood. Much of the work described in these pages cries out for follow-up. A common reaction of reviewers of the manuscripts was to wish that they could know what happened next. When the community becomes more a part of the curriculum, what are the long-term effects on students? How will the young teachers who considered the deeper meaning of mathematics and bears, or who grapple with the thought of Krishnamurti, teach in their own classrooms? What became of the abused teenagers who passed through their powerful program with Tom Smith? What difference does the absence of service learning from a teacher education program make after ten years? Longitudinal investigations are unpopular in a society that seeks instant gratification and quick fixes, and consequently, we know very little about how today's exciting experiential program contributes to the rest of a student's life.

Major consideration needs to be given to overhauling the practices of student evaluation. Stories of practice show that conventional patterns of evaluation and grading are irrelevant and inimical to experiential education. There is much creative, and largely secret, sidestepping of institutional evaluative demands as a response of teachers determined to do their best with their students, regardless. There is a grave need for researchers and teachers to work together as fellow learners to uncover existing imaginative practices and refine them for public consideration and trial.

To this end, it will be necessary to develop a different conception of curriculum itself. From the middle of the 20th century, curriculum was seen as a set of objectives to be achieved. In a bold stroke, Kieran Egan (1986) suggested that, at least for younger children, curriculum could be considered a set of stories to be told. Egan follows this fundamental proposition to its logical end, showing how curriculum would necessarily be changed to reflect a very different starting point. Egan's work foundered on the problem of how to evaluate pupils. The contents of this book suggest that serious conceptual consideration should be given to the starting point that curriculum is a set of experiences to be had and to be learned from. Most of the ideas and practices in this book would fall into such a concept of curriculum, but the evaluation problem would persist because we do not have recognized, tried ways of assessing a person's learning and meaning from their lived experiences. I think that this is a central problem because sensible teachers everywhere want their students to do well, and to be seen to do well in the eyes of the world. The evaluation tail does wag the curriculum dog, and if experience is to be a significant part of curriculum, then the evaluation problem must be solved, or dissolved.

There is also need for work in program evaluation. Lyn Shulha and Jeff Piker show the dilemmas of doing everything the right way in determining a program's efficacy, only to find that the key decision-makers do not need that kind of information. Tom Smith demonstrates an effective model to marry education and therapy, only it is set in the wrong place and draws down too rapidly the strength and energy of staff members. Throughout the broad arena of experiential education, new programs are born out of enthusiasm and die unrecognized and unfunded. The field needs its researchers to better study the parameters for program evaluation, and to develop different expectations for objectivity.

Social Change

The nature of this book reflects the turmoil and transition of its times. The last decades of the 20th century and the early decades of the 21st are seen by many to be a period of profound change in social values and structures. These transformations are documented by writers like Morris Berman and Conor Cruse O'Brien. Berman (1981) traces the history of Western thought from an earlier stage of participating consciousness, through the golden years of scientific detachment and alienation from the world, to a transition zone around the turn of the century in which new efforts are being made to weaken the hegemony of scientific objectivity and regain some new form of participation in the world.

O'Brien (1994) uses his formidable powers of scholarship and eloquence to describe the erosion and collapse of Enlightenment values in Western culture. Writing in 1994, he vividly describes political and military shifts which are entirely contrary to the earlier, unquestioned commitment to the Enlightenment as enshrined in the Western democracies. O'Brien predicts that these changes will continue into the third millennium of the Christian era, and will result in quite unpredictable, and possibly unpleasant, transformations.

These high and great matters may seem, at first glance, to be totally removed from issues of experience in the curriculum. But they aren't. Education is both a victim of change and a contributor to change. Schools are a central participant in the social fabric and are caught up in whatever turbulence or stability society provides. Three particular aspects of change and transition in the larger culture relate to this book. First is the question of how and what we know. When science is not the only recognized way of acquiring and understanding knowledge, there are critical implications for what counts as learning in schools and colleges. Second is the tension between the conservative and transformative functions of education in a culture. In a stable culture, education clearly works to sustain that culture by exercising the young in the cultural norms. But in transition, education has the capability of influencing change, of generating dissatisfaction with the status quo, and of providing stimulus and provocation for alternatives. Third, there is an axis of tension between individual learning and communal learning. In the following sections, I will consider each of these three topics in the light of the essays in this book.

Ways of Knowing

The old Peoples had ways of knowing that became largely lost from the 17th century onward. Our times are now dominated by the way of knowing which characterizes modern science. The material benefits, if such they are, that flow from knowledge obtained by the methods and attitudes of science are so great that scientific knowledge has come to dominate all knowing. The price we pay for this kind of knowledge is alienation from the world and from ourselves. Berman (1981) calls this a loss of enchantment. A number of factors are at work to erode the dominance of science as the best of all ways of knowing. The upshot of these is that, in some quarters, objectivity is valued less than it used to be. Those things that can be numbered are not valued more highly than those things that can not. Knowledge which has emotional and spiritual content is coming to be recognized as legitimate. There are forces at work which will restore enchantment in human relations with the rest of the world.

One of the great gifts of science was print. The emergence of print and literacy gave learning via reading a primacy over learning via other routes, for example, oral accounts, dreams, or direct experience. To sustain the scientific way of knowing, to enhance the necessary personal detachment from the objects of study, learning from print became more important than learning from the world itself. In this way emerged a curriculum expressed in textbooks rather than in the lived experiences of students.

When lived experience enters the curriculum, as illustrated by this book, the value of the scientific way of knowing, with all its entailments, is not denied. Rather, it is put into a larger context of being human. The school can become more than a factory where teachers are seen as tools and students as products. Explanations couched in terms of machines and reason alone become enlarged by the inclusion of soul and emotion. The dominant education can become more inclusive and more easily compatible with traditional cultural knowledge, such as that possessed by aboriginal and tribal people. For example, the Mohawks of Ahkwesahsne have developed a science and mathematics curriculum which is grounded in the culture and tradition of the Longhouse people (Wendt, 1995). Arthur Solomon, Ojibwa Elder and spiritual teacher, writes:

> We propose to surround our children with a total educational environment whereby the teachers and the parents and the elders provide an education that is fashioned not only by those who teach but also by the ones who learn. We will again become each other's teachers as it always was. (Solomon, 1990, p. 99)

As the accepted ways of knowing expand, the structure of research expands and, consequently, there is hope for a sound body of inquiry to support experience in the curriculum. As the nature of knowledge takes on new structures, the context for schools, curriculum, and the training of teachers changes.

Should Curriculum Lead or Follow?

Curriculum can have two kinds of influence on social structures. It can be conservative, working to maintain and transmit social and cultural values and norms from one generation to the next, or it can be transformative, contributing to change in society. Given that both directions coexist, curriculum is not likely to be able to bring about radical change. Indeed it is unlikely, in my view, that schools can take the lead in promoting change unless parallel change is already beginning in other sectors of the culture.

The Association for Experiential Education (1995) has adopted "positive social change" as part of its vision statement, although it is not stated what "positive" means. I interpret the vision statement to mean that the experiential educators who are part of that Association wish to emphasize the transformative power of curriculum. The essays in this book support that wish by showing how it can be done, why it works, and some of the pitfalls along the way. The transformative perspective is not practised to the exclusion of the more normal conservative one. Almost all of the stories in this book come from school and college teachers who are embedded in conventional institutions with essentially conservative perspectives.

The transformative aspect of curriculum is present, and may even be nurtured, in conventional settings. This is both a hopeful and an uncomfortable state of affairs.

The direction of change is not clear. At first glance, it seems strange that the Association for Experiential Education would espouse social change and not clearly specify the direction. But perhaps this turns out to be the path of wisdom. It is clear that social values are in transition, that there is conflict among a clamour of voices. It may be best not to be specific when there are many possible choices. It may be better to broadcast many varieties of seeds and allow those forces over which we have no control to sort out the survivors. To be fair, the Association's vision statement does refer to justice and compassion as desirable elements of the world. But it remains to be seen how these qualities will be understood in changing times.

Planting seeds is exactly what placing experience in the curriculum does. Experience in the curriculum makes demands on the young (and anyone who wishes to learn) to pay attention to the particulars of life and construct meaning from them. It demands that the meanings fit each person's frame of reference, including both existing transmitted cultural structures and newly emerging ones. It demands that meaning and understanding change as new experiences and new times come along. Such a curriculum provides tools of awareness, thought, and feeling which arise out of the most useful of traditions and the most promising of emergent novelties. It seems to me that a person educated in this way could hardly be better prepared for an uncertain, unpredictable future.

The Individual in Community

Experiential education tends to place emphasis on individual growth, development, and learning. Much experiential education is done in small groups with distinct communal elements, yet, at the end, individual gains are what count. Even the most intensely focused learning communities are dismantled when the course is over. In fact, groups in experiential education are very short-lived. This term's classmates are not the same as next term's classmates. Consequently, although experiences may be shared and interpreted on a group basis, individual right to idiosyncratic interpretation and individual responsibility for learning are the abiding values. Individuals are the atoms of the dominant Western culture — mobile, transferable, and even interchangeable.

Part of the change that is swirling about the arrival of the 21st century is the recognition of indigenous knowledge, the knowledge, wisdom, and understanding residual in aboriginal peoples all over the world. Indigenous knowledge is one of the factors affecting the climate of change in ways of knowing and possible new directions for education. I raise it here, because it sheds light on the puzzling tension between individual and communal knowledge. Indigenous people have a way of placing the individual much more firmly in community than is done in dominant industrialized societies. There are many extremes in tribal variations, but a general characteristic is that an individual's prowess and accomplishment is for and of the community. Knowledge is communal property, after a fashion. One of the powerful ways of expressing this relationship is through service (Hall, 1991).

The practice of experiential education, as exemplified in this book, does not have this kind of emphasis on community. There are traces of its presence, as in Bill Patterson's work and in Rena Upitis's observation that family and friends were important elements in her students' struggles with their independent projects. At this stage in its development, the practice of experiential education contains only rudiments of learning as a communal enterprise. By contrast, the corporate sector may be better developed, in this respect. Corporations are encouraging and training their employees to think in terms of community and to understand that phenomenon called "corporate learning." This is the ultimate stage in the personification of corporations. It is ironic that while some branches of experiential education are active in corporate training, the curriculum in many schools and colleges has not yet embraced experiential methods.

Conclusion

The authors of this book demonstrate the diversity of views and practice which contributes to experiential education. The field is not clearly bounded, nor is it highly developed. All the same, there are clear common elements of practice and there are skilled practitioners. It has been recognized that the ablest practitioners are not necessarily the most articulate. It has also been recognized that committing to action with students is so consuming that there is little energy left for writing. Nevertheless, according to Page (1990), if we are not to join the decline of the progressive movement, it is critically important that teachers themselves make thoughtful reports about their practice.

Thoughtful teachers going public with their interpretations of experience in the curriculum have an impact on teacher education and research. These accounts reveal teachers reflecting and learning, as professionals should do. By going public, the gritty particulars of practice as well as the ideological and curriculum contexts are made available for other teachers and would-be teachers. There are opportunities to discuss, debate, appreciate, and even disapprove within school communities. Numerous questions and issues calling for research are exposed. Giving voice to that which has previously been largely silent is a very creditable activity.

O'Brien (1994) predicts, darkly, that during the 21st century "the advanced world may well be like, and feel like, a closed and guarded palace, in a city gripped by the plague" (p. 141). He powerfully documents that prediction by showing the erosion of Enlightenment values such as democracy, the rule of law, and freedom of expression. Experience in the curriculum is a grand antidote for such a grim image. Not because experiential education can stop the plague or guard the palace, but rather, it can prepare ordinary people to make sense of their lives whatever the circumstances. Indeed, in O'Brien's terms, an experiential curriculum might even be construed as part of the plague, and that would be an appropriate construction since the plague is where the action is. Survival in a changing world means more than hanging on. It also means participating in the changes. Using experience to discover the immanent possibilities in the world is a way to avoid being locked up in the guarded palace.

No one has said that any part of it is easy.

References

Association for Experiential Education. (1995, February). *The AEE Horizon*, p. 2.

Berman, M. (1981). *The reenchantment of the world.* Ithaca, NY: Cornell University Press.

Connelly, J. M., & Clandinin, D. J. (1994). Telling teaching stories. *Teacher Education Quarterly 21*(1), 145-158.

Dewey, J. (1938). Experience and education. New York: Collier.

Egan, K. (1986). Teaching as story telling. An alternative approach to teaching and curriculum in the elementary school. London, Ontario: The Althouse Press.

Ewald, M. (1970). Salem school 1919-33: Foundation and expansion. In H. Rohrs & H. Tunstytall-Behrens (Eds.), *Kurt Hahn.* London: Routledge and Kegan Paul

Hall, M. (1991). *"...something shining like gold—but better." The National Indian Youth Leadership model: A manual for leaders.* Gallup, NM: National Indian Youth Leadership Project.

O'Brien, C. C. (1994). *On the eve of the millennium.* Concord, Ontario: The House of Anansi Press.

Page, M. (1990). Active learning: Historical and contemporary perspectives. (ERIC RIE ED 338 389)

Patterson, B. (1995). The TAMARACK program. *Green Teacher, 42,* 25-28.

Perkins, R. (1983). *Against straight lines. Alone in Labrador.* Boston: Little, Brown.

Solomon, A. (1990). *Songs for the people: Teachings on the natural way.* Toronto: NC Press Limited.

Schön, D. (1983). *The reflective practitioner: How professionals think in action.* New York: Basic Books.

Wendt, K. (1995). Ahkwesahsne science and math pilot project: A native approach to learning. *Pathways: The Ontario Journal of Outdoor Education, 8*(3), 14-19.

Whitehead, A. N. (1929). *The aims of education and other essays.* New York: Macmillan.

Wigginton, E. (1986). *Sometimes a shining moment. The Foxfire experience.* Garden City, NY: Anchor Press/Doubleday.

AFTERWORD

Keith V. King

The Magic Ways of Learning

> *Whatever you can do, or dream you can, begin it.*
> *Boldness has genius, power and magic in it.*
> W. H. Murray

I suggest ... to sug.gest' v. to bring (a thought, problem, desire, etc.) to the mind for consideration.

I wonder ... to won'der v. to have doubt and curiosity about; to want to know.

I wonder ... about the boldness, genius, power, and magic necessary for good teaching.

I suggest ... some of the magic lies in the learner's interest in the outcome of the process.

... some of the magic lies in the location in which the learning takes place. If in the eyes of the learner, the situation is real, I suggest there is some of that magic in it.

... some of the magic depends upon the learner's ownership in the situation. There is magic when the learner feels responsibility and has input in the outcome.

... a major part of the magic of learning is dependent upon the opportunity and skill of reflective thinking

... there is magic present if the consequences of the learner's actions are immediate, true, and a direct result of the learner's decisions.

... there is much magic if, in the eyes of the learner, there is risk.

... the adventure of it all, the unknown outcome, creates magic.

... there must be a feeling of trust on the part of the learner in order for the magic to be present.

... the feeling of the chance of success is a critical factor in that magic.

... the excitement, along with the adventure, along with the newness of the challenge, makes the magic work.

... there is a great deal of magic created by the knowledge there will be support for me and my screwy ideas and goofs, oops, mistakes, no matter what.

I wonder ... are there other magic ingredients of good teaching?

I wonder ... if you, the reader, have realized the verb "to teach" or the noun "teacher" is used only twice in the above listing? Also, have you realized the word "experiential" has not been used once?

INDEX

ADDITIONAL BOOKS from
The Association for Experiential Education
Published by Kendall/Hunt

THE THEORY OF EXPERIENTIAL EDUCATION, THIRD EDITION
Karen Warren, Mitchell Sakofs, and Jasper S. Hunt, Jr., editors
ISBN #0-7872-0262-2
The third edition of this groundbreaking book looks at the theoretical foundations of experiential education from a philosophical, historical, psychological, social, and ethical perspective. The aim of the book is to encourage readers to think about *why* they are doing *what* they are doing. It has become a generally accepted truth in experiential education that one must always combine action with reflection in order to have a full human experience. This book shows the reflection side of the experience of experiential educators.
AEE Member price $30.00 / Non-member $38.95

EXPERIENTIAL LEARNING IN SCHOOLS AND HIGHER EDUCATION
Richard Kraft and Jim Kielsmeier, editors
ISBN #0-7872-0183-9
A new edition of *Experiential Education and the Schools,* this updated and expanded anthology contains some of the best articles published in the *Journal of Experiential Education* to address the role of experiential education at all levels of schooling. General theory, service learning, research and evaluation, cultural journalism, the environment, and practical ideas are just some of the subjects covered. This book is a must for educators, school board members, administrators, professors, and researchers who are striving to improve education for all our children, young people, and adults.
AEE Member price $30.00 / Non-member $38.95

ADVENTURE THERAPY: THERAPEUTIC APPLICATIONS OF ADVENTURE PROGRAMMING

by Michael A. Gass, Ph.D.

ISBN #0-8403-8272-3

This valuable resource book contains writings by Dr. Gass and other respected practitioners in the growing field of therapeutic adventure programming. The book's 39 chapters address such issues as why adventure therapy works; programming considerations; the theory of adventure therapy; current research in the field; examples of effective programs; and future directions of the field.

AEE Member price $23.95 / Non-member $29.95

ETHICAL ISSUES IN EXPERIENTIAL EDUCATION, SECOND EDITION

by Jasper S. Hunt, Jr.

ISBN #0-8403-9038-6

An examination of the current ethical issues in the field of adventure programming and experiential education. Examples of topics include: ethical theory, informed consent, sexual issues, student rights, environmental concerns, and programming practices. This book encourages experiential education practitioners to reflect carefully on the ethical issues inherent to their profession.

AEE Member price $16.00/ Non-member $23.00

BOOK OF METAPHORS, VOLUME II

Michael A. Gass, Ph.D.

ISBN # 0-7872-0306-8

The use of metaphors in adventure programming often serves as the key for producing lasting functional change for clients. This book is a compilation of presentations designed to enhance learning for those participating in adventure-based programs, in which practitioners share how they prepare experiences for presentation. Topics covered include steps for framing experiences, verbal introductions, debriefing, and methods for facilitating adventure experiences.

AEE Member price $23.00 /Non-member $28.95

To order a title, call Kendall/Hunt Publishing Company at (800) 228-0810.